A Mariner's Miscellany

Peter H. Spectre

Sheridan House
Seafarer Books

Published 2005 in the United States of America
by Sheridan House Inc.
145 Palisade Street
Dobbs Ferry, NY 10522

and in the United Kingdom
by Seafarer Books
102 Redwald Road
Rendlesham, Woodbridge
Suffolk IP12 2TE

Library of Congress Cataloging-in-Publication Data
Spectre, Peter H.
A mariner's miscellany: things forgotten, recalled; things known, illuminated / by Peter H. Spectre.
        p. cm.
Includes bibliographical references and index.
ISBN 1-57409-195-6 (alk. paper)
1. Boats and boating—Miscellanea. I. Title.
GV777.3.S64 2005
797.1—dc22
                    2004021307

British Library Cataloguing in Publication Data
Spectre, Peter H.
A mariner's miscellany
1.Seamanship—Miscellanea 2.Sailing 3. Sailing—Miscellanea
I.Title
623.8'8
ISBN 0 95470 621 8

Design by Lindy Gifford

US ISBN 1 57409 195 6
UK ISBN 0 95470 621 8

Printed in the United States of America

You think at times you hear the distant call of a ship.
But what would that be? Something in the mind.
It happened long ago....
                                        —H.M. Tomlinson

Acknowledgements

Heartfelt thanks to Llewellyn Howland III, bookman, for suggesting the concept for this work many years ago; Kathleen Brandes, editor, for showing me things I could not see; Lindy Gifford, designer, for fitting it all together; Oscar Lind, bookman, for encouraging me at a critical moment; and Lothar Simon, publisher, for going out on a limb.

Contents

Introduction

The roots of this book are in my *Mariner's Book of Days,* published annually since 1992. A desk diary, it combines data about what happened on each day of the year throughout maritime history with encyclopedic information, both historical and contemporary, concerning the nautical world. The *Mariner's Book of Days* didn't just arise out of thin air. The roots of it are in the *Mariner's Catalog,* a multivolume series coedited by George Putz and me in the 1970s. Generally, the *Mariner's Catalog* was a resource book, a guide to such tangibles as equipment, tools, hardware, gear, boats, etc. The *Mariner's Book of Days,* on the other hand, is about intangibles: history, traditions, concepts, literature, the romance of the sea.

This book is an amalgam of the two, a combination of the tangible and the intangible—practical information about boats, anchors, rope, and ballast, cheek by jowl with poetry, legend, lore, superstitions, language of the sea, art, thoughts about literature, and more.

Nautical literature, especially, has held a fascination for me ever since I was a boy with romance-of-the-sea on the brain. Awhile back, I heard a radio interview with a country-style mandolin player who described in great detail the roots of his music. He said he had become involved with bluegrass as a young boy, when he met Bill Monroe, the Father of Bluegrass. Monroe touched him, both literally and figuratively, and as a result his musical direction, he said, was forever fixed. I was reminded of Carl Lane, whose effect on me was the same, though the subject was different.

The first non-juvenile book I ever read was by Carl Lane, and even though I was only about eight or nine years old at the time, I can still remember the circumstances in detail. I had pulled some outrageous stunt or other around the house, and my mother banished me to my room for the day. When I complained that there wasn't anything to do up there, she said yes there was, that I could read, and that I would be a better person for it.

I don't know where it came from—certainly no one in my family had any interest at all in boats—but in a corner of my room was a book called *The Boatman's Manual.* I picked it up, became intrigued by the illustrations, and began to read. Of course, for a boy of my age it was a difficult slog. When I came to a word I didn't understand, I'd yell downstairs to my mother. She'd ask me to spell it. "B-o-w-s-p-r-i-t," I'd say. "Never heard of it," my mother would say. Which made the book all the more fascinating: Here was something my mother, the smartest person in the whole, wide world, didn't know anything about. I can trace my fascination with boats, ships, and the sea to that day and that book.

The Boatman's Manual was by Carl Lane, and over the years, whenever I came across another book by him, I'd drop everything and read it. His writing was clear, direct, opinionated, accurate, and captivating. (An example: "No boat need strand on a strange coast if the skipper is a navigator and seaman in fact, not theory. No boat need suffer a 'licking' at sea if the skipper is a seaman and sailor in fact, not theory. No boat need suffer any form of shipwreck if her skipper has fitted her out and equipped her for the purposes of her use, wisely and generously.") His illustrations—pen-and-ink sketches—were as clean, simple, and concise as his writing.

As I gained actual experience with boats, spurred on by Lane's writing, I came to understand that his style was boaty, not yachty, and that he belonged to a school of nautical writers of the 1930s, 1940s, and 1950s that included Hervey Garrett Smith, William and John Atkin, Clifford Ashley, and John G. Hanna, among many others. No yacht club posturing here. None of the class distinctions inherent in yachting of that time. Just unadulterated boatiness, with emphasis on the happy, almost childlike appreciation of the traditions of the sea. These men, in turn, were inspired by writers and editors who preceded them, and those were inspired by the crowd that came before them. Under their influence, I began a long march back in time through Alf Loomis, C.S. Forester, C.G. Davis, Felix Riesenberg, W.P. Stephens, Thomas Fleming Day, Basil Lubbock, Joseph Conrad, Claud Worth, Joshua Slocum, Richard Henry Dana, Jr., Captain Frederick Marryat, Henry David Thoreau, Robert Southey, and no end of others.

This book is published in homage to that continuum of writers and editors. It is published, also, in the hope that its contents will be found relevant today and will carry a new generation of enthusiasts into the future with a grounding in what William McFee called "harbors of memory" and C.G. Davis called "the ways of the sea."

Peter H. Spectre
Spruce Head, Maine

A sea of dreams

*T*here's an ache in my heart, and I can't tell why,
Something to do with the sea and sky.   —Bill Adams

A Wanderer's Song
by John Masefield

A wind's in the heart of me, a fire's in my heels,
I am tired of brick and stone and rumbling wagon-wheels;
I hunger for the sea's edge, the limit of the land,
Where the wild old Atlantic is shouting on the sand.

Oh I'll be going, leaving the noises of the street,
To where a lifting foresail-foot is yanking at the sheet;
To a windy, tossing anchorage where yawls and ketches ride,
Oh I'll be going, going, until I meet the tide.

And first I'll hear the sea-wind, the mewing of the gulls,
The clucking, sucking of the sea about the rusty hulls,
The songs at the capstan at the hooker warping out,
And then the heart of me'll know I'm there or thereabout.

Oh I am sick of brick and stone, the heart of me is sick,
For windy green, unquiet sea, the realm of Moby Dick;
And I'll be going, going, from the roaring of the wheels,
For a wind's in the heart of me, a fire's in my heels.

The feel of it, according to Michael Scott

I went aft, and mounted the small poop and looked forward towards the rising moon, whose shining wake of glow-worm coloured light, sparkled in the small waves that danced in the gentle wind on the heaving bosom of the dark-blue sea, was right ahead of us, like a river of quicksilver with its course diminished in the distance to a point, flowing towards us, from the extreme verge of the horizon, through a rolling sea of ink, with the waters of which, for a time, it disdained to blend. Concentrated, and shining like polished silver afar off—intense and sparkling as it streamed down nearer, but becoming less and less brilliant as it widened in its approach to us, until, like the stream of the great estuary of the Magdalena, losing itself in the salt waste of waters, it gradually melted beneath us and around us into the darkness.

I looked aloft—every object appeared sharply cut out against the dark firmament, and the swaying of the mastheads to and fro, as the vessel rolled, was so steady and slow, that they seemed stationary, while it was the moon and stars which appeared to vibrate and swing from side to side, high overhead, like the vacillation of the clouds in a theatre, when the scene is first let down.

The masts and yards, and standing and running rigging, looked like black pillars, and bars and wires of iron, reared against the sky, by some mighty spirit of the night; and the sails, as the moon shone dimly through them, were as dark as if they had been tarpaulins. But when I walked forward and looked aft, what a beauteous change! Now each mast, with its gently swelling canvas, the higher sails decreasing in size, until they tapered away nearly to a point, through topsail, topgallant-sail, royal and skysails, showed like towers of snow, and the cordage like silver threads, while each dark spar seemed to be of ebony, fished with ivory, as a flood of cold, pale, mild light streamed from the beauteous planet over the whole stupendous machine, lighting up the sand-white decks, on which the shadows of the men, and of every object that intercepted the moonbeams, were cast as strongly as if the planks had been inlaid with jet.

There was nothing moving about the decks. The look-outs aft, and at the gangways, sat or stood like statues, half bronze, half alabaster. The old quarter-master, who was conning the ship, and had perched himself on a carronade with his arm leaning on the weather nettings, was equally motionless. The watch had all disappeared forward, or were stowed out of sight under the lee of the boats; the first lieutenant, as if captivated by the serenity of the scene, was leaning with folded arms on the weather-gangway, looking abroad upon the ocean, and whistling now and then, either for a wind or for want of thought. The only being who showed sign of life was the man at the wheel, and he scarcely moved, except now and then to give her a spoke or two, when the cheep of the tiller-rope, running through the well-greased leading blocks, would grate on the ears as a sound of some importance; while in daylight, in the ordinary bustle of the ship, no one could say he ever heard it.

Three bells!—"Keep a bright look-out there," sung out the lieutenant.

"Ay, ay, Sir," from the four look-out men, in a volley.

Then from the weather-gangway, "All's well," rose shrill into the night air.

The romance of the sea is a strange thing. It manages to cling to some extent to everything that floats. —C. Fox Smith

Buy a boat, and you buy the sea

And so by adventure he [Sir Launcelot] came by a strand, and found a ship, which was without sail or oar. And as soon as he was within the ship, there he felt the most sweetness that ever he felt; and he was fulfilled with all things that he thought on or desired.
—from *Le Morte d'Arthur*, Sir Thomas Malory

To my mind, unless one's spirit soars at the sight of a boat, unless one instantly sees oneself at its helm under a blue sky with porpoises leaping alongside, it just won't do. —Arthur Beiser

**Why there's pleasure in messing about in boats,
according to Ratty in Kenneth Grahame's *Wind in the Willows***
In or out of 'em, it doesn't matter. Nothing seems really to matter, that's the charm of it. Whether you get away or whether you don't; whether you arrive at your destination or whether you reach somewhere else or whether you never get anywhere at all, you're always busy, and you never do anything in particular; and when you've done it there's always something else to do…

You are not going to find the ideal boat. You are not even going to have it if you design it from scratch. —Carl Lane

But you can still try, and here's how
Study the area in which you will be sailing.
Select a boat that suits it.

4

You have a great deal of pleasure before you
Go poking around until you find just the boat you want. This one will not be on the market. Keep on until you find another. The price on this will be just twice what you want to pay. The fifth boat, somewhere near your requirements, may be for sale at a reasonable price. Go over her carefully, keeping before you your ideal, and try to convince yourself that this boat is it. Usually you can do this. Remember how well you hope she will look swinging off your favorite club and don't look too closely at her timbers.

Poke around her garboards and butts with a penknife. If the knife goes in so far you can't get it out, you may assume the wood is soft. A little streak of rust down the side means a nail is rusting, but then, think how many other nails are in her. Ask your wife how she likes the cabin decoration finish. Then ask her what finish she wants put on in place of what is there. Ask the yard owner how much this will cost. Ask the former owner why he is selling the boat. Make him sign something to this effect. Ask him how fast she goes. Divide by 1.3. Ask him how much gas she burns. Multiply by 1.3. Ask him what he really expects to get for the boat. Laugh, and walk away. —Colonel O.C. Pelletier

*How serious could a man become about boats and still function and
succeed in everyday society?* —Anthony Bailey

E.F. Knight's general principles, published in 1894, on the buying of a yacht

The size has to be determined upon; but this can soon be done by refer-
ring to the length of the purse out of which the funds for keeping the
yacht in commission are to be supplied.... Though the original outlay
may have been small ... it would be dear at any price should money not
be forthcoming to meet the annual expenditures.

Find out what kind of yachtsman the owner of the yacht for sale is—
that is, if he is a man who has made yachts and yachting his sole hobby, and
has therefore been in the habit of keeping his vessels in the best condition.

One way to determine the right boat for you is to buy the wrong one.

—anon.

How to determine which boat is for you

Ask around the waterfront.

Read a range of books by a range of authors.

Sail on a variety of boats, owned by a variety of sailors, in a variety of
conditions.

Listen to your inner ear, then discount half of what you hear.

How NOT to determine which boat is for you

Consider the word of the yacht broker as absolute.

Believe the results of a "boat test" published in a popular boating consumer
magazine.

Take literally the claims in advertisements.

It is easier to buy a boat than to sell one.
—William Atkin

Assessing a boat with a view toward purchase

Be suspicious if the paint is new, especially at the end of the season.

Close all openings—hatches, ports, ventilators, etc.—for a few hours.
Then go below decks. If the air smells bad, the boat is probably bad.

Determining whether a boat being considered for purchase leaks
If the bilgewater is fresh and clear, she leaks.
If the bilgewater is dirty and dank, she doesn't.

Determining if the bilgewater in a leaky boat afloat in salt water is coming from above or below
Taste it.
If it is very salty, it is coming through the bottom.
If it is fresh, it is coming down from the deck.
If it is brackish, it is coming from both directions.

A few boat-buying NEVERs, according to Carl Lane
Never buy a boat that is too large or too expensive for your purse.
Never buy a boat designed for fresh water for use on salt water.
Never buy a boat whose length, beam, or underwater shape has been tampered with.
Never buy a boat that has suffered from dry rot for any length of time.
Never buy a boat without knowing her history.
Never buy a boat without interviewing people who have sailed her.
Never buy a boat without checking for liens and attachments.
Never buy a boat without surveying her.
Never buy a boat without taking her for a trial sail.

A few thoughts on buying a used boat
The best time to buy a boat is at the end of the summer, when the sellers are looking to avoid winter layup and storage expenses.

Look first at boats you know, or ones that are owned by people you know.

If a boat is not the size and type for you—if she is an open boat, for example, and your heart is set on one with accommodations—walk away and don't look back. No matter how charming she may be, she is not for you and never will be.

Before responding to advertisements, visit as many boatyards as possible and examine the boats offered for sale that interest you.

Pay special attention to boats that are new to the market.

Boats old to the market are likely to have problems that have precluded their sale; on the other hand, their owners are more likely to negotiate a lower price.

The higher-priced boats may very well be the cheapest in the long run.

Generally speaking, an older boat of excellent design and construction will be more worthy of consideration than a new boat of mediocre or poor design and construction.

A boat owned by someone who knows boats and takes good care of them will always be worth more than one owned by someone who does not.

Try to find out why the present owner is selling, as it will say a great deal about the boat.

Examine the boat thoroughly.

Seek advice, check out the source of the advice, look into the history of the boat, ask around.

Do not succumb to the heat of the moment.

Do not surrender to pressure from the seller. Especially do not fall for the classic story—usually bogus—that there's another buyer about to write a check.

The condition of the mechanical gear is often an indication of the amount of care a boat has been given. Look at the shackles, blocks, windlass, winches, the fittings of the head. If they have been freshly greased and oiled, the owner has been paying attention to routine maintenance.

When you make an offer on a boat, indicate in writing that the purchase is contingent on a survey and on financing, if necessary. Make clear that any deposit must be returned if the survey is not satisfactory, and that you, the buyer, will be the final judge of what constitutes "satisfactory." Then, if the offer is accepted, have the boat surveyed.

If the boat is in the water, have the boat hauled and surveyed out of the water.

Do not accept the results of a previous survey—that is, one commissioned by the seller or a buyer who subsequently backed out.

The choice of a surveyor is as important as the choice of a boat to buy. Hire only a surveyor who has been recommended by several people you trust. Do not rely only on the recommendation of the yacht broker representing the seller. Do not allow the seller to select the surveyor.

If you trust the surveyor enough to hire him, heed what he says.

Let your mind make the final decision, not your heart.

A few thoughts on yacht brokers and surveyors

The yacht broker is involved in the sale of the boat, not the determination of its condition.

The surveyor is involved in the determination of the condition of the boat, not its sale.

Never confuse one with the other. Take with a grain of salt the broker's word on the condition of the boat and the surveyor's estimate of the value of the boat.

A conventional yacht broker represents the seller, not the buyer. When push comes to shove, the seller's interest will always come first in the mind and actions of the broker. As a buyer, never fool yourself into thinking otherwise.

A buyer's broker represents the buyer, not the seller. If you engage the services of a buyer's broker, put the agreement in writing.

A surveyor represents the person who hires him. When buying a boat, always hire your own surveyor; do not ask the broker to hire one for you.

Surveyors are paid by fee, usually based on an hourly or daily rate, plus expenses. The fee is payable whether or not the sale goes through.

Yacht brokers are paid by commission as a percentage of the sale price. No sale, no commission. The greater the sale price, the larger the commission.

The yacht broker's commission is paid by the seller, not the buyer.

As a buyer, when in doubt about conflicting reports on the condition of a boat from the broker and the surveyor, take the word of the surveyor.

The three basic types of boat survey

Pre-survey survey—A superficial look at the boat where she lies. Undertaken by the prospective buyer if knowledgeable, or a trusted adviser if not, to determine if the boat is worth buying and therefore justifies the expense of hiring a professional surveyor. It would include at the least looking into all the lockers, below all the floorboards, behind bunks and other cabin furniture, into the engine compartment, forepeak, lazarette, etc.

Simple structural survey—This would involve hauling the boat to inspect the keel, deadwood, stem, rudder, and propulsion gear. Also lifting some of the fixed floorboards, ceiling, etc.

Complete survey—Undertaken by a professional to determine the true condition of all aspects of the boat (hull, rig, accommodations, engine, electrical and plumbing systems, etc.) and whether that condition justifies the purchase price. Includes, if necessary, pulling and inspecting keelbolts, removing plank fastenings, and dismantling engines and other machinery.

DO NOT buy a boat on the basis of a pre-survey survey or simple structural survey alone.

Surveying tools recommended by Ian Nicolson
Brad awl (use the handle for tapping)
Cork for protecting yourself from the tip of the brad awl
Long, thin electrician's screwdriver
Medium-weight ball-peen hammer
Lightweight (4 oz) tack hammer
Plug-in portable mechanic's light with long cord
Heavy-duty flashlight
Chalk or felt-tip pen with washable ink for marking defects
DO NOT USE A POCKET KNIFE and go easy with the pointy end of the brad awl.

A few options if you must have a yacht that is too large for your means
Buy and maintain her in partnership with one or two others.
Charter her out for part of the season.
Use her one season, charter her out for the next.

Keep this in mind
The bigger the boat,
The deeper the draft,
The fewer the waters available to her.

The most desirable characteristics of a yacht, generally speaking
Coastal cruising—speed and windward ability
Offshore passagemaking—seaworthiness and seakindliness

For comfortable cruising on a limited budget, you want
A comfortable bunk
Tight decks
Dry stowage space
A good galley stove

For comfortable cruising on a limited budget, you don't want
A generator
Air-conditioning
Television
Pressure hot water

The length of a man's boat should equal his age.

—anon.

All boats are compromises. A good boat makes good compromises;
a bad one does not.

—Fred Brooks

Buying from fads, according to Thomas Fleming Day

I once knew a lady who would not buy a house, because she did not like the way in which the halls between the rooms were painted. Some yachtsmen are just as bad. Last year I met a young fellow who wanted a knockabout with a white enameled cabin. He refused to take several, because they lacked this inside coating. Others will be caught by a lot of brass or gaudy cushions and curtains. Nicely varnished spars, parceled backstays, and immaculate sail covers are other and successful traps. Others will buy a boat because a friend has one like it.

Which brings to mind this ...

Finish is one thing; performance is another. To be satisfying to a sailor, a good boat should provide comfort, elbow room, a reasonable turn of speed, handling ease, and safety. That's because when push comes to shove, the boat itself will see you through a foul day at sea—not the depth of the varnish, or the brightness of the brass, or the freshness of the paint.

Many times, beauty is the difference

N̶othing can deface the beauty of a ship.
                                    —Joseph Conrad

Ever in my ears roared the bow-wave
And pattered the water-drops blown ahead along the sea,
As the cutwater swung high into the air,
And then plunged crashing onwards and down.
I thought, "A ship is a very beautiful thing,
Wrought by man's hands indeed,
But beloved of God for its beauty."
                —from "A Ship Seen from the Jib-boom," by H.G. Dixey

Just as beauty in woman creates allure and inspires affection, so it does
in a boat.   —William Snaith

The most beautiful work, according to Basil Lubbock
There have been many discussions as to which of Nature's beauties
should be awarded the palm. Some have lauded the snow-capped mountain peak; others the giant forest tree; others again the glories of sunrise
or sunset, the charm of running water or the grandeur of the breaking
wave. But as regards the works of man, all old-time votes were invariably
given to the sailing ship.

The practical side of beauty, according to L. Francis Herreshoff
Perhaps the greatest difference between the beautiful yacht and the plain
one is the way their crews treat them, for the crew of the beautiful yacht
usually gives her tender loving care. They realize that all of their work will
show to advantage, while the crew of the plain yacht has learned from
experience that nothing they can do will help much, for the sailorman at
heart is still a romanticist. The beautiful yacht is handled most carefully
by the yard men when she is hauled out and launched. She is stored in
the best location in the yard, so that after ten or fifteen years the handsome yacht may sell for almost as much as she cost new, while her plainer
sister is nearly junk.

*The perfection of a yacht's beauty is that nothing should be there for
only beauty's sake.* —John MacGregor

These things create beauty in a boat
Continuously curving lines
Harmonious proportions
Symmetry
Deck furniture and houses in proportion and character with the hull type
Harmonious color combinations
The rake of the masts
The shape of the stern
The shape of the bow

The bow of a boat, as seen by John Ruskin
One object there is still, which I never pass without the renewed wonder of childhood, and that is the bow of a Boat. Not a racing-wherry, or revenue cutter, or clipper yacht; but the blunt head of a common, bluff, undecked sea-boat, lying aside in its furrow of beach sand. The sum of Navigation is in that. You may magnify it or decorate it as you will: you do not add to the wonder of it. Lengthen it into hatchet-like edge of iron—strengthen it with complex tracery of ribs of oak—carve it and gild it till a column of light moves beneath it on the sea—you have made no more of it than it was at first. That rude simplicity of boat plank, that can breast its way through the death that is the deep sea, has in it the soul of shipping. Beyond this, we may have more work, more men, more money; we cannot have more miracle.

It is undeniable that the beauty of a yacht depends more on her sheer than on any line in the ship.   —Douglas Phillips-Birt

The different types of sheer
Normal, or concave—the sheerline starts high at the bow, sweeps low at or near amidships, and rises to the stern.
     Straight—the sheerline is straight or nearly so.
     Hogged, or convex, or reverse—the sheerline starts low at the bow, rises high at or near amidships, and declines to the stern.
     Powderhorn—the sheerline starts low at the bow, rises high about one-third the length aft of the bow, sweeps low to about two-thirds of the distance aft, and then either runs straight or rises slightly from there to the stern.
     No matter the type, a sheerline cannot be beautiful if it is not fair.

A small sailing craft is not only beautiful, it is seductive and full of strange promise and the hint of trouble.   —E.B. White

When the seven wise men of Greece delivered the oracular dictum that there are only two beautiful things in the world, women and roses, and only two good things, women and wine, they spoke according to their limited experience—they had never seen a racing yacht under sail.

—Sir Edward Sullivan

The satisfaction of beauty, according to L. Francis Herreshoff

While it may be true that some naval architects today think the secret of success is to get orders and collect commissions, I advise the young designer to create something beautiful as a much surer means of success, for not only will this give him the finest of all advertisements but, best, it will give him lasting satisfaction.

No one likes an ugly boat, however cheap or fast.

—Roger Duncan

The number of yacht designers able to turn out a beautiful boat can be counted on the fingers of one hand.   —Hervey Garrett Smith

The most beautiful of all, the nineteenth-century clipper ship

*N*ever, *in these United States has the brain of man conceived, or the hand of man fashioned, so perfect a thing as the clipper ship. In her, the long-suppressed artistic impulse of a practical, hard-working race burst into flower. The* Flying Cloud *was our Rheims, the* Sovereign *of the* Seas *our Parthenon, the* Lightning *our Amiens; but they were monuments carved from snow. For a brief moment of time they flashed their splendor around the world, then disappeared with the sudden completeness of the wild pigeon.* —Samuel Eliot Morison

When I saw her first there was a smoke of mist about her as high as her foreyard. Her topsails and flying kites had a faint glow upon them where the dawn caught them. Then the mist rolled away from her, so that we could see her hull and the glimmer of the red sidelight as it was hoisted inboard. She was rolling slightly, tracing an arc against the heaven, and as I watched her the glow upon her deepened, till every sail she wore burned rosily like an opal turned to the sun, like a fiery jewel. She was radiant, she was of an immortal beauty, that swaying, delicate clipper.... She came trembling down to us, rising up high and plunging; showing the red lead below her waterline; then diving down till the smother bubbled over her hawseholes. She bowed and curveted; the light caught the skylights on the poop; she gleamed and sparkled; she shook the sea from her as she rose. —John Masefield

**The beauty of the American clipper ships,
according to Captain Arthur H. Clark, writing in 1910**
Judged by any standard of beauty, the American clipper ships were handsome, noble-looking vessels. During the past fifty years I have seen many fleets of men-of-war and merchant ships, besides naval reviews, and at various times the squadrons of yachts that gather each summer in Cowes Roads and Newport Harbor, but I have never seen a collection of vessels which could compare in stately beauty with the fleet of American clipper ships which lay in the harbor of Hong-kong during the autumn of 1858.

*Built for freight, and yet for speed,
A beautiful and gallant craft.*
　　　　　　　—Henry Wadsworth Longfellow

**The four principal imperatives leading to the development
of the clipper ship**
Opium
Tea
Silk
California gold

The four types of nineteenth-century clipper ship
Baltimore clipper
American-built China clipper
American-built California clipper
British-built tea clipper

The eight major American clipper shipbuilding centers
New York, New York
Boston, Massachusetts
Medford, Massachusetts
Newburyport, Massachusetts
Portsmouth, New Hampshire
Portland, Maine
Bath, Maine
Rockland, Maine

Origin of the word "clipper"

The noun "clipper" is generally thought to have originated in the verb
"to clip," as in, to move swiftly ("clip right along").

The first recorded use of the word "clipper" in reference to a sailing
vessel was in 1819, when a waterman, on seeing the yacht *Transit* under
sail on the River Thames, London, England, exclaimed, "My God, what
a clipper!"

Contemporary [1850s] definition of a clipper ship

Clean, long, smooth as a smelt. Sharp arching head. Thin, hollow bow;
convex sides; light, rounded and graceful stern. A genuine East India-
man or Californian. Aloft, large built, iron-banded lower masts; taunt,
tapering smaller masts, long-proportioned spars from lower to skysail
yards. Above board, she towers up with strong, fibrous arms spreading a
cloud of canvas to the gale.

The clipper *Ariel*, according to her skipper, John Keay

Ariel was a perfect beauty to every nautical man who saw her: in symmetrical grace and proportion of hull, spars, sails, rigging and finish, she sat-
isfied the eye, and put all in love with her without exception. The curve of
stem, figurehead, and entrance, the easy sheer and graceful lines of the
hull, seem grown and finished as life takes shape and beauty: the proportion and stand of her masts and yards were all perfect. On deck there was
the same complete good taste: roomy flush decks with pure white bul-
wark panels, delicately bordered with green and minutely touched in the
center with azure and vermilion. She had not topgallant bulwarks (her
main rail was only three feet high), but stanchions of polished teak, protected by brass tubing let flush.

Accommodations aboard the clipper ship *Challenge* of 1851, in her day considered one of the most splendid of all sailing ships

The great cabin contains six staterooms, &c., and is wainscotted with
oak and rose-wood, set off with elliptically arched panels, relieved with
oak pillared pilasters, and enameled cornices, ornamented with exquisite
carving. The corners of the beams are also fringed with beautiful carving,
and edged with gold. The transom forms a semi-circular sofa, and forward there is another sofa, both covered with rich green and gold bocatel.
In the forward partition is a splendid mirror, which gives a reflected view
of the cabin abaft it. In every stateroom there is a deck and side light, and
the cabin furniture throughout is in perfect keeping with her other
appointments....   —from the Boston *Daily Atlas*

A really fast clipper

Much has been made of the speed through the water of the clipper ships, but little is said about the sometimes frantic speed of building many of these vessels. The great demand for clippers in the years 1850 to 1855, primarily caused by the California Gold Rush, put tremendous pressure on the shipyards. The 1,100-ton *John Bertram*, for example, was launched by the Ewell & Jackson yard of East Boston, Massachusetts, sixty-one days after her keel was laid; a month later, she was on her way from Boston to San Francisco with a full cargo.

Fast as a whippet and comfortable to boot,
from a contemporary description of the clipper ship *Flying Cloud*

We can only say that more comfortable luxury, more tasteful and costly furniture, more ample ventilation and comfort of every kind, we never knew even in an earth-built packet ship or steamer.

The *Flying Cloud* is just the kind of vehicle, or whatever else it may be called, that a sensible man would choose for a ninety days voyage.

The color scheme of the clipper ship *Flying Cloud*

Black—bowsprit, channels, hull above the copper sheathing
White—deckhouses, rail cap and monkey rail, inside the bulwarks, small boats
Light blue—waterways, tops of deckhouses
Scraped and/or varnished—masts, jibboom beyond bowsprit end, yards, decks

The rapid evolution of clipper ships, bigger and more expensive

1850—*Stag Hound*, 1,534 tons, approximate construction cost $45,000
1851—*Flying Cloud*, 1,782 tons, approximate construction cost $50,000
1852—*Sovereign of the Seas*, 2,421 tons, approximate construction cost $95,000
1853—*Great Republic*, 4,555 tons, approximate construction cost $300,000

A few specifications relating to Donald McKay's clipper ship
Great Republic, as originally built the largest of them all

Length, 325 feet
Extreme beam, 53 feet
Depth of hold, 39 feet
Complete decks, 4
Stowage capacity, 6,000 tons
Hard pine used in her construction, 1,500,000 board feet

White oak, 2,056 tons
Iron, 336.5 tons
Copper (not including sheathing), 56 tons
Canvas for sails, 15,653 yards
Time to build, 50,000 man-days
Crew, 100 men and 30 boys

Clipper ships required sizable crews; the *Sovereign of the Seas* carried
1 captain
4 mates
2 boatswains
2 carpenters
3 stewards
2 cooks
10 boys
80 able-bodied seamen

Books about the clipper ships, the great trio
The Clipper Ship Era: An Epitome of the Famous American and British Clipper Ships, Their Owners, Builders, Commanders and Crews, 1843–1869, by Captain Arthur H. Clark, 1910

American Clipper Ships, 1833–1858, by Octavius T. Howe and Frederick C. Matthews, vol. 1, 1926; vol. 2, 1927

Greyhounds of the Sea: The Story of the American Clipper Ship, by Carl C. Cutler, 1930

A famous captain's famous father
The captain of the British tea clipper *Cutty Sark* was Jock Willis, son of Captain "Old Stormy" Willis, beloved of his crew and immortalized in the halyard chanty "Stormalong":

Stormy's dead, that good old man,
*   To my ay, Stormalong;*
Stormy he is dead and gone,
*   Ay, ay, ay, Mister Stormalong.*

Stormy's dead and gone to rest,
*   To my ay, Stormalong;*
Of all the skippers he was best,
*   Ay, ay, ay, Mister Stormalong.*

We dug his grave with a silver spade,
*   To my ay, Stormalong;*
His shroud of softest silk was made,
*   Ay, ay, ay, Mister Stormalong.*

I wish I was old Stormy's son,
*   To my ay, Stormalong;*
I'd build a ship a thousand ton,
*   Ay, ay, ay, Mister Stormalong.*

I'd load her deep with wine and rum,
*   To my ay, Stormalong;*
And all my shellbacks should have some,
*   Ay, ay, ay, Mister Stormalong.*

***Cutty Sark*'s cargo capacity**

1,375,000 pounds of tea
    or
5,300 bales of wool
    or
1,180 tons of coal
    or
26,300 cases of case oil

Whence the name

The name *Cutty Sark*, Gaelic for "short shirt" or "short shift," comes from Robert Burns's poem "Tam o' Shanter" and refers to the garment worn by the witch Nannie. The vessel's figurehead depicts Nannie in her short shift, her arm outstretched to catch the tail of the horse on which a farmer, the subject of the poem, is trying to escape.

Her cutty sark, o' Paisley harn
That while a lassie she had worn
In longitude tho's sorely scanty
It was her best, and she was vauntie.
            —Robert Burns

In the nineteenth century, the word "cutty" alone referred to a short, stumpy smoking pipe, as:

Hey, sailor, what do you smoke?
"In harbors and in fine weather I smoke a long pipe; in fresh weather I
    smoke a cutty, and when it blows a gale of wind I chew."
And, we hope, spits to leeward.

Clipper ships achieved high speeds at sea when certain conditions coincided, according to Carl Cutler

The vessel was lightly loaded to her best sailing marks.
    and
The ship's bottom was clean and smooth.
    and
The ship was blessed with a steady, following wind with a smoothly
    rolling, powerfully driving sea.

The swift clippers left the ocean behind them with the fine clean wake of a surgeon's scalpel, marking the smoothness of their passage. Art, and supreme art it was, and nerve and skill, went into their sailing.

—Felix Riesenberg

The fastest clipper ships, nautical miles per hour

22 knots—*Sovereign of the Seas,* 1854, on a voyage between London, England, and Sydney, Australia

21 knots—*James Baines,* June 18, 1856, several hundred miles west of Cape Horn

20 knots—*Champion of the Seas,* December 12, 1854, average speed over twenty-four hours

The fastest clipper ships, average nautical miles per hour sustained over a ten-day period

15½ knots—*Lightning,* August 1854, east of Australia

11 knots—*Sea Witch,* May–June 1847, on a passage from China to New York

The fastest clipper ships, nautical miles run in twenty-four hours

465 miles—*Champion of the Seas,* December 12, 1854, west of Cape Horn

449 miles—*Flying Scud,* November 6, 1854, South Atlantic

438 miles—*Marco Polo,* January 7, 1854

436 miles—*Lightning,* March 1, 1854, North Atlantic

The magnificent clipper ship *Lightning* gets up to speed, according to a contemporary description

Not a ripple curled before her cutwater, nor did the water break at a single place along her sides. She left a wake straight as an arrow, and this was the only mark of her progress. There was a slight swell, and as she rose, one could see the arc of her forefoot rise gently over the sea as she increased her speed.

***Lightning*'s specifications**

Length, 244 feet overall

Beam, 44 feet

Depth, 23 feet

Length of poop, 92 feet

Length of main saloon, 86 feet

Headroom between decks, under the beams, 8 feet

Mainmast, deck to truck, 164 feet high

Main yard, 95 feet long

Sail area, 13,000 square yards

**The afterguard on the *Lightning* lived well,
according to a contemporary description**

There is a spacious house over the wheel, designed, in part, for a smoking room, and it also protects a staircase on the starboard side, which leads to the captain's stateroom and the after cabin. The after cabin is 34 feet long, 12 wide, and 7 high, and is wainscotted with mahogany, enamel, polished ash, and other fancy woods, relieved with rosewood pillars, papier maché cornices, and flowered gilding.... A more beautiful cabin or one more richly furnished we have never seen.

**From the clipper ship *Lightning*'s abstract log on the day
of her record run**

March 1 [1854]—Wind S., strong gales; bore away for the North Channel, carried away the foretopsail and lost jib; hove the log several times, and found the ship going through the water at the rate of 18 to 18½ knots per hour; lee rail under water, and the rigging slack; saw the Irish land at 9:30 p.m. Distance run in the twenty-four hours, 436 miles.

"Speed on the ship!"

—John Greenleaf Whittier

Factors contributing to speed
Long waterline length
Low wetted surface
Smooth, clean hull
Hydrodynamic appendages
Properly cut, set, and trimmed sails
Steady hand on the helm
Knowledgeable and well-trained crew
Skipper with a cool head and steely nerves

Conjecture versus scientific measurement, according to Claud Worth
A few days before starting on a cruise we dined with Green's uncle, a
retired Naval officer. We told him about a very smart run which *Foam* had
made from Weymouth to the Needles, and Green estimated the speed at
eight and a half knots. A day or two afterwards a box arrived at Green's
lodgings containing a log-ship [chip log] with line, reel, and sand-glass.
Foam was faster than most yachts of her size. All day, with a strong southwest wind she travelled at very nearly her maximum speed. We hove the
log several times. On one occasion only her speed just reached six knots.
A log-ship is a most instructive instrument.

The chip log, for determining speed
A light line 150 fathoms long is rolled on a reel.
    Fastened to the end of the line with a bridle is a chip—a pie-shaped

sector of wood, a quarter of a circle with a radius of about 6 inches, weighted on the circular side, and fitted with a socket and toggle.

A piece of bunting is tied to the line at a point 15 fathoms from the chip; this segment of line from the chip to the bunting is called the stray line.

From the bunting, the line is marked at 47-foot, 3-inch intervals with a knot for each division; i.e., the first division is marked with 1 knot; the second, at 96 feet, 3 inches, with 2 knots, etc. These main divisions are called knots.

Within the main divisions, there are five subdivisions, each representing two-tenths of a knot, marked off with white bunting.

Three men are required to heave the log.

One man holds the reel so the line can run freely, one man heaves the chip over the stern and tends the line, and one man watches the log glass.

The log glass is a sandglass timed to 28 seconds.

The log line runs out over the stern of the vessel. When the bunting at the end of the stray line crosses the taffrail, the log glass is inverted to begin the timing sequence. When the sand runs out in the glass, the log line is seized at the taffrail.

The mark at the taffrail at this very moment indicates the speed of the vessel in knots and, by interpolation, tenths.

For example, if the mark is between 3 and 4 knots, halfway between the second and third pieces of white bunting, the speed of the vessel is 3.5 knots.

When running before a heavy sea, the vessel will make greater speed than indicated; add 1 mile for every 10 knots run out.

Driving into a heavy sea, the vessel will make less speed than indicated; subtract 1 mile for every 10 knots run out.

To retrieve the chip, the line is given a sharp jerk, which frees the toggle from the socket and causes the chip to lie flat on the water; the line can now be hauled in and reeled up.

The Dutchman's log, for determining a small boat's speed
Choose an arbitrary point at the bow and another at the stern, and measure the distance between them.

Drop a chip—a small block of wood—in the water at the point at the bow and, using a watch with a second hand, determine the amount of time required for the point at the stern to pass the chip.

Plug the numbers into the formula: distance in feet, divided by time in seconds, times .6, equals speed in knots.

Thus, if the distance between points is 18 feet, and the time to pass the chip is 3 seconds, the speed is: 18 divided by 3, times .6, equals 3.6 knots.

Quick-and-dirty determination of speed
Tie a block of wood to the end of a string that is precisely 84.4 feet long. Toss the block overboard while holding tight to the bitter end of the string. With a stopwatch, determine the time in seconds it takes for the string to go taut.
The number of seconds divided into 50 will indicate speed in knots. (For example, if the elapsed time is 10 seconds, the speed is 5 knots.)

To count seconds without a watch
Construct a simple pendulum with light line and a small, heavy weight. A 9.8-inch pendulum (measured from the point of suspension to the center of the weight) will produce a swinging period, over and back, of one second. The swinging period of a 39.1-inch pendulum will be two seconds.

Speed-time-distance formulas
Distance = Speed x Time
Speed = Distance/Time
Time = Distance/Speed

Speed, in rough terms
1 knot = 33 yards per minute
2 knots = 66 yards per minute
3 knots = 100 yards per minute
4 knots = 130 yards per minute
5 knots = 165 yards per minute

Speed in feet per minute x .01 = knots
Speed in yards per minute x .03 = knots

Knots versus knots per hour

Sticklers for accuracy never say "knots per hour," but such sticklers are rarely, if ever, nautical men. The seasoned seaman says "knots per hour" without a blush. And we can well now consider that "knot" is merely another term for "sea-mile." —Geoffrey Prout, *Pocket-Book for Yachtsmen*, 1930

Speed conversions

To convert	Into	Multiply by
kilometers/hour	knots	0.5396
knots	statute miles/hour	1.151

Formula for determining the theoretical top speed of a displacement hull

1.4 x Load Waterline (in feet) = maximum speed in knots

Speed in small craft

The reason a sailing dinghy is faster than other craft of comparable size is that her crew acts as shifting ballast and the crew often weighs more than the dinghy itself.

A few winning average speeds for the unofficial Blue Riband, which signified the fastest engine-powered Atlantic Ocean passenger liner of the day

8.2 knots—*Great Western,* westbound, 1838
10.75 knots—*Acadia,* eastbound, 1840
13 knots—*Baltic,* westbound, 1849
14.5 knots—*City of Brussels,* eastbound, 1869
15.5 knots—*Germanic,* westbound, 1876
16.75 knots—*Alaska,* eastbound, 1882
19 knots—*Oregon,* westbound, 1884
21 knots—*City of Paris,* westbound, 1893
22 knots—*Lucania,* eastbound, 1893
25.01 knots—*Lusitania,* westbound, 1909
26.06 knots—*Mauretania,* westbound, 1909
27.91 knots—*Europa,* westbound, 1929
30.34 knots—*Normandie,* eastbound, 1935
35.59 knots—*United States,* eastbound, 1952

The faster the mile, the more it costs.
                                    —R.D. "Pete" Culler

Cut back a bit, save a lot, says Weston Farmer

I point out to you a simple fact: There is no known form of locomotion that pays back such large fuel savings for cutting down speed as does a powered vessel. In most cases, if you cut down speed in a boat by a knot or two, you can usually double your cruising range. Twice as far on a gallon, or half the fuel—think of it either way. What is more, spectacular improvement in fuel economy frequently follows proper load balance. It is perfectly surprising to me how many boat owners haven't the slightest knowledge of why this is true. They'll operate a boat for years with little thought to what makes the craft behave the way she does.

Fast times across the Atlantic, monohull sailing yachts, nineteenth century

21 days—1851, schooner *America,* New York to Le Havre
16 days, 12 hours—1851, sloop *Silvie,* New York to Le Havre
13 days, 21 hours, 55 minutes—1866, schooner *Henrietta,*
    Sandy Hook to Cowes
12 days, 9 hours, 36 minutes—1869, schooner *Sappho,*
    New York to Queenstown

Fast times across the Atlantic, sailing yachts, twentieth century

Year	Yacht	Skipper	Time	Avg. Speed
1905	*Atlantic*	Charlie Barr	12d 4h 1m	10.02 kts
1980	*Paul Ricard*	Eric Tabarly	10d 5h 14m	11.94 kts
1981	*Elf Aquitaine I*	Marc Pajot	9d 10h 6m	12.94 kts
1984	*Jet Services II*	P. Morvan	8d 11h 36m	14 kts
1986	*Royale II*	L. Caradec	7d 21h 5m	15.39 kts
1987	*Fleury Michon VIII*	P. Poupon	7d 12h 49m	16.16 kts
1988	*Jet Services V*	S. Madec	7d 6h 30m	16.71 kts
1990	*Jet Services V*	S. Madec	6d 13h 3m	18.63 kts

All were multihulls, with the exception of the *Atlantic,* a three-masted monohull schooner.

March of the record for nautical miles run in twenty-four hours by a sailing yacht

508.6 (21.19 knots, avg.)—1984, *Crédit Agricole*, catamaran
522.7 (21.78 knots, avg.)—1990, *Jet Services*, catamaran
540 (22.5 knots, avg.)—1994, *Primagaz*, trimaran
580 (24.17 knots, avg.)—1999, *Playstation*, catamaran
687.17 (28.63 knots, avg.)—2001, *Playstation*, catamaran

All these were multihulls. The best distance run in twenty-four hours by a monohull was 467.7 nautical miles (19.49 knots, avg.) by *Armor Lux–Foie Gras Bizac* in 2001.

By contrast, any of the mid-nineteenth-century clipper ships, if they could be resurrected (with their skippers and crews), would still be competitive with today's best multihull and monohull yachts. The clipper-ship record of 465 miles was set on December 12, 1854, by *Champion of the Seas* in the Southern Ocean west of Cape Horn—quite an achievement for a commercial vessel.

March of the record for sailing around the world nonstop in a crewed yacht

1993–94, *Explorer,* catamaran—79 days, 6 hours, 15 minutes,
        56 seconds; average speed 11.35 knots
1994–95, *Enza,* catamaran—74 days, 22 hours, 17 minutes,
        22 seconds; average speed 12 knots
1997, *Sport Elec,* trimaran—71 days, 14 hours, 22 minutes,
        8 seconds; average speed 12.66 knots
2000–1, *Innovation Explorer,* catamaran—64 days, 22 hours,
        32 minutes; average speed 18.45 knots

By contrast, the first person to sail alone around the world nonstop was Robin Knox-Johnston in the ketch *Suhaili*, 312 days (1968–69); average speed 3.6 knots.

The lure of speed

There came a screeching, screaming, piercing whine of an engine worked far beyond its legitimate tolerances. A line of flying spray passed suddenly before us. The noise stopped. The spray fell in sheets to the water's surface. A long, sleek motorboat was revealed in the bright sunlight, rocking gently in the swell. Droplets of water slid down the boat's gleaming black sides; a purple haze hung over it like an ethereal cloud. Sitting in the cockpit, staring straight ahead, was a stranger dressed from head to foot in a hooded jumpsuit of black leather.

—from *The Further Adventures of Expansion Man*,
attributed to C. Mulford Scull, the South Jersey speed demon

The progress of powerboat speed

First over 75 mph—1921, *Miss America II*, driven by Gar Wood, 80.567 mph

First over 100 mph—1931, *Miss America IX*, driven by Gar Wood,
     102.256 mph

First over 125 mph—1937, *Bluebird K3*, driven by Malcolm Campbell,
     126.32 mph

First over 150 mph—1950, *Slo-Mo-Shun IV*, driven by Stanley Sayres,
     160.323 mph

First over 175 mph—1952, *Slo-Mo-Shun IV*, driven by Stanley Sayres,
     178.497 mph

First over 200 mph—1962, *Miss U.S.A.*, driven by Roy Duby,
     200.419 mph

First over 225 mph—1956, *Bluebird K7*, driven by Donald Campbell,
     225.63 mph

First over 250 mph—1959, *Bluebird K7*, driven by Donald Campbell,
     260.33 mph

First over 275 mph—1964, *Bluebird K7*, driven by Donald Campbell,
     276.3 mph

First over 300 mph—1978, *Spirit of Australia*, driven by Ken Warby,
     317.6 mph

Note: In January 1967, Donald Campbell's *Bluebird* broke the 300-mph barrier by achieving 328 mph on Coniston Water, Cumbria, England, but the boat disintegrated at speed and Campbell was killed.

This is what Kenneth Grahame would have written in *The Wind in the Willows* if the Water Rat and the Mole had been in a Gar Wood speedboat instead of a rowing skiff

"Is it so nice as all that?" asked the Mole shyly, though he was quite prepared to believe it as he leaned back in his seat and surveyed the hand-stitched leather upholstery, the instrumentation, the steering wheel, and all the fascinating fittings, and felt the engine's growl vibrate through the hull as the Water Rat flicked the throttle control.

"Nice? Are you kidding? Do you realize what one of these machines can do to you?" yelled the Water Rat with enthusiasm as the boat leaned violently into a high-speed turn. "Believe me, my young friend, there is nothing—absolutely nothing—half so much worth doing as simply blasting around with the engine screaming like a cornered she-lion, the spray gathering astern into shimmering roostertails, and the rushing airstream looping over the windshield to peel back your eyelids and flatten your ears to the side of your head."

The speed at which you travel is a measure of your discomfit.
                                                              —Uffa Fox

The search for comfort afloat

The speed–comfort continuum
More speed = less comfort.
More comfort = less speed.

Why comfort is more than a simple matter of luxury
While a boat might be extremely seaworthy, sooner or later it will
encounter a situation in which it will be badly battered. In such a situation, the comfortable boat will mitigate the inevitable strain on the crew;
the uncomfortable boat will not.

**Generally speaking, what are considered good accommodations
for a cruising boat are usually divided thus**
After part—working
Amidships—sleeping
Fore—personal hygiene and storage

Comfort on a cruising boat
Uncomplicated cabin layout
Provision for privacy, even if only temporary screening
Well-laid-out and -equipped galley
Standing headroom in the galley
Guardrail on the galley stove
Large, easily accessible icebox with a proper drain

Enclosed head, or an open one that can be rigged for privacy, with room
    for the average person to turn around
Stowage space for everything
Wet locker for foulweather gear
Provision for airing bedding and drying clothes
Adequate ventilation of the living space
In cold climates, a solid-fuel heating stove
Screening against insects
Good lighting, both natural and artificial
Plenty to read
Bunks for everyone, with plenty of length and width
Chart table and easily accessible storage for charts
Enough food and water for everyone on board for the expected duration
    of the cruise, with a 25 percent reserve

The nub of it, however, is
A tight deck
A dry bunk
A stove that works

When a lot is too much
In some circumstances, accommodations that are too generous can be a
disadvantage. An extra-wide berth can be a luxury when at anchor in a
snug harbor; at sea in a gale, it can be too wide for you to wedge yourself
in securely. So, too, an open-plan galley—room to roam at anchor, but no
surfaces against which to brace yourself when being tossed around by
high seas.

Cabin layout and decoration, according to Frederic A. Fenger
One should attain the feeling of coziness without turning one's cabin into
a marine hock shop.

*The only way to secure true comfort in one's abode is to have very little or
nothing in it.*   —Weston Martyr

**The evolution of increased accommodation space on sailing yachts,
least to most**
Flush deck
Flush deck with skylights

Short cabinhouse
Long cabinhouse
Cabinhouse with doghouse
Raised deck

Space under all of the above can be further improved with reverse-curve sheer, greater deck camber, or a combination of both. But remember this: When working out an accommodation plan on paper, the outline of the deck in plan view can provide a deceptive vision of the actual available space in the three-dimensional hull.

A solution to the standing-headroom problem, according to E. F. Knight
If one wishes to assume an erect position, one can go on deck.

A headroom rule of thumb
Headroom under the main boom is worth much, much more than headroom in the cabin.

A companionway rule of thumb

An offset companionway is worth much, much more than a companionway on the centerline, as one is much less likely to become brained by the boom when emerging from the hatch.

An equipment rule of thumb

Unnecessary stuff equals unnecessarily constricted space.

A cramped-cabin rule of thumb

Neatness equals roominess.

The living room afloat

Our yachts, with but few exceptions, are simply objects of speed and beauty—there is no demand for strong, healthy and trustworthy craft, but a great demand for fancy work, gewgaw and gimcrack cabin work; all gilt and velvet, nice marble mantelpieces, silver sets, and, in short, all manner of luxurious but nautically useless trash.　　　　　　　—C.P. Kunhardt, 1872

The 146-foot late-nineteenth-century schooner *Ambassadress*, owned by William Astor, from a contemporary description

The main saloon is reached by a broad mahogany stairway, and is one of the most elegant apartments that can possibly be provided on shipboard. Its dimensions are 22 by 24 feet, and it is furnished in walnut, maple, mahogany, and cherry; furniture of a very elaborate description in the way of sofas, lounges, chairs, sideboard, etc., in blue upholstery adorn the room. The carpet is Wilton; the mainmast from floor to ceiling is panelled with mirrors; the smoking room, aft of the saloon, is 11 by 17 feet, finished in maple and oak.

The forecastle of a typical North American deepwater merchant sailing ship in the 1830s, according to W.S. Lindsay, who served his apprenticeship in one

At all times it was a foulsome and suffocating abode, and in bad weather the water and filth that washed about the deck, and among the chests and casks, created the most intolerable and loathsome stench.

Here, however, these fourteen sailors and apprentices slept, washed, dressed, and had their food, except in fine weather, when they took their meals on deck, their food consisting almost entirely of inferior salted pork, beef which was sometimes nearly as hard and unpalatable as the kids [containers] in which it was served, and brown biscuits too often mouldy and full of maggots. To make matters worse, the forecastle of the ship was full of rats, and I have the most vivid recollection of one of these animals on more than one occasion finding its way into the hammock where I slept.

Personal space

No-fooling-around headroom—6 feet, 2 inches
Sort-of headroom—6 feet
Stooping headroom—4 feet, 3 inches
Sitting headroom—at least 3 feet, 6 inches above the seat cushion
Doorway, minimum width of opening—1 foot, 8 inches
Orientation of berth—fore and aft
Width of single berth—21 inches minimum, 36 inches maximum,
     30 inches average
Length of berth, no-fooling-around—6 feet, 2 inches
Length of berth, sort-of—6 feet
Space above berth—21 inches minimum
Seat—at least 16 inches wide, 12 inches above sole
Height of seat back—2 feet, 1 inch
Furniture used while standing—34 to 40 inches above sole
Per-person storage space, minimum—3 feet of shelf, 2 cubic feet of drawer,
     4 inches of hanging locker
Enclosed head—26 inches wide minimum; at least 27 inches from the
     bulkhead in front of the head to the center of the seat

A matter of priority, according to William Atkin

I once designed a big boat for a very wealthy man. In the engines he took a mild interest. In the materials he seemed little interested. In the painting he acquiesced in the whims of his wife. In the furnishing the words of an interior decorator were those of wisdom. But when it came to the toilet rooms, boy, then he shone! Sort of a hobby of his were the toilet rooms: tiled, fitted with showers, hot and cold water, salt or fresh, and push buttons to start the water flowing.

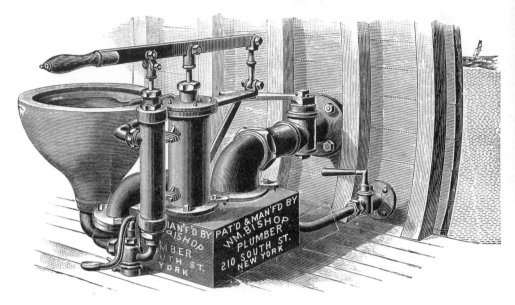

Eliminating wastes, the simplest method to the most complex
Backside over the rail (best on a vessel with no tumblehome)
In a bucket, then over the rail
Seat with a hole in it, mounted outboard, usually in the bow
     (hence the word "head")
Mechanical head with a hand pump
Mechanical head with an electric pump
Conventional toilet above the waterline with shoreside-type plumbing

**Why the marine head is an abomination,
according to L. Francis Herreshoff**
Perhaps I can best describe to you what I think of below-the-waterline
water closets in small boats by quoting a few lines of that poem "A
Sailor's Yarn" by J.J. Roche.
They bored a hole below her line to let the water out,
But more and more, with awful roar, the water in did spout.
     A good pump water closet represents a substantial investment in
money after it is installed with proper copper pipe, fittings, sea cocks,
and all. It requires quite a lot of annual overhauling to prevent freezing
and insure the tightness of all valves and joints. But worst of all, no matter
how much you scrub and polish up around them, they will still have a
certain suggestive odor perhaps from their metal parts or rubber and
leather valve and packings on which the salt water is having a chemical
action. To sit, eat, and sleep beside the toilet is too much for me.

The First Law of the Mechanical Marine Head
Never, Ever, deposit anything in the head that hasn't been eaten first.

The Second Law of the Mechanical Marine Head
Never, Ever, leave the boat unattended with the intake and discharge sea-cocks open; the head can sink your boat.

The Third Law of the Mechanical Marine Head
Never, Ever, go to sea with a head of doubtful condition, as the condition above obtains (the head can sink your boat); when in doubt, have it rebuilt or ditch it.

The Fourth Law of the Mechanical Marine Head
Unless you have a cast-iron stomach, Never, Ever, take the head apart for repairs when you can convince someone else to do it for you, and hang the expense.

Maintaining the head
To revive the seals in a marine head, as well as lubricate the mechanical parts and joints, pour a quarter of a cup of hydraulic oil or cooking oil into the bowl and then flush it.

Six days shalt thou labor
And do all thou art able,
And on the seventh,
Holystone the decks and scrape the cable.

—anon.

Cleaning Ship
by Charles Keeler

Down on your knees, boys, holystone the decks,
Rub 'em down, scrub 'em down, stiffen out your necks,
For we're gettin' near t' home, lads, gettin' near t' home,
With a good stiff breeze and a wake o' shining foam.
Up on th' masts, boys, scrape 'em white an' clean,
Tar th' ropes an' paint th' rails an' stripe her sides with green,
For we're gettin' near t' home, lads, gettin' near t' home,
With a good stiff breeze an' a wake o' shining foam.

The religious doctrine of holystoning the decks

Holystones, also known as ecclesiastical bricks, were used to clean and smooth wooden decks. Legend has it that at one time Britain's Royal Navy performed this task with stone fragments from the ruined St. Nicholas Church in Great Yarmouth, England—hence the name.

Holystoning produced a handsome, snow-white surface on pine decks, but because the technique wore away at the wood, too much of it, too often, eventually made the deck too thin and ruined it structurally.

The larger stones, used for open spaces, were called "bibles."

The smaller ones, for getting into corners and working along the edges of the deck furniture and the rails, were called "prayer books."

The act of holystoning—when the sailors got down on their hands and knees with the stones—was known as "praying."

"Our knees became sore from constant praying," wrote Felix Riesenberg, a hand on the American full-rigged ship *A. J. Fuller* at the turn of the twentieth century, "and the skin on our hands was worn down thin. To overcome the hardness of the deck, we rigged up pieces of board to which three cleats were nailed and a strip of old canvas stretched over them. This afforded a yielding cushion to kneel on and kept our legs out of the water swishing about with the rolling of the ship."

Before the era of detergents and sponges

Sand, to wear away the dirt
Rope-yarn, to apply it with

Cleaning up in the eighteenth century

We scraped our decks and gave our ship a thorough cleansing; then smoked it between decks, and after all washed every part well with vinegar. These operations were extremely necessary for correcting the noisome stench on board, destroying the vermin; for from the number of our men, and the heat of the climate, both these nuisances had increased upon us to a very loathsome degree.   —Captain George Anson

Modern "soogee," the traditional exterior washdown solution

Add a cup of detergent and a cup of bleach to a pail of fresh, hot water. Dip a stiff brush in the soogee and wash down. Clean up with a cotton mop, then flush with cold water.

To whiten decks
Mix one pound oxalic acid with one gallon fresh water.
Apply the solution with a mop, taking care not to get it on nearby
paintwork.
Wash off with fresh water immediately.

To remove a rust stain from a deck
Make a solution of 1 part muriatic acid and 3 parts fresh water. Lay it on
the stain with a brush. Allow to stand for a few hours, then rinse with
clean, fresh water.
—or—
Lay on the stain a clean, absorbent cloth dipped in a 10 percent solution
of hydrochloric acid. Allow the cloth to sit for half an hour, then rinse the
spot with clean, fresh water. The stain will not entirely disappear, but its
intensity will be reduced.

To bleach a wooden deck
Wash with a solution of 1 pound oxalic acid in 2 gallons warm, fresh water.
Before the solution has a chance to dry, rinse the deck with salt water.

To remove an oil spot from a wooden deck
Cover the spot overnight with a dollop of cornstarch. In the morning,
sweep the spot clean. (The cornstarch absorbs the oil.)

To clean the decks of a small boat on an ocean passage, according to Colin Mudie
First you wait for a day on which the seas wash over them. Then take off
your shoes and climb onto the foredeck with a bottle or packet of detergent. Sprinkle the detergent on the deck. The next wave produces a lath-
er and the next sweeps it clean.

Captain Pete Culler's deck oil, for maintaining an uncoated wood surface
1 gallon boiled linseed oil
1 pint turpentine
1 pint pine tar
Mix thoroughly.
Apply liberally with a brush.

To make your own teak oil
Mix equal amounts in volume of 100 percent tung oil and turpentine. Apply with a brush or a soft cloth. Allow to soak in for fifteen minutes, then wipe off excess with a clean, absorbent cloth.

To clean salt off windows
Wash with a mild solution of vinegar and warm water (best), or ammonia and warm water. Windex is also effective.

To maintain plexiglass
Wash with a solution of mild soap and water, using a clean, soft cloth. Do not use abrasive cleaners. Wax the plexiglass to protect it from scratches. Eliminate shallow scratches by rubbing with a soft cloth dipped in jeweler's rouge or toothpaste.

To clean fiberglass
Use nonabrasive cleansers (such as Bon-Ami, and NOT Ajax), a brush with soft synthetic bristles, and a plastic or nylon scrubber.

To remove stains from fiberglass
Rub with a pad dipped in a paste of baking soda and water.

To clean and brighten copper
Rub with a pad dipped in a paste of lemon juice, salt, and flour.

To clean chrome
Wash with apple cider vinegar.

To brighten chrome
Polish with a pad dipped in baby oil.

To remove spots from stainless steel
Wash with vinegar.

To brighten stainless steel
Rub with a pad dipped in baking soda or mineral oil.

To clean and brighten aluminum
Wash with a solution of 2 tablespoons cream of tartar in 1 quart warm water.

A sloppy, ill-kept ship is ever the mark of a poor sailor and an indication of indifference or ignorance or both. —Hervey Garrett Smith

Positioning brass work to facilitate polishing
On square-based fixtures, align the screw heads so the slots all lie in the same direction.

On round- or oval-based fixtures, align the screw heads so the slots lie parallel to the perimeter.

Polish the base of the fixture in the direction of the slots.

(If the screw slots run in all directions, the heads will tear threads from the polishing cloth and the polish will not wipe off cleanly.)

Polishing metal quickly
Dip a clean, soft rag in oil.

Sprinkle the rag with powdered pumice or rottenstone.

Rub the surface briskly.

To remove rust, substitute kerosene for the oil.

Two ways to clean and polish brass that has been unattended for a long time
1. Wash with a solution of 1 part muriatic acid and 1 part water; flush thoroughly with fresh water; polish.
2. Wash with Worcestershire sauce; flush thoroughly with fresh water; polish.

Truly stubborn stains can be helped along with fine bronze wool.

To preserve the shine on newly polished brass and bronze
At sea, buff the surface with automobile paste wax, or any other wax rated for exterior use. The shine should last 50 percent longer than it would if the surface were left unwaxed.

For winter storage, polish the brass when the boat is hauled, then coat it with Vaseline or light machine oil, or spray it with WD-40.

Until you do it all yourself you cannot have any idea of the innumerable minutiae to be attended to in the proper care of a yacht.
—John "Rob Roy" MacGregor

To remove mildew
Make up a solution of 3 parts water, 1 part liquid chlorine bleach (Clorox). Apply with a stiff brush.

To protect against mildew
Spray all surfaces with a colorless germicide, such as Lysol. Ventilate, let the sunshine in, and don't put away anything when it is damp or wet.

Cleanliness and comfort go together in a boat, and scrubbing-brush and swab should not be allowed to get dry-rot by disuse.
—Captain A.J. Kenealy

Sing while you clean, boys, and time will pass faster.
—from an old sea song

The music of the sea

The two types of seagoing music
Sea song—sung when off duty, for entertainment
Chanty—sung during work

A sea song

As I through Sandwich town passed along,
I heard a brave Damsel singing of this song,
In the praise of a Saylor she sang gallantly,
Of all sorts of tradesmen a Seaman for me.

I gave good attention unto her new ditty,
My thoughts it was wonderful gallant and pretty,
With a voice sweet and pleasant most neatly sung she,
Of all sorts of tradesmen a Seaman for me.

Come, all you fair maidens in country and town,
Lend your attention to what is pen'd down;
And let your opinions with mine both agree,
Of all sorts of tradesmen a Seaman for me.

—from "The Seaman's Renown," by T. Lanfiere

The sea chanty
The sea chanty is simply a musical device for keeping time while working on repetitive tasks. Since there are two types of repetitive tasks on board ship—those that require pauses in the rhythm and those that do not—

there are essentially two types of sea chanty. Heaving on the halyards, for example, requires effort and then a pause, effort and then a pause. Pushing on the capstan, on the other hand, requires continuous effort.

And pronounce the word properly

The "ch" sound in chanty is not the same as that in chain or chandlery. Rather, the word is pronounced as if it were spelled shanty, as in a crude shack, and it rhymes with scanty.

The value of the chanty, according to Laura Alexandrine Smith

The chanty is not recreation, it is an essential part of the work on shipboard, it mastheads the topsail yards when making sail, it starts and weighs the anchor, it brings down the main-tack with a will, it loads and unloads the cargo, it keeps the pumps a-going; in fact, it does all the work where unison and strength are required. I have heard many an old salt say that a good chanty was worth an extra hand.

A halyard chanty

O Sally Brown of New York City,
Ay ay, roll and go;
O Sally Brown of New York City,
I'll spend my money on Sally Brown.

O Sally Brown, you are very pretty,
Ay ay, roll and go;
O Sally Brown, you are very pretty,
I'll spend my money on Sally Brown.

Your cheeks are red, your hair is golden,
Ay ay, roll and go;
Your cheeks are red, your hair is golden,
I'll spend my money on Sally Brown.

A windlass chanty

Far aloft amongst the rigging
Stretches out each snowy sail,
Like a bird with outspread feathers
Flies our ship before the gale.
And the billows sweeping past us
Seem to whisper as they flee,
There's a welcome sweet awaits you
In the land where you would be.

Rolling home, rolling home,
Rolling home across the sea,
There's a welcome sweet awaits you
In the land where you would be.

In the event you were thinking that knowledge of sea chanties was dead and gone—a bibliography

The Early Naval Ballads of England, by J.O. Halliwell, Cambridge, England, 1841
Naval Songs, by S.B. Luce, New York, 1883
The Music of the Waters, by Laura A. Smith, London, 1888
Songs of Sea and Sail, by Thomas Fleming Day, New York, 1898
Old Sea Chanties, by J. Bradford and A. Fagge, London, 1904

Sailors' Songs or Chanties, by Ferris Tozer and F.J. Davis, London, 1906
Sea Songs and Shanties, by Captain W.B. Whall, 1910
Shanties and Forebitters, by Mrs. Clifford Beckett, London, 1914
Songs of Sea Labour, by Frank T. Bullen and W.F. Arnold, London, 1915
King's Book of Chanties, by Stanton H. King, Boston and New York, 1918
Capstan Chanteys, by Cecil K. Sharp, London, 1919
Pulling Chanteys, by Cecil K. Sharp, London, 1919
Deep Sea Chanties, by Owen Trevine, London, 1921
The Shanty Book, Part I, by R.R. Terry, London, 1921
Sea Songs and Ballads, C. Fox Smith, London, 1923
Roll and Go: Songs of American Sailormen, by Joanna C. Colcord,
    Indianapolis, 1924
Sea Chanties, by Geoffrey Toye, London, 1924
Songs of the Sea and Sailors' Chanteys, by Robert Frothingham,
    Boston, 1924
Ballads and Songs of the Shanty-Boy, by Franz L. Rickaby, Boston, 1926
The Shanty Book, Part II, by R.R. Terry, London, 1926
The Seven Seas Shanty Book, by John Sampson, London, 1927
A Book of Shanties, by C. Fox Smith, London, 1927
Salt Sea Ballads, by R.R. Terry, London, 1931
American Sea Songs and Chanteys, by Frank Shay, New York, 1948
Shantymen and Shantyboys: Songs of the Sailor and the Lumberman, by
    W.M. Doerflinger, New York, 1951
The Shell Book of Shanties, London, 1952
Sea Songs of Sailing, Whaling and Fishing, by Burl Ives, New York, 1956
*Shanties from the Seven Seas: Shipboard Work-Songs from the Great Days
    of Sail,* by Stan Hugill, London, 1961
Sailor's Songs and Shanties, by Michael Hurd, London, 1965
Shanties and Sailors' Songs, by Stan Hugill, London, 1969

*The three great elemental sounds in nature are the sound of rain,
the sound of wind in a primeval wood, and the sound of outer ocean
on a beach.*   —Henry Beston

The sound of the beach, according to Henry David Thoreau
If I were required to name a sound the remembrance of which most perfectly revives the impression which the beach has made, it would be the dreary peep of the piping plover *(Charadrius melodus)* which haunts

there. Their voices, too, are heard as a fugacious part in the dirge which is ever played along the shore for those mariners who have been lost in the deep since first it was created. But through all this dreariness we seemed to have a pure and unqualified strain of eternal melody, for always the same strain which is a dirge to one household is a morning song of rejoicing to another.

"The Sound of the Sea"
by Henry Wadsworth Longfellow

The sea awoke at midnight from its sleep,
And round the pebbly beaches far and wide
I heard the first wave of the rising tide
Rush onward with uninterrupted sweep;
A voice out of the silence of the deep,
A sound mysteriously multiplied
As of a cataract from the mountain's side,
Or roar of winds upon a wooded steep.
So comes to us at times, from the unknown
And inaccessible solitudes of being,
The rushing of the sea-tides of the soul;
And inspirations, that we deem our own,
Are some divine foreshadowing and foreseeing
Of things beyond our reason or control.

The voice of the sea, according to Henry Beston
The sea has many voices. Listen to the surf, really lend it your ears, and you will hear in it a world of sounds: hollow boomings and heavy roarings, great watery tumblings and tramplings, long hissing seethes, sharp, rifle-shot reports, splashes, whispers, the grinding undertone of stones, and sometimes vocal sounds that might be the half-heard talk of people in the sea.

The music of the rigging, according to John Masefield
The noise of the wind booming, and the clack, clack, clack of the sheet-blocks, and the ridged seas roaring past us, and the groaning and whining of every block and plank, were like tunes for a dance.

The whole package, according to Sir Arthur Quiller-Couch
Patter of reef-points, creak of cordage, hum of wind, hiss of brine—I think at times that she has found a more human language.

Classical music inspired by the sea

Nelson Mass, by Franz Joseph Haydn (1732–1809)

The Water Music, by Georg Friedrich Handel (1685–1759)

Der fliegende Hollander (The Flying Dutchman),
        by Richard Wagner (1813–1883)

La Mer, by Claude Debussy (1862–1918)

Sadko, by Nikolay A. Rimsky-Korsakov (1844–1908)

Ocean Symphony, by Anton Rubinstein (1829–1894)

Sea Interludes in the operas *Peter Grimes* and *Billy Budd,*
        by Benjamin Britten (1913–1976)

Sea Pictures, by Edward Elgar (1857–1934)

Sea Symphony, by Ralph Vaughan Williams (1872–1958)

Oceanides, by Jean Sibelius (1865–1957)

Une Barque sur l'océan, by Maurice Ravel (1875–1937)

There is no music that man has heard
        Like the voice of the minstrel Sea,
Whose major and minor chords are fraught
        With infinite mystery,
For the Sea is a harp, and the winds of God
        Play over his rhythmic breast,
And bear on the sweep of their mighty wings
        The song of a vast unrest.
                    —from "A Sea Lyric," by William Hamilton Hayne

"And what is the sea?"...

"The sea!" cried the miller. "Lord help us all, it is the greatest thing God made! That is where all the water in the world runs down into a great salt lake. There it lies, as flat as my hand and as innocent-like as a child; but they do say when the wind blows it gets up into water-mountains bigger than any of ours, and swallows down great ships bigger than our mill, and makes such a roaring that you can hear it miles away upon the land. There are great fish in it bigger than a bull, and one old serpent as long as our river and as old as all the world, with whiskers like a man, and a crown of silver on her head." —from *The Merry Men,* by Robert Louis Stevenson

I will go back to the great sweet mother,
    Mother and lover of men, the sea.
        —Algernon Charles Swinburne

And I have loved thee, Ocean!
        —Lord Byron

H.M. Tomlinson, essayist, on loving the sea
"I love the sea," a beautiful woman once said to me. (We then stood looking out over it from a height, and the sea was but a sediment of the still air, the blue precipitation of the sky, for it was that restful time, early October. I also loved it then.)

I was thinking of this when the floor of the cabin nearly became a wall, and I fell absurdwise, striking nearly every item in the cabin. Was this the way to greet a lover?

Henry David Thoreau on the sea and the shore

We do not associate the idea of antiquity with the ocean, nor wonder how it looked a thousand years ago, as we do of the land, for it was equally wild and unfathomable always. The Indians have left no traces on its surface, but it is the same to the civilized man and the savage. The aspect of the shore only has changed. The ocean is a wilderness reaching around the globe, wilder than the Bengal jungle, and fuller of monsters, washing the very wharves of our cities and the gardens of our seaside residences.... To go to sea! Why, it is to have the experience of Noah—to realize the deluge. Every vessel is an ark.

The lonely sweep of the sea, according to Juan Baader

If one assumes that two yachts are unable to see each other if they sail 10 miles apart, the oceans of the world would hold one million sailing yachts, which would be unable to see each other if they were correctly spaced out.

The Seven Seas are actually oceans

North Atlantic
South Atlantic
Arctic
Antarctic
North Pacific
South Pacific
Indian

We *are* the sea, says John F. Kennedy

All of us have in our veins the exact same percentage of salt in our blood that exists in the ocean, and, therefore, we have salt in our blood, in our sweat, in our tears. We are tied to the ocean. And when we go back to the sea, whether it is to sail or to watch it, we are going back from whence we came.

The constituents of the average sample of seawater

Chloride, 55.04 percent
Sodium, 30.61 percent
Sulfate, 7.69 percent
Magnesium, 3.69 percent
Calcium, 1.16 percent
Potassium, 1.10 percent
Bicarbonate, 0.41 percent
Bromide, 0.19 percent
Boric acid, 0.07 percent

PASSENGERS ARE REQUESTED NOT TO SPEAK TO THE MAN AT THE WHEEL

Strontium, 0.04 percent
Fluoride, 0.003 percent
Trace elements, less than 0.01 percent

The zones of the ocean

Epipelagic—surface to 650 feet depth, the zone of light penetration
Mesopelagic—650 feet to 6,500 feet, the zone of twilight
Bathypelagic—6,500 feet to 21,000 feet, the zone of darkness
Abyssopelagic—21,000 feet and lower, the zone of blackness

The great irony of the sea
The sea supports the vessels that ply it.
The sea destroys the vessels that ply it.
　　　Contrary to popular thought, the greatest danger to vessels is not
on the open sea, but near the shore, in sight of land.

The opaque beauty of the deep sea, according to Charles Kingsley
Very remarkable and unexpected was the opacity and seeming solidity of
the ocean when looked down on from the bows. Whether sapphire under
the sunlight, or all but black under the clouds, or laced and streaked with
beads of foam, rising out of the nether darkness, it looks as if it could
resist the hand; as if one might almost walk on it; so unlike any liquid, as
seen near shore or inland, is this leaping, heaving plain, reminding one,
by its innumerable conchoidal curves, not of water, not even of ice, but
rather of obsidian.

The sea is the center of everything, according to Xenophanes
The sea is the source of the waters, and the source of the winds. Without
the great sea, not from the clouds could come the flowing rivers or the heav-
en's rain; but the great sea is the father of clouds, of rivers and of winds.

It's not a garbage dump, says Rachel Carson
Although man's record as a steward of the natural resources of the earth
has been a discouraging one, there has long been a certain comfort in the
belief that the sea, at least, was inviolate, beyond man's ability to change
and to despoil. But this belief, unfortunately, has proved to be naive.

And we have much making-up to do, says Alex A. Hurst
"Uglification" is the ugliest word ever coined, but none is more apt to
describe man's effect on the world in the twentieth century and, as he has
despoiled his cities and his countryside, so, on the altars of the Gods of
Progress, he has despoiled his sea.

One doesn't really love the sea itself. It's too impersonal.
It's the ships we love.　　　　　　　　　　—"Peter Gerard" (Dulcie Kennard)

A ship!

Onward she comes, in gallant combat with the elements, her tall masts trembling, and her timbers starting on the strain; onward she comes, now high upon the curling billows, now low down in the hollows of the sea, as hiding for the moment from its fury; and every storm-voice in the air and water cries more loudly yet, "A ship!"

—from *Martin Chuzzlewit,* by Charles Dickens

She seemed to laugh as she ran; seeming to sing, to ripple, as she flew, scattering sea beauties about her, gleaming as stars gleam when frosts are white along far inland meadows. She was a ship.   —Bill Adams

The talk was of ships, says William McFee
The house might not be a ship but it was filled with pictures of ships, with talk of ships, and occasionally with the captains of ships. They would come home with my father as evening fell, these gray-whiskered ship-masters, and the dining room would fill with a blue fog as they drank brandy and water and smoked their pipes and discussed the one subject in which they were interested—ships.

Comparative tonnages of some famous ships
1492, *Santa Maria,* circa 100 tons
1514, *Henri Grâce à Dieu* ("Great Harry"), circa 1,200 tons
1577, *Golden Hind,* circa 120 tons
1609, *Half Moon,* 60 tons

1620, *Mayflower,* 180 tons

1628, *Vasa,* 1,300 tons

1637, *Sovereign of the Seas,* 1,522 tons

1765, HMS *Victory,* 2,164 tons

1768, James Cook's *Endeavour,* 368 tons

1779, *Bonhomme Richard,* circa 900 tons

1789, HMS *Bounty,* 230 tons

1797, USS *Constitution,* 2,200 tons

1831, HMS *Beagle,* 241 tons

1834, Richard Henry Dana's *Pilgrim,* 180 tons

1841, whaler *Charles W. Morgan,* 351 tons

1843, steamer *Great Britain,* 3,270 tons

1846, clipper *Sea Witch,* 907 tons

1851, clipper *Flying Cloud,* 1,782 tons

1851, schooner-yacht *America,* 170 tons

1853, clipper *Great Republic,* 4,555 tons

1860, battleship HMS *Warrior,* 9,210 tons

1869, tea clipper *Cutty Sark,* 921 tons

1874, revenue cutter *Bear,* 1,675 tons

1890, battleship USS *Maine,* 6,650 tons

1895, Joshua Slocum's oyster sloop *Spray,* 12.71 tons

1902, bark *Preussen,* 5,081 tons

1902, seven-masted schooner *Thomas W. Lawson,* 5,218 tons

1906, battleship HMS *Dreadnought,* 17,940 tons

1909, six-masted schooner *Wyoming,* 3,730 tons

1912, liner *Titanic,* 46,329 tons

1914, liner *Leviathan,* 59,957 tons

1923, aircraft carrier USS *Lexington,* 30,000 tons

1932, liner *Normandie,* 79,280 tons

1934, liner *Queen Mary,* 81,237 tons

1938, liner *Queen Elizabeth,* 83,673 tons

1941, battleship *Yamato,* 63,720 tons

1944, battleship USS *Missouri,* 45,000 tons

1951, liner *United States,* 53,000 tons

1962, tanker *Manhattan,* 103,000 tons

1970s, ultra-large crude carriers, circa 475,000 tons

1990s, largest oil tanker in the world, *Jahre Viking* of Norway, 564,000 tons

2004, largest luxury liner in the world, *Queen Mary 2,* 151,400 tons

There is little man has made that approaches anything in nature, but a sailing ship does. There is not much man has made that calls to all the best in him, but a sailing ship does.
—Alan Villiers

The ship as cradle, according to William Wood, 1634

Whoever shall put to sea in a stout and well-conditioned ship, having an honest master and loving seamen, shall not need to fear, but he shall find as good content at sea as on land. It is too common with many to fear the sea more than they need, and all such as put to sea confesses it to be less tedious than they ever feared or expected. A ship at sea may well be compared to a cradle rocked by a careful mother's hand, which though it be moved up and down it is not in danger of falling.

Sailing ships are enchanting, according to John Ruskin

There is not, except the very loveliest creatures of the living world, anything in nature so absolutely notable, bewitching, and, according to its means and measure, heart-occupying, as a well-handled ship under sail in a stormy day.

They are nasty but lovable, says Rex Clemens

The sailing ship was an exacting mistress to serve. She was all that; she was a heartbreaking wench at times, yet none the less a Cleopatra among the sisterhood of the sea, inspiring an affection the lady-like liner is powerless to evoke.

And they are living beings, says Captain Arthur H. Clark

A sailing ship is an exceedingly complex, sensitive, and capricious creation—quite as much so as most human beings. Her coquetry and exasperating deviltry have been the delight and despair of seamen's hearts, at least since the days when the wise, though much-married, Solomon declared that among the things that were too wonderful for him and which he knew not, was "the way of a ship in the midst of the sea."

You give me the choice of my wife or the vessel, I take the vessel.
—Captain William R. Krueger

"Ships!" exclaimed an elderly seaman in clean shore togs. "Ships"—and his keen glance, turning away from my face, ran along the vista of magnificent figure-heads that in the late seventies used to overhang in a serried rank the muddy pavement by the side of the New South Dock—"ships are all right; it's the men in 'em...." —Joseph Conrad

If you wish to study ships, you must also study the men who sail them.
—T. C. Lethbridge

A kiss of a sea-man is worth two of another

—anon., seventeenth century

The sooner [intellectuals] become aware that ships are manned by human beings and not by Hairy Apes the sooner we shall understand each other.
—William McFee, marine engineer and novelist

I yam what I yam.
—Popeye

The making of a sailor, according to Lord Brassey
It is not in books or at the library table that the art of the seaman can be acquired. Quickness of eye, nerve, promptitude of judgment, are the indispensable gifts, which must be gained by long and varied experience at sea.

When we sail with a freshening breeze,
*   And landsmen all grow sick, sir,*
The sailor lolls with his mind at ease.
*   And the song and glass go quick, sir.*
*   Laughing here,*
*   Laughing there,*
*   Steadily, readily,*
*   Cheerily, merrily,*
Still from care and thinking free,
Is a sailor's life at sea.

When the sky grows black and the winds blow hard,
*   And landsmen skulk below, sir,*

The sailor mounts to the topsail yard,
* And turns his quid as he goes, sir.*
*   Hauling here,*
*   Bawling there,*
*   Steadily, readily,*
*   Cheerily, merrily,*
* Still from care and thinking free,*
* Is a sailor's life at sea.*

> —from an old sea song

A good sailor, according to Hervey Garrett Smith

A good sailor hates loose gear, be it rope, boat hook, or bobby pins. He knows that at all times every item of gear not in actual use should be stowed away or secured. He has learned that sheets and halyards must be ready to run clear in an instant, without fouling. He knows he may have to pay out 100 feet of cable in a hurry in a dark night, and is prepared to do so. He realizes that if and when he needs life jackets there will be no time for pawing around in the forepeak or dismantling a made-up berth to get at them. He has a place for everything, and he *keeps* them there, with a catalog in his head. In the most accessible places are the items he will need quickly, and he is darned sure they are ready for instant use.

Hearts of Oak are our ships, Hearts of Oak are our men.

> —from an old sea song by David Garrick

Boy meets the sea for the first time

He hired a rowboat and, while I sat in the stern eating bananas, rowed all up and down the docks. And to me there came a feeling of release, of great freedom. Under the figureheads of ships we passed—figureheads representing women, and warriors, and goddesses. One ship had a red and yellow dragon for a figurehead, I mind. There was scrollwork about the ships' bows, in gold and bright colors. And some of the ships' names were in gold lettering. There was a scent of tar, of cordage, of brine. Sails hung to dry flapped gently in a little breeze. Men high on masts called to one another, in words unintelligible to me. And as we passed under the bow of one great ship a sailor seated beneath her boom called down to me, "Hey, shipmate! How about one of them bananas?" I tossed him one. He caught it, peeled it with a quick jerk, and crammed it whole into his mouth. *"Shipmate!"* A sailor had called *me* "Shipmate"! Ah, I cannot tell you how it was that I felt then!

> —Bill Adams

The true sailor, according to L. Francis Herreshoff

The true sailor is a born artist, a sportsman, and above all a man of good instinct. If this were not so, he neither would have ventured on the water nor could he have stayed above it. His instinct and artistic ability enable him to recognize a good vessel when he sees it, just as a lover of horses can recognize a thoroughbred when he sees it.

The ersatz sailor, Mark Twain model

My traveling outfit [by sea to Hawaii] began with a naval uniform, continued with a case of wine, a small assortment of medicinal liquors and brandy, several boxes of cigars, a bunch of matches, a fine-tooth comb and a cake of soap, and ended with a pair of socks.

A sure sign of a good seaman is the roving eye. The man whose eyes rove is always a good observer. The first thing to look for in a seaman or naviga-tor is the eye, then the hand.
—Conrad Miller

Keep 'em busy, says Richard Henry Dana, Jr.

Nothing is more common than to hear people say, "Are not sailors very idle at sea? What can they find to do?" This is a natural mistake, and, being fre-quently made, is one which every sailor feels interested in having correct-ed. In the first place, the discipline of the ship requires every man to be at work upon something when he is on deck, except at night and on Sundays. At all other times you will never see a man, on board a well-ordered vessel, standing idle on deck, sitting down, or leaning over the side. It is the offi-cers' duty to keep every one at work, even if there is nothing to be done but to scrape the rust from the chain cables. In no state prison are the convicts more regularly set to work, and more closely watched.

The American versus the European sailor, early nineteenth century, according to Alexis de Tocqueville

The European sailor navigates with prudence; he only sets sail when the weather is favorable; if an unfortunate accident befalls him, he puts into port; at night he furls a portion of his canvas; and when the whitening bil-lows intimate the vicinity of land, he checks his way and takes an observa-tion of the sun. But the American neglects these precautions and braves these dangers. He weighs anchor in the midst of tempestuous gales; by night and day he spreads his sheets to the winds; he repairs as he goes along such damage as his vessel may have sustained from the storm; and when at last approaches the term of his voyage, he darts onward to the shore as if he already descried a port. The Americans are often ship-wrecked, but no trader crosses the sea so rapidly. And as they perform the same distance in a shorter time, they can perform it at a cheaper rate.

The English sailors are generally savages.
—Spanish Ambassador to the Court of Henry VII

The five general classifications of European sailors, as defined by themselves, in the age of sail

Limeys—from the British Isles
Dutchmen—of Teutonic origin
Squareheads—from the north
Dagos—from the south
Russian Finns—from the eastern regions of the Baltic

The three categories of men before the mast in the age of sail, in order of rank, lowest to highest
Boys, green hands, and landsmen
Ordinary seamen
Able seamen

Character, above all, says Basil Lubbock
No cleverness of brain or dexterity of finger can make a great painter or musician, and it is the same when you come to deal with the ship and the horse. Whether you are handling a fiddle or the tiller, a bridle or a paint brush, you need certain almost indefinable qualities of character to be really successful; and if you lack these qualities you remain a piano thumper, a paint dauber, a wrecker of ships and a spoiler of horses.

Don't you see the ships a-coming?
        Don't you see them in full sail?
Don't you see the ships a-coming
        With the prizes at their tail?
Oh! my little rolling sailor,
        Oh! my little rolling he
        Blithe and merry might he be.

Sailors, they get all the money,
        Soldiers they get none but brass;
I do love a jolly sailor,
        Soldiers they may kiss my arse.
Oh! my little rolling sailor,
        Oh! my little rolling he;
I do love a jolly sailor,
        Soldiers may be damned for me.

—from an eighteenth-century sea song

An oft-quoted conversation—perhaps apocryphal, perhaps not— between a minister and a sailor
Minister: How long have you been at sea?
Sailor: Twenty years.
Minister: Was your father a sailor?
Sailor: Yes.

Minister: What happened to him?

Sailor: He was drowned at sea.

Minister: And your grandfather?

Sailor: He was a sailor. He was also lost at sea.

Minister: But this is an awful prospect for you, my poor man. Are you not
    afraid to go to sea?

Sailor: Afraid, parson? Where did your father die?

Minister: In bed, of course, like a good Christian.

Sailor: And your grandfather?

Minister: He died in his bed, too.

Sailor: That's bad, parson. Are you not afraid, then, to go to bed?

The sailor's despair and discontent defined

There are two expressions of despair and discontent which come readily
from the lips of a sailorman when things are at their blackest and nothing
seems to come right; when decks are awash and you have spent the whole
of your watch below shortening sail; when the temperature is approaching
freezing-point and the weather door of the galley has been smashed in,
which means no food or hot coffee; when the temperature is round about a
hundred and the fresh water is running short—then some bright specimen
is sure to remark: "The man who goes to sea for pleasure would go to hell
for pastime"; or "Who wouldn't sell a farm and go to sea?"

—Alexander H. Bone

A sailor must be many things, says Herman Melville

He must be a bit of an embroiderer, to work fanciful collars of hempen
lace about the shrouds; he must be something of a weaver, to weave mats
of rope-yarns for lashings to the boats; he must have a touch of millinery,
so as to tie graceful bows and knots, such as Matthew Walker's roses, and
Turk's heads; he must be a sort of jeweler, to set dead-eyes in the standing
rigging; he must be a carpenter, to enable him to make a jury-mast out of a
yard in case of emergency; he must be a sempstress, to darn and mend
sails; a ropemaker, to twist marline and Spanish foxes; a blacksmith, to
make hooks and thimbles for the blocks: in short, he must be a sort of
Jack of all trades, in order to master his own.

The seaman of today, according to William McFee

With his daily newspaper and radio entertainment, his fresh provisions
and comfortable quarters, his library of books and his short waking
hours, his feeling of economic solidarity with all other seafaring men in
the world, his voyages so short by comparison that he is never aware of

the solitude that was the blessing—or the curse—of sea life in the old days, the seaman of today has more ideological identity with the operator of a truck or train than with the Ancient Mariner and Captain Ahab.

Four commonly perceived principal desires of Jolly Jack Tar, the sailorman

Women
Tobacco
Rum
More rum

Bread is the staff of life; rum is life itself

—old sailors' saying

Sailor's rum, defined

Rumbullion—the original word for rum, distilled from molasses,
a byproduct of the refinement of sugar

Bumboo—rum, water, sugar, and nutmeg

Rumfustian—beer, gin, rum, raw eggs, sugar, cinnamon, and nutmeg,
all heated together

Hangman's blood—rum, gin, brandy, and dark beer

Tarantula juice—water, alcohol, burnt peaches, and plug tobacco,
all seasoned in a keg

Screech—water, molasses, yeast, and plug tobacco, all fermented in a keg

Beer, swipes, rum, and grog in the Royal Navy

Before the eighteenth century, sailors in the Royal Navy were given a gallon of beer per day: a quart in the morning, at noon, at the end of the afternoon, and at supper.

Eventually, the beer was watered down—some say to reduce drunkenness, others say to save money. The name for this thin beer was "swipes."

During the eighteenth century, rum was substituted for beer.

Watered-down rum, which became standard in the mid-eighteenth century, was first issued in 1740 by Vice Admiral Edward "Old Grog" Vernon of the British Royal Navy. The admiral's nickname came from grogham, the material of his cloak; the name for his watered rum came to be known as "grog." Officially, in the Royal Navy, grog was the daily one-half-pint rum ration diluted by one quart of water. (From 1850 to 1970, the rum ration was one-quarter pint.)

For grog is our starboard, our larboard,
Our mainmast, our mizen, our log—
At sea, or ashore, or when harbour'd,
The mariner's compass is grog.

—from an old sailor's song

Some sailors named their grog by the points of the compass, thus—
North—pure rum.
North nor'west—two-thirds rum, one-third water
Nor'west—half rum, half water
West nor'west—two-thirds water, one-third rum
West—water, no rum

All hands to the two-by-four, and be snappy about it
The weather grew colder and colder.... The Captain issued rum to all hands outside the charthouse, a large wooden spoonful to each man. This rum was like no other I had ever tasted. It was four over proof and had the same effect as a blow from a heavy stick.   —Eric Newby

Modern grog
Mix together in a medium-size mug:
1 teaspoon molasses
1 tablespoon lemon juice
1½ ounces dark rum
     Top up the mug with boiling water and garnish with a twist of lemon peel and a dusting of nutmeg or cinnamon.

A capitayn sholde lyve in sobrenesse.
—Geoffrey Chaucer

The private cellar of the captain of the Royal Navy ship Argo in 1761
Messina: 1 butt, and 3 kegs containing 40 gallons each
Port: 2 hogsheads
Cyprus: 2 kegs, 1 demijohn and 2 bottles
Champagne: 6 dozen bottles
Burgundy: 12 dozen bottles
Claret: 12 dozen and 7 bottles
Frontenac: 6 bottles

Montepulciano: 1 chest
Florence: 8 chests and a half
Malvasia: 2 chests
Rum: 1 dozen and nine bottles
Beer: 3 dozen and six bottles

The private cellar, a total of more than 600 gallons, of the captain of the Royal Navy ship *Harwich* in 1749
Madeira: 2 pipes, 2 puncheons, and 2 hogsheads
Arrack: 1 puncheon, 3 hogsheads, 1 half-leaguer, and 4 third-leaguers
Rum: 27 gallons, 2 quarts in bottle and cask
Brandy: 20 gallons

Traditional toasts in the Nelsonian era
Sunday night, "Absent friends."
Monday night, "Our ships at sea."
Tuesday night, "Our men."
Wednesday night, "Ourselves (as no one is likely to concern themselves with our welfare)."
Thursday night, "A bloody war or a sickly season."
Friday night, "A willing foe and sea-room."
Saturday night, "Sweethearts and wives (may they never meet)."

On getting the ladies
Candy
Is dandy
But liquor
Is quicker.
    —Ogden Nash

"Sam Swipes"
by Captain Frederick Marryat

Sam Swipes, he was a seaman true,
As bold and brave a tar
As e'er was dressed in navy blue
On board a man-of-war.

One fault he had—on sea or land
He was a thirsty dog;
For Sammy never could withstand
A glass or so of grog.

He always liked to be at sea;
For e'en on shore, the rover,
If not as drunk as he could be,
Was always half seas over.

The gunner, who was apt to scoff,
With jokes most aptly timed,
Said Sam might any day go off,
'Cause he was always primed.

Sam didn't want a feeling heart,
Though never seen to cry;
Yet tears were always on the start—
The drop was in his eye.

At fighting Sam was never shy,
A most undoubted merit;
His courage never failed, and why?
He was so full of spirit.

In action he had lost an eye,
But that gave him no trouble;
Quoth Sam, "I have no cause to sigh:
I'm always seeing double."

A shot from an unlucky gun
Put Sam on timber pegs;
It didn't signify to one
Who ne'er could keep his legs.

One night he filled a pail with grog,
Determined he would suck it;
He drained it dry, the thirsty dog!
Hiccupped, and kicked the bucket.

*To the question, "When were your spirits at their lowest ebb?" the obvious
answer seemed to be, "When the gin gave out."*
                    —Sir Francis Chichester, on his solo circumnavigation of the globe

*Whiskey is the life of man,
    Whiskey, Johnny;
Oh, I'll drink whiskey when I can
    Whiskey for my Johnny.
Yes, whiskey made me sell my coat
    Whiskey, Johnny;
Oh, whiskey's what keeps me afloat
    Whiskey for my Johnny.*
                            —from an old chanty

Drink, in the words of the sailor
Binder—one for the road
Black varnish—bottled stout
Bottle the tot—save the drink for later
Brown food—beer, ale, stout
Bug juice—cocoa
Cape Horn rain; also Nelson's blood; also stagger juice—rum
Chai—tea
Cow—milk
Dead marine—empty bottle
Devil's toothbrush—half brandy, half gin
Giggle water—cocktail
Gimlet—gin and lime
Goffer—any drink with fizz
Gunfire—morning tea
Horse's neck—brandy and ginger ale
Kye—cocoa
Monkey piss—lime juice
Panther piss; also tiger piss—beer
Round-the-world—sherry, gin, whiskey, and brandy, together
Sluggers—sloe gin
Swipes—near beer

Switchel—molasses, vinegar, and water
Thickers—strong tea
Tonsil varnish—low-grade tea
Wallop—beer

Drunk, in the words of the sailor
Anchored in Sot's Bay
Back teeth awash
Bonkers
Carry three red lights (from the lights shown by a vessel not under control)
Cockbilled
Deado
Sewn up
Stitched
Three sheets to the wind
Trimmed down
Under full sail

Serious liquid measures (in imperial gallons)
Pipe of Port, 115
Pipe of Tenerife, 100
Pipe of Marsala, 93
Pipe of Madeira and Cape, 92
Pipe of Lisbon and Bucellas, 117
Butt of Sherry and Tent, 108
Aum of Hock and Rhenish, 30
Hogshead of Claret, 46
Hogshead of Port, 57
Hogshead of Sherry, 54
Hogshead of Madeira, 46
Hogshead of Ale, 54
Butt of Ale, 108

Only fools and passengers drink at sea.
> —Alan Villiers

Demon rum, New England style
It is indispensably become my duty to represent to their lordships that the custom of supplying New England rum to his majesty's ships is in my humble opinion highly prejudicial to the state. The use of it destroys the

health and faculties of the people and debilitates them surprisingly. The seamen always continue healthy and active when drinking spruce beer; but in a few days after New England rum is served, although mixed with four or five waters, the hospital is crowded with sick, and those on board are pallid, weak, and incapable of doing half their duty. I appeal to the captains of the squadron that this is always the consequence of their crews having New England rum.

—from a letter by Vice Admiral Samuel Graves,
Royal Navy, to the Admiralty, September 22, 1775

Serpent's Breath, enough for the entire crew

1 bottle dark rum
1 bottle light rum
1 bottle Cognac
7 cups tea
3 cups lemon juice
1½ cups sugar

Stir the sugar and the lemon juice into the tea, then add the hard stuff. Allow the ingredients to meld for two hours—if you can wait that long.

Ode to the end, in August 1970, of the Royal Navy's daily tot of rum

Most farewell messages try
To jerk a tear from the eye
But I say to you lot
Very sad about tot
But thank you, good luck and good-bye.

—First Sea Lord, to all units of the Royal Navy

A cup of Josephus Daniels

Josephus Daniels was appointed Secretary of the Navy by President Woodrow Wilson in 1913. Among his naval reforms were inaugurating the practice of making 100 Sailors from the Fleet eligible for entrance into the Naval Academy, the introduction of women into the service, and the abolishment of the officers' wine mess. From that time on, the strongest drink aboard Navy ships could only be coffee and over the years, a cup of coffee became known as "a cup of Joe."   —from an official U.S. Navy explanation

Let's talk coffee, in the language of the sailor
Java
Jamoke
Joe
Murk
Mud
Shot
Shot-in-the-arm
Black and bitter—no sugar or cream
Black and sweet—with sugar
Blonde and bitter—with cream
Blonde and sweet—with cream and sugar
Tinned teat—condensed milk

Ersatz coffee
Burnt bread, boiled in water, sweetened with sugar; known by nineteenth-century sailors as "Scotch coffee."

Perfect coffee
To make perfect coffee, just two ingredients are necessary, and only two. These are water and coffee. It is owing to the bad management of the latter that we drink poor coffee.   —Nessmuk (George Washington Sears)

It is hard to make a landsman understand what a cup of coffee means to a sailor at five o'clock on a cold, stormy morning.   —Isaac Hibbard

Coffee, and then some
Breakfast of coffee, eggs, coffee, homemade biscuits, coffee, pancakes, coffee, French toast, coffee, sausage and bacon, coffee. It was a wonder anybody had the strength to get up from the table. Wired from the caffeine? If we had a generator on board we could have hooked everybody up and produced enough juice to operate the ship-to-shore radio for a month.
          —from *A Passage in Time*

If you like your coffee with sand for dregs,
A decided hint of salt in your tea,
And a fishy taste in the very eggs—
By all means choose the Sea.
          —from "A Sea Dirge," by Lewis Carroll

Coffee and the weather, according to the U.S. War Department, 1883
When the bubbles of coffee collect in the center of the cup, expect fair
    weather.
When they adhere to the cup, forming a ring, expect rain.
If the bubbles separate without assuming any fixed position, expect chang-
    ing weather.

Two types of tobacco used at sea during the age of sail
That which was smoked
That which was chewed
    By far the preference among the crew was pipe smoking when it
was permitted and chewing when it was not. Cigars were favored by the
officers, with the pipe running a close second. In the last days of sail, cigarettes, almost always hand rolled, gained a hold on all classes of sailors.
Given the difficulties in keeping specialized varieties on hand, the same
tobacco was often used for pipes, cigarettes, and chewing. This was
almost always "plug" tobacco, sometimes pressed cake, and was personally prepared by the user and wrapped in canvas. The chewer would simply cut off a piece of appropriate size with his rigging knife. The smoker
would cut the plug or cake into thin slices and rub it out between the
palms of his hands—coarse flakes for the pipe, fine flakes for cigarettes.

How plug tobacco was made
Tobacco leaves were soaked in honey, molasses, or other flavored syrup.
A hole was drilled into a baulk of wood—hickory was preferred, but other
species served in a pinch—and the sodden tobacco was forced into it
(hence the word "plug"). Once the tobacco had cured, the plug was
pulled from the hole and wrapped in canvas, ready for use.

A good, all-around seagoing pipe-tobacco blend
Burley, 72 percent
Virginia, 25 percent
Latakia, 3 percent
    To prevent the tobacco from burning too rapidly in windy conditions
at sea, the cut should be coarse—cube, or moderately thick flake. Sliced-
plug or pressed-cake pipe tobacco should not be rubbed out too much.

The finest ersatz tobacco, according to Rex Clements

Tobacco never tastes so good as in the salt air on ship-board, and is almost a necessity of existence in a hard-case "lime-juicer." A pipe of tobacco has often to serve in place of a meal and, rammed well down and glowing red in the bowl of a short clay, makes the cheeriest of companions in the long night watches. [Near the end of the voyage] we felt the loss of it very keenly; the last few plugs changed hands at fancy prices, and when they were all gone our search for substitutes was exhaustive. Ropeyarns, whether manila or hemp, ravelled out, were tried and found very hot and heady; tea-leaves had their votaries, and some hardy spirits experimented with some of the green weed that decorated our waterline, dried in the sun. But the most popular smoke was a combination of ropeyarns, coffee-grounds and the bark off a pork-barrel, rubbed up small and mixed in equal quantities. If it had not the flavour of best Virginia it filled a place and we were thankful.

Nautical books, memorable opening lines

On the day we lost the Cereal Account I finally decided to go to sea.
— *The Last Grain Race,* by Eric Newby, 1956

Houses are but badly built boats so firmly aground that you cannot think of moving them. —Racundra's *First Cruise,* by Arthur Ransome, 1928

"Hello, ship," Jake Holman said under his breath.
The ship was asleep and did not hear him.
— *The Sand Pebbles,* by Richard McKenna, 1962

Proverbially it is not easy to blow and swallow at the same time. So also it is not easy to combine mountaineering and sailing.
—Mischief *in Patagonia,* by H.W. Tilman, 1957

As evening closed in it looked as if we might be in for a dirty night.
— *Swatchways and Little Ships,* by Maurice Griffiths, 1971

We saw her first from the top of the cliff. She turned at her chains to every attack of wind, swaying, airy, and buoyant, as though cut of fragile porcelain on the sea below. She was a two-masted schooner....
— *The Saga of* Cimba, by Richard Maury, 1939

Once upon a time I built a schooner.
— *The Southseaman,* by Weston Martyr, 1926

It was a strange and pleasant life for me all summer, sailing entirely alone by sea and river....
— *The Voyage Alone in the Yawl* Rob Roy, by John MacGregor, 1867

Maritime power is the means whereby we control the sea for our own purposes and deny such control to the enemy.
— *White Ensign,* by Captain S.W. Roskill, RN, 1960

I start from the premise that no object created by man is as satisfying to his body and soul as a proper sailing yacht.
— *The Proper Yacht,* by Arthur Beiser, 1978

Squire Trelawney, Dr. Livesey, and the rest of these gentlemen having asked me to write down the whole particulars about Treasure Island, from the beginning to the end, keeping back nothing but the bearings of the island, and that only because there is still treasure not yet lifted, I take up my pen.... — *Treasure Island,* by Robert Louis Stevenson, 1883

Call me Ishmael.
— *Moby-Dick,* by Herman Melville, 1851

It is as hard to describe the fascination of the sea as to explain the beauty of a woman, for, to each man, either it is self-evident, or no argument can help him see it. — *Yacht Cruising,* by Claud Worth, 3rd ed., 1926

In my part of New England there is a saying that some of the best deals are those you do not make. There is no doubt in my mind that some of the best boats are those which, fortunately, you manage not to buy.
            —*The Thousand Dollar Yacht*, by Anthony Bailey, 1967

I bought a Friendship sloop in the early spring of 1938. She was lying in a boatyard in Flushing, Long Island. Her name was Princess. It was neatly lettered on her transom in the arc of an eyelid. "New York" formed the lower lid. Where you might imagine an eyeball there was a two-inch iron pipe that broke through the lovely oval of her counter. She had been crying, too; the rusty stains dripped down to her water line.
            —Princess–*New York*, by Joe Richards, 1956

The Cup is in fact not a cup at all as its bottom is open.
            —*The America's Cup*, by Ian Dear, 1980

It is the appointed lot of some of History's chosen few to come upon the scene at the moment when a great tendency is nearing its crisis and culmination.
            —*The Life of Nelson*, by Captain Alfred Thayer Mahan, USN, 1897

If you were to discover that someone was attempting to teach the fine points of horsemanship with water buffaloes or camels for mounts, you might be amused or indignant, depending upon your regard for the equestrian art. A not entirely dissimilar situation now obtains in this country with respect to rowing.   —*Building Classic Small Craft*, by John Gardner, 1977

It is perhaps difficult to realize that the true clipper-ship, the fruit of centuries of maritime experiment, was conceived, born, flourished, degenerated and passed away forever, all within the span of an average lifetime.
            —*The Tall Ships Pass*, by W.L.A. Derby, 1937

The Harry F. Sinclair, Jr. *was still afloat and burning a week after she had been torpedoed. Her fo'c'sle was free from flame. Yet men were burned to death because they jumped overboard, and they jumped overboard because they were not prepared.*
            —*How to Abandon Ship*, by Phil Richards and John J. Banigan, 1942

Read all about it

**Watershed nautical literature—sixteen books and two poems that
influenced history or styles, or changed perceptions**
*The Principall Navigations, Voyages, Traffiques and Discoveries of the
       English Nation,* by Richard Hakluyt, 1589
Architectura Navalis Mercatoria, by Fredrik Henrik af Chapman, 1768
An Universal Dictionary of the Marine, by William Falconer, 1768
The New American Practical Navigator, by Nathaniel Bowditch, 1802
Life of Nelson, by Robert Southey, 1813
"Old Ironsides," by Oliver Wendell Holmes, 1830
Two Years Before the Mast, by Richard Henry Dana, 1840
Moby-Dick, or the White Whale, by Herman Melville, 1851
The Physical Geography of the Sea, by Lt. Matthew Fontaine Maury, USN,
       1855
The Voyage Alone in the Yawl Rob Roy, by John MacGregor, 1867
A Manual of Yacht and Boat Sailing, by Dixon Kemp, 1878
The Influence of Sea Power Upon History, 1660–1783, by Captain Alfred
       Thayer Mahan, USN, 1890
Sailing Alone Around the World, by Joshua Slocum, 1900
"Sea Fever," by John Masefield, 1902
The Riddle of the Sands, by Erskine Childers, 1903
Traditions and Memories of American Yachting, by W.P. Stephens, 1946
American Small Sailing Craft, by Howard I. Chapelle, 1951
Rushton and His Times in American Canoeing, by Atwood Manley, 1968

"Old Ironsides"
by Oliver Wendell Holmes (1830)

Ay, tear her tattered ensign down!
*   Long has it waved on high,*
And many an eye has danced to see
*   That banner in the sky;*
Beneath it rung the battle shout,
*   And burst the cannon's roar;—*
The meteor of the ocean air
*   Shall sweep the clouds no more!*

Her deck, once red with hero's blood,
*   Where knelt the vanquished foe,*
When winds were hurrying o'er the flood,
*   And waves were white below,*
No more shall feel the victor's tread
*   Or know the conquered knee;—*
The harpies of the shore shall pluck
*   The eagle of the sea!*

O better that her shattered hulk
*   Should sink beneath the wave;*
Her Thunders shook the mighty deep,
*   And there should be her grave;*
Nail to the mast her holy flag,
*   Set every threadbare sail,*
And give her to the god of storms,
*   The lightning and the gale!*

First-rate seagoing anthologies

Prose
The Call of the Sea, compiled by F.G. Aflalo, 1907
Great Sea Stories of All Nations, edited by H.M. Tomlinson, 1930
A Sailor's Reader, edited by George Macy, 1943
The Book of the Sea, edited by A.C. Spectorsky, 1954

Prose and poetry
The Book of the Sea, edited by Aubrey de Selincourt, 1961
The Flowers of the Sea, edited by Captain Eric Wheeler Bush, RN, 1962
The Oxford Book of the Sea, edited by Jonathan Raban, 1992

Poetry
A Sailor's Garland, selected and edited by John Masefield, 1906
A Book of the Sea, selected and arranged by Lady Sybil Scott, 1918
    (with some prose)
The Eternal Sea, edited by W.M. Williamson, 1946

*Most boating books and magazines of today [1926] are at least 51
percent bunk.*
                                      —John G. Hanna

**Some complaints about the deficiencies of boating magazines
are timeless**
We sadly need good and intelligent descriptions of new yachts and alter-
ations of old ones. Elaborate descriptions of upholstery and mahogany
fittings are all very well, but we want to learn the peculiarities of the
yacht, whether in model or rig, height and position of spars, area of canvas, weight of ballast, and other information which will readily suggest
itself to anyone conversant with the subject.
                           —from a letter by Tom Cringle to
                The Aquatic Monthly and Nautical Review, 1872

Definition of a boating magazine, according to George Putz
Two hundred and seventy pages of ads and thirty pages of editorial, the
latter composed of:
1. An interview with Gosh Hithere, winner of last year's South Shetlands
    to Iceland gas-guzzling Kidney Stomp.
2. A pictorial essay on the *Eagle.*
3. Useful gewgaws you can build yourself with matches and hankies.

4. New Designs, this month featuring the *Yawn,* which showed real
   promise in the Six-Pac.
5. How to retire on your own boat for just $200,000.
6. A list of sail-training programs to which to send your ungrateful brat.
7. Some floozy wearing nothing, holding a stern bearing.

The two major English-language scholarly journals of maritime history
The American Neptune, Peabody Essex Museum, East India Square,
   Salem, MA 01970
The Mariner's Mirror, the International Journal of the Society for
   Nautical Research, c/o National Maritime Museum, Greenwich,
   London SE10 9NF, England

A nautical writer Hall of Fame, twentieth century
All-Century, Cannot Be Topped—Joseph Conrad
Best American, Boating—Joe Richards
Best British, Boating—Maurice Griffiths
Most Entertaining—L. Francis Herreshoff
Most Enthusiastic—William Atkin
Most Inventive—E.H. Morgan
Best Sea Stories, American—Lincoln Colcord
Best Sea Stories, British—"Shalimar" (F.C. Hendry)
Most Entertaining Braggart—Weston Farmer
Brightest Technical Prose—David C. "Bud" McIntosh
Dullest Technical Prose—Howard I. Chapelle
Best Historical, the Grand Sweep—Samuel Eliot Morison
Best Historical, Small Craft—John Gardner
Best Historical, Naval Architecture—Howard I. Chapelle
Best Expository—Hervey Garrett Smith
Hippest—George J. Putz
Artiest—Rockwell Kent
Saltiest—Carl Lane
Most Co-Authors, Books—Basil Greenhill
Most Prolific, Good Books—Alan Villiers
Most Prolific, Bad Books—Bill Robinson
Best Father-and-Son Team—William and John Atkin
Hairiest Chest, Deserved—Uffa Fox

Hairiest Chest, Undeserved—Sterling Hayden
Best Novels, Nineteenth-Century Naval—C.S. Forester
Best Novels, Twentieth-Century Naval—Nicholas Monsarrat
Best Novels, Tugboats—Jan de Hartog
Most Novels, Good But Impossible to Finish—William McFee
Most Novels, Mediocre But Impossible to Put Down—Alistair MacLean
Best Current Reputation, Deserved—Patrick O'Brian
Best Current Reputation, Undeserved—Tom Clancy

The compass of nautical literature

According to a study conducted in the mid-1970s, a catalog at the Naval
Library of the Ministry of Defence in London, England, listed 21,000
marine authors. The library of the National Maritime Museum in Greenwich, England, contained 45,000 books and more than 100,000 plans
and manuscripts; the Nationaal Scheepvaartmuseum, Antwerp, Belgium,
contained 16,000 books, 20,000 plans, and 5,000 maps and manuscripts; the Peabody Museum of Salem (now the Peabody Essex Museum) contained 40,000 books; and the Mariners' Museum, Newport
News, Virginia, contained 45,000 books.

And the curators of those institutions considered their collections
to be far from complete!

A long winter's night's reading list

Down to the Sea, by "Shalimar" (F.C. Hendry), 1937. Short stories of life
at sea; marvelously written and technically accurate.
Cape Cod, by Henry David Thoreau, 1865. A seaside walking tour when
the Cape was the saltiest place on earth.
The Distant Shore, by Jan de Hartog, 1951. Heart-rending World War II
love story involving a Dutch tugboat skipper, an Englishwoman,
and an apartment key.
London River, by H.M. Tomlinson, 1921. Essays on the tidal River
Thames, the docklands, and merchant mariners.
An L. Francis Herreshoff Reader, by L. Francis Herreshoff, 1978. Name a
nautical subject and LFH had an opinion on it.
Endurance, by Alfred Lansing, 1959. Shackleton's self-rescue from
Antarctica; if you think *your* times are tough, drop everything and
read this book.
Three Men in a Boat, by Jerome K. Jerome, 1889. Hilarity aboard a river-
cruising rowboat in Victorian times.
The Seven Seas, by Rudyard Kipling, 1896. Poetry in the swaggering ballad
tradition ("The earth is full of anger, the seas are dark with wrath....")

"The Coastwise Lights"
by Rudyard Kipling

Our brows are wreathed with spindrift and the weed is on our knees;
Our loins are battered 'neath us by the swinging, smoking seas.
From reef and rock and skerry—over headland, ness, and voe—
The Coastwise Lights of England watch the ships of England go!

Through the endless summer evenings, on the lineless, level floors;
Through the yelling Channel tempest when the siren hoots and roars—
By day the dipping house-flag and by night the rocket's trail—
As the sheep that graze behind us so we know them where they hail.

We bridge across the dark and bid the helmsman have a care,
The flash that wheeling inland wakes his sleeping wife to prayer;
From our vexed eyries, head to gale, we bind in burning chains
The lover from the sea-rim drawn—his love in English lanes.

We greet the clippers wing-and-wing that race the Southern wool;
We warn the crawling cargo-tanks of Bremen, Leith, and Hull;
To each and all our equal lamp at peril of the sea—
The white wall-sided war-ships or the whalers of Dundee!

Come up, come in from Eastward, from the guardports of the Morn!
Beat up, beat in from Southerly, O gipsies of the Horn!
Swift shuttles of an Empire's loom that weave us, main to main,
The Coastwise Lights of England give you welcome back again!

Go, get you gone up-Channel with the sea-crust on your plates;
Go, get you into London with the burden of your freights!
Haste, for they talk of Empire there, and say, if any seek,
The Lights of England sent you and by silence shall ye speak!

The Ten Best Books of the Sea, according to a vote taken at the National Marine Exposition in New York, 1920
1. *Treasure Island,* by Robert Louis Stevenson
2. *Two Years Before the Mast,* by Richard Henry Dana, Jr.

3. *The Sea Wolf,* by Jack London
4. *Captains Courageous,* by Rudyard Kipling
5. *Twenty Thousand Leagues Under the Sea,* by Jules Verne
6. *The Cruise of the* Cachalot, by Frank Thomas Bullen
7. *Under Sail,* by Felix Riesenberg
8. *Mr. Midshipman Easy,* by Captain Frederick Marryat
9. *Lord Jim,* by Joseph Conrad
10. *The Nigger of the* Narcissus, by Joseph Conrad

The best books of the sea, according to Felix Riesenberg, master mariner in sail and steam, essayist, editor, and novelist

The Wreck of the Grosvenor, by Clark Russell: a "bully sea story."
Robinson Crusoe, by Daniel Defoe: "Might well be added to the Bible."
Mr. Midshipman Easy, *Peter Simple*, and *The Phantom Ship,* by Captain
     Frederick Marryat: "Read all of Frederick Marryat."
Westward Ho! by Charles Kingsley
Hard Cash, by Charles Reade
Ninety-three and *The Toilers of the Sea,* by Victor Hugo
Casuals of the Sea, by William McFee: "A masterpiece of descriptive fiction."
Two Years Before the Mast, by Richard Henry Dana, Jr.: "The true relation-
     ship between fancy and fact."
Miles Wallingford, by James Fenimore Cooper
Moby-Dick, by Herman Melville: "The soul of the great fish and the secret
     of the sea he lived in and much of the secret perversity of man."
The Mirror of the Sea, Typhoon, Lord Jim, The Nigger of the Narcissus,
     Youth, and *The Shadow Line,* by Joseph Conrad: "He would have
     written great books even if he had never seen the sea."
The Cruise of the Cachalot and *With Christ at Sea,* by Frank T. Bullen
The Brassbounder and *Broken Stowage,* by David Bone
The Windjammers, by T. Jenkins Hains
Sinful Peck, by Morgan Robertson
From Forecastle to Cabin, by Captain Samuel Samuels: "Full of authentic
     romance."
The Passage of the Bark Sappho, by J.E. Patterson: "Sailing very close
     indeed to genius."
Round the Horn Before the Mast, by Basil Lubbock: "A stout, seaworthy
     book."
Blue Water, by Arthur Hildebrand
The Cruise of the Alerte, by E.F. Knight
Treasure Island, by Robert Louis Stevenson: "Richer in the treasures of art."

The three great early American navigational reference works
The American Coast Pilot, by Captain Lawrence Furlong, 1796
The New American Practical Navigator, by Nathaniel Bowditch, 1802
The Physical Geography of the Sea, by Lt. Matthew F. Maury, USN, 1855

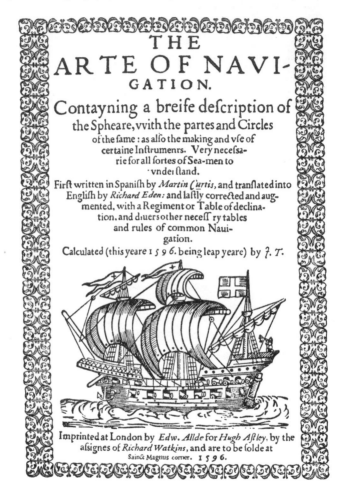

THE
ARTE OF NAVI-
GATION.

Contayning a breife defcription of
the Spheare, vvith the partes and Circles
of the fame : as alfo the making and vfe of
certaine Inftrumenrs. Very necefsa-
rie for all fortes of Sea-men to
·vndei ftand.

Firft written in Spanifh by *Martin Curtis,* and tranflated into
Englifh by *Richard Eden:* and laftly correcfted and aug-
mented, with a Regiment or Table of declination, and diuers other necefſ ry tables
and rules of common Naui-
gation.

Calculated (this yeare 1 5 9 6. being leap yeare) by *J. T.*

Imprinted at London by *Edw. Allde* for *Hugh Aftley,* by the
afsignes of *Richard Watkins,* and are to be folde at
Sainct Magnus corner. 1 5 9 6.

"One of the excellentest artes that ever hath bin devised is the arte of navigation."

—Martin Frobisher

Bowditch's *American Practical Navigator*
The first edition of the *American Practical Navigator*, by Nathaniel Bowditch, was published in 1802 by Edmund Blunt, a printer in Newburyport, Massachusetts. The book was actually entitled *The New American Practical Navigator,* as it was a complete revision of John Hamilton Moore's *Practical Navigator.* Now familiarly known as "Bowditch," it is published by the Defense Mapping Agency of the U.S. government (H.O. Pub. No. 9, DMA Stock No. NVPUB9V1) in two volumes. Over the years, more than 900,000 copies have been printed in approximately seventy editions.

As long as ships shall sail, the needle point to north, and the stars go through their wonted courses in the heavens, the name of Dr. Bowditch will be revered.
—Salem Marine Society

The principal methods of navigation
Piloting—fixing position within sight of land or aids to navigation; aka
    coastal navigation
Celestial—fixing position by reference to the sun, the moon, various
    planets, and various stars
Dead (deduced, or ded.) reckoning—determining approximate position
    by plotting courses and distances from the last positive position
    determined by either piloting or celestial navigation
Electronic—fixing position by such electronic devices as radar, GPS,
    and others

Bowditch on dead reckoning

Dead reckoning is the determination of position by advancing a known
position for courses and distances. It is reckoning relative to something stationary or "dead" in the water, and hence applies to courses and speeds
through the water. Although of less than the desired accuracy, dead reckoning is the only method by which a position can be determined at *any* time
and therefore might be considered *basic* navigation, with all other methods
only appendages to provide means for correcting the dead reckoning.

The three Ls of dead reckoning in ancient times

Log—to estimate the distance traveled
Leadline—to steer through reefs and shoals
Lookout—to guard against hazards

U.S. Navy and Coast Guard rules regarding the maintenance of a dead-reckoning plot

Every hour on the hour
At the time of every course change
At the time of every speed change
At the time of obtaining a single line of position
At the time of obtaining a fix or a running fix

The three basic tools for chartwork

Protractor—for measuring angles
Dividers—for measuring distance
Parallel rulers—for advancing lines

The three principal elements of navigation

Position—where you are
Course—how to get where you are going
Distance—how far away your destination is

The three-minute rule

In three minutes a vessel will travel a distance in hundreds of yards equal
to her speed in knots. For example, if your speed is 6 knots, you will travel
600 yards (1,800 feet) in three minutes.

The three deterrents to steering a straight course

Tidal set—a tidal current running at an angle to your intended course
Leeway—the sideways movement of the boat by the pressure of the wind
          on the hull, sails, and rigging
Careless helmsmanship

The three types of log, or diary, kept aboard vessels

Rough log—an account of everything that occurs on board, routine or
  otherwise, kept by the officers

Smooth log—a copy of the rough log, written in ink, kept by the chief officer

Official log—names of the crew and information about their conduct, the
  vessel's freeboard and draft, births, deaths, marriages, illnesses,
  crimes and punishments, accidents, etc., kept by the master.

Abbreviations used for navigational notes

AM—before noon
C—course
Corr—corrected
DR—dead reckoning
Dev—deviation
M—miles
PM—after noon
Rfix—running fix
S—speed
Var—variation
Yd(s)—yard(s)

Simple code for recording the state of the weather in a vessel's log

b—blue sky
c—cloudy
d—drizzle
f—fog
ff—thick fog
g—gloomy or dark
h—hail
l—lightning
m—mist or haze
o—overcast
p—passing showers
q—squalls
r—continuous rain
s—snow
t—thunder
u—ugly or nasty
v—distant objects clearly seen
S—smooth sea
M—moderate sea

L—long sea
R—rough sea
C—cross sea
H—heavy sea
VH—very heavy sea

A line under a letter is used to indicate that the condition is significant. A dot under the line indicates that the condition is significant and
has been continuous for a long period of time.

The letters can be used in combination to indicate the complete
state of the weather, such as dffgpuHC—drizzle, thick fog, gloomy, passing
showers, heavy cross sea—in other words, a thoroughly ugly, nasty day.

Navigational tools, minimal kit

Piloting, small boats

Accurate compass whose deviation is known
Up-to-date chart
Parallel rulers, dividers, pencil, and eraser
Common sense
Electronic aid: GPS

Piloting, yachts

Compass
Pelorus
Charts
Plotting equipment
Means for measuring speed or distance
Logbook
Tide and tidal current tables
Light list
Coast pilot or sailing directions
Hand lead
Binoculars
Flashlight
Stopwatch
Fog signal apparatus
Barometer
Thermometer
Electronic aids: radar, GPS, depth sounder

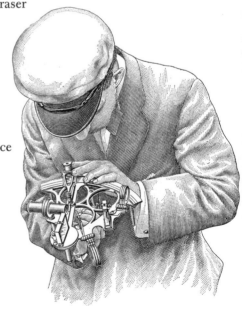

Offshore work
All of the above, plus:
Sextant
Accurate timepiece
Nautical almanac
Sight reduction tables
Star finder

You never can have too much navigational equipment
If there is doubt as to advisability of including some item of equipment,
the safer decision is to include it. It is better to have unused equipment
than to risk danger of becoming lost because of lack of needed equipment.
— *The American Practical Navigator*

GPS is fine, but...
The receiver is a delicate instrument that depends on electricity to keep it
    functional.
Use it with the understanding that sooner or later it will go on the fritz.
Therefore, ALWAYS KEEP A DEAD-RECKONING PLOT.

**Coastal navigation before radio, radar, GPS, depth sounder, et al.,
from the *French Coasting Pilot* of 1805**
If you are to pass between St. Michael's island and St. Catherine, when
you perceive the corner wall of St. Catherine's garden in one with a white
house that stands in the middle of Nezenel town; steering in the direction
of this mark, you come athwart the southernmost end of St. Catherine,
and then you range along the whole of the place in such a manner as to
leave ⅔ of the Channel towards St. Michael, and ⅓ towards St. Catherine; this track is to be followed till you discover a little wood in the neigh-
bourhood of Port Louis, called Querbel, through the hole of a stone
bridge or causey, which communicates from St. Catherine to the main;
in steering thus, Pangarne rock beacon is left on the starboard side; and
when you have passed it a ship's length, you steer for the road of Penne-
mane.... When you have proceeded so far as to bring a fountain on the
beach of Gavre in a line with a single tree on the same part of the penin-
sula to the N. eastward of the village, then you are to steer keeping Larmor windmill on with the two houses which are nearest to the extreme
point of Larmor.

The day's work
On board ship, the term "the day's work" refers to the calculation and recording at noon of the courses and distances made good for the previous twenty-four hours. The official logbook contains a summary of each day's work, including the courses and distances run, with the leeway, variation, and deviation applicable to each. It also includes positions of the ship—computed by dead reckoning, celestial observation, and electronic means—and all other significant happenings on board.

An old rule of thumb for sailing from the British Isles to the Caribbean
South 'til the butter melts, then west.

The by-guess and by-gosh method
There are two methods of finding a ship's position on the face of the waters: (1) by scientific calculation; (2) by empirical guess; and, though no scientist or certified navigator will ever admit it, there are points about No. 2 which mark it superior in many respects to No. 1.

—Weston Martyr

Navigating by the seaweed line
In the seventeenth century, Spanish vessels homeward bound from the Philippines sailed due east across the Pacific to a point near but out of sight of the California coast, then turned south for Cape Horn. The navigators knew it was time to turn south when they saw what they called *porra,* a type of floating seaweed.

In the Atlantic Ocean, a good navigator has this quality, says Alf Loomis
The ability to distinguish sunrise from sunset, then to steer toward the sunset until a large continent looms in sight.

Contrary to popular perception, the sun does not rise in the east
Except during those rare times when its declination is 0 degrees; i.e., when it will become straight overhead at midday.
At all other times, it will rise north of east when the sun is north of the equator and south of east when the sun is south of the equator.

The fool at sea judges his position by what he conceives to be his nearness to a given object, but the prudent man insists on two bearings. —anon.

The basics of position fixing

Line of position—you are somewhere on a line.

Circle of position—you are somewhere on a circle.

Two lines of position—you are at the intersection of the lines.

Two or more circles of position—you are at one of two points where the circles intersect each other; if the circles are tangent, you are at the point of tangency.

Distance

Nautical mile, 6,080 feet

Statute mile, 5,280 feet

Kilometer, 3,280 feet

Angular measure translated into distance

1 degree of latitude equals 60 nautical miles.

1 minute of latitude equals 1 nautical mile.

1 degree of longitude equals 60 nautical miles only on the equator. (All meridians of longitude converge at the poles, so the farther north or south one travels from the equator, the less the distance between the meridians.)

Distance and weather

When the atmosphere is clear and the sun is shining on an object, the object appears closer than it really is.

When the atmosphere is hazy and the light is dim, the opposite is true.

Judging distance at sea, clear day, height of eye five feet

2.5 miles, approximately—the line of the horizon; a ship whose bow wash is just visible; a moderate-size sailboat whose hull is just visible.

2 miles, approximately—a beacon whose base is just below the horizon; a rock whose waterline is just visible.

1.5 miles, approximately—a navigational buoy that can be seen, but the color and shape of which cannot be determined.

1 mile, approximately—a walking person on the shore or on the deck of a vessel appears as a moving black dot.

.5 mile, approximately—a walking person appears as a moving vertical black line.

400 yards, approximately—the movement of the legs of a walker and the arms of a rower are just discernible.

300 yards—the face of a person is just discernible.

To determine distance off a cliff or large object by timing the echo

$.18/2$ x time in seconds = distance off in miles

But keep this in mind: 99 percent of the time, the cliff or object will be set back from the edge of the shore; in that event, the shore itself will be closer to your position than the echo may indicate.

To determine distance off with your thumb

Hold your thumb in front of you at arm's length. For the average person, the ratio of the length between the thumb tip and the first knuckle, and the distance of the thumb from the eye, is 1:15. Therefore, by measuring a distant object of known height with your thumb, you can determine your distance off.

Using a sextant to determine whether you are gaining on, or losing ground to, another vessel

Measure the vertical angle of the masthead, or funnel-head, to the water-line several times. If the angles increase, you are gaining; if the angles decrease, you are losing ground.

Leeway

The angle between the course a vessel steers and the course she actually makes through the water. Leeway is caused by wind and current.

A quick determination of leeway

Take the reciprocal (opposite) bearing of the course the vessel is steering. Take another bearing of the wake the vessel is making in the water astern. The difference between the two, measured in degrees, is leeway.

To offset leeway

Adjust the vessel's course, by addition or subtraction—whichever is appropriate—by the amount of leeway determined by observation.

The rule of leeway under sail

Wind on the starboard side, allow for leeway to port; wind on the port side, allow for leeway to starboard.

Staying on course in a sailboat at night

Steer by the compass, or

Steer by the wind if it is steady—sense the direction by the feel of the wind on your cheek or your neck, or

Steer by the tremor of the luff of the sail, or

Steer by the North Star if the night is clear.

Compass direction

The direction the compass indicates is toward the north pole. This can deviate from the real direction of magnetic north because of the magnetic influence of objects near the compass. Compass direction differs from true direction by compass error (the algebraic sum of variation and deviation).

Variation

The angle of difference, expressed in degrees east or west, between true direction and magnetic direction.

Deviation

The angle of difference, expressed in degrees east or west, between magnetic direction and compass direction. Deviation is caused by metal objects in a vessel, such as the engine, the galley stove, etc. It varies according to the heading of the vessel.

Magnetic direction

The direction of the magnetic pole. In the Northern Hemisphere, the magnetic north pole lies in the vicinity of 74 degrees N, 101 degrees W. Magnetic direction differs from compass direction by deviation and from true direction by variation.

True direction

The direction of the geographic north pole. True direction differs from magnetic direction by variation and from compass direction by compass error (the algebraic sum of variation and deviation).

Reciprocal

The reciprocal of a course is its opposite. The reciprocal of a course of due East (090) is due West (270). To find the reciprocal of a course given in degrees:

If the course is less than 180 degrees, add 180 to it.

If the course is more than 180 degrees, subtract 180 from it.

    —or—

Add 180 degrees to it. If the sum is greater than 360 degrees, subtract 360.

Remembering the points of the compass

Cardinal points
North
East
South
West

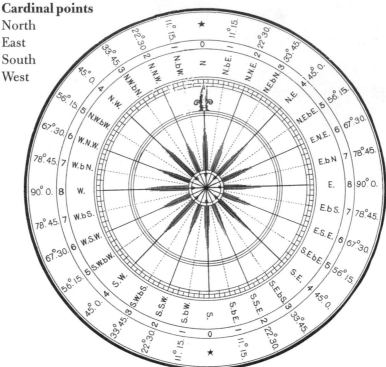

Intercardinal points	**"By" points**
North East	North by East
South East	North East by North
South West	North East by East
North West	East by North
Three-name points	East by South
North North East	South East by East
East North East	South East by South
East South East	South by East
South South East	South by West
South South West	South West by South
West South West	South West by West
West North West	West by South
North North West	West by North
	North West by West
	North West by North
	North by West

Every sailor should have the compass engraved upon his brain.
—Felix Riesenberg

Relative bearings

Relative bearings indicate the angular distance of an object in relationship to the heading of a vessel. They can be measured in degrees or points. Points are usually used for reporting visual bearings when precise measurement is not required.

Relative bearings are called out as follows:

Ahead
1 point on the starboard (or port) bow
2 points on the starboard (or port) bow
3 points on the starboard (or port) bow
Broad on (or off) the starboard (or port) bow
3 points forward of the starboard (or port) beam
2 points forward of the starboard (or port) beam
1 point forward of the starboard (or port) beam
Starboard (or port) beam (abeam or abreast)
1 point abaft the starboard (or port) beam
2 points abaft the starboard (or port) beam
3 points abaft the starboard (or port) beam
Broad on (or off) the starboard (or port) quarter
3 points on (or off) the starboard (or port) quarter
2 points on (or off) the starboard (or port) quarter
1 point on (or off) the starboard (or port) quarter
Astern

Collision and the relative bearing

If another vessel appears to be on a converging course with yours, and if the relative bearing of that vessel remains unchanged over a period of time, then what appears to be a converging course is even worse than that: it is a collision course.

Maneuvering at night near a vessel whose riding lights can be seen

When meeting another vessel

When all three lights are seen ahead,
Starboard wheel and show your red.

When passing another vessel

Green to green or red to red,
Means perfect safety, go ahead.

When in a crossing situation with another vessel
If on your starboard red appear,
It is your duty to keep clear.
To act as you may think it proper,
To port or starboard—back or stop her.
But when upon your port is seen,
A steamer's starboard light of green,
There's nothing else for you to do,
But see that she keeps clear of you.

"Ships That Pass in the Night"
by Henry Wadsworth Longfellow

Ships that pass in the night, and speak each other in passing,
Only a signal shown and a distant voice in the darkness;
So on the ocean of life we pass and speak one another,
Only a look and a voice, then dirtiness again and a silence.

The language of the sea

*T*here is really something strangely cheering to the spirits in the
meeting of a ship at sea.   —Benjamin Franklin

"The Meeting of the Ships"
by Thomas Moore

When, o'er the silent seas alone,
For days and nights we've cheerless gone,
Oh, they who've felt it know how sweet,
Some sunny morn a sail to meet!

Sparkling at once is every eye,
"Ship ahoy! ship ahoy!" our joyful cry;
While answering back the sounds we hear,
"Ship ahoy! ship ahoy! what cheer? What cheer?"

Then sails are backed; we nearer come:
Kind words are said of friends and home;
And soon, too soon, we part with pain,
To sail o'er silent seas again.

The majesty of a ship hove-to, according to W. Clark Russell
A full-rigged ship never looks more majestic I think than when she is hove
to under all plain sail, that is, when all canvas but stun'sails is piled upon
her and her main topsail is to the mast, with the great main course hauled
up to the yard and windily swaying in festoons. She is then like a noble

mare reined in; her very hawse pipes seem to grow large like the nostrils of some nervous creature impatiently sniffing the air; she bows the sea as though informed with a spirit of fire that maddens her to leap the surge, and to rush forward once more in music and in thunder, in giddy shearing and in long floating plunges on the wings of the wind. Never does a ship show so much as a thing of life as when she is thus restrained.

The gam

In the days of sail when a ship could voyage on lonely seas for weeks and months at a time without seeing another, the custom when falling in with another ship was to heave-to and engage in what was known as a gam—that is, a conversation among strangers as if they had been friends for a lifetime. To facilitate this, the ship to windward would back her mainyards and the ship to leeward would back her foreyards. If wind and sea conditions allowed, and enough time was available, boats would be put over for shipboard visiting. If not, news and comment would be passed by shouting directly from ship to ship.

Greetings at sea, mid-nineteenth century, according to Richard Henry Dana, Jr.

There is a settled routine for hailing ships at sea: "Ship a-hoy!" Answer, "Hulloa!" "What ship is that, pray?" "The ship *Carolina,* from Le Havre, bound to New York. Where are you from?" "The brig *Pilgrim,* from Boston, bound to the coast of California, five days out." Unless there is leisure, or something special to say, this form is not much varied from.

The gam, defined by Herman Melville

Gam. Noun—A social meeting of two (or more) Whale-ships, generally on a cruising-ground; when, after exchanging hails, they exchange visits by boats' crews: the two captains remaining, for the time, on board of one ship, and the two chief mates on the other.

"To gam"… is a substitute for the verbs "to visit," "to gossip." It expresses the garrulity of the sea, and is a pleasant break in the monotony of the life.
                                                                    —Jack London

The pleasures of a gam in the great age of sail, according to Basil Lubbock

Neither the passengers nor crew of a modern steamship know the pleasures of boating on the long swell of a Line calm, when a ship showed from the tiny boat in all her beauty with hull, sails and rigging reflected in the transparent blue of the deep sea, in very truth "a painted ship upon a painted ocean." When porpoises or bonito sported round the oar blades,

flying fish in clouds burst out of the water from under the boat's stem,
and sea birds, such as the frigate, the bosun or the booby, circled overhead or swooped and dived alongside. The wonderful charm of such a
sea picture can hardly be described, nor yet the delight of a "gam," as
whalesmen termed it, between two ships, which had been cut off from all
news of the land for perhaps weeks—or even months.

The gam, alas, is over

The time was when ships passing one another at sea backed their topsails
and had a "gam," and on parting fired guns; but those good old days have
gone. People have hardly time nowadays to speak even on the broad
ocean, where news is news, and as for a salute of guns, they cannot afford
the powder. There are no poetry-enshrined freighters on the sea now; it
is a prosy life when we have no time to bid one another good morning.

—Joshua Slocum

But we can still speak properly

Sea speech is so rich, and can express such fine shades of meaning, that to avoid using it nearly always sacrifices some nice distinction. Consider, for example, how, in Naval language, the varying degrees of giving freedom to a rope which bears a strain may be expressed:

"Check," that is, let out a very little and stop it at once. "Ease," let out a little more than is implied in "check" if the rope referred to is the sheet of a sail; but "ease handsomely" in lowering a weight means lower very slowly and delicately and stand by to take a turn, i.e., to make fast, at once. "Pay out" and "veer" sometimes mean almost the same thing, and express continued action: "pay out" suggests the actual handling of the rope in the process of veering. "Let go" is final and implies that responsibility ceases with obeying the order. —Alan Moore

**To the seaman these common words of the landsman
mean something else**

Arm—the part between the crown and the flukes of an anchor

Bank—a large shoal with sufficient depth of water for navigation

Caboose—a cookhouse on the deck of a sailing ship

Dead head—a mostly submerged spar or log floating on end

Earring—a line used to bend a sail to a spar

Fox—several rope-yarns twisted together

Groin—a breakwater

Hog—the condition of a vessel in which the bow and stern have drooped

Indian head—a type of turn-of-the-twentieth-century New England fishing schooner distinguished by the curve of the stem

Jackass—a canvas bag filled with oakum, stuffed in the hawsehole to make it watertight at sea

Kid—a tub or pan for serving food

Leech—the after side of a fore-and-aft sail; the outer sides of a squaresail

Mole—a breakwater, usually of masonry, used also as a landing stage

Nose—the stem or cutwater of a vessel

Ordinary—a naval vessel that is laid up in reserve but still in commission

Pea—the point of an anchor's palm

Quarter—the section of the side of a vessel from the aftermost chainplate to the stern

Roach—the curve in the side of a sail

Sheet—a line used to control a sail

Throat—the part of a gaff near the mast

Up—the position of the helm that will allow a sailing vessel to fall off the wind

Vast—a variation of avast, an order to stop or cease

Whack—a sailor's food allowance

Xray—the universal phonetic pronunciation for the letter X in wireless transmissions

Yankee—a jib topsail

Zulu—a lug-rigged fishing boat indigenous to Scotland

Rest assured when reading Kipling, says William McFee, novelist and marine engineer

One of our eminent literary critics, who was writing a book on Kipling, but who had no knowledge of ships or machinery, once inquired of me if all that technical stuff in Kipling's stories had any real accuracy. It was a pleasure to reassure that eminent critic. To my knowledge Kipling never made a mistake. Some of his detail, when one remembers he was a journalist by profession, was clairvoyant.

From *Captains Courageous,* by Rudyard Kipling

She might have been the very Flying Dutchman, so foul, draggled, and unkempt was every rope and stick aboard. Her old-style quarter-deck was some four or five feet high, and her rigging flew knotted and tangled like weed at a wharf-end. She was running before the wind—yawing frightfully—her staysail let down to act as a sort of extra foresail,—"scandalised," they call it,—and her foreboom guyed out over the side. Her bowsprit cocked up like an old-fashioned frigate's; her jib-boom had been fished and spliced and nailed and clamped beyond further repair; and as she hove herself forward, and sat down on her broad tail, she looked for all the world like a blouzy, frouzy, bad old woman sneering at a decent girl.

Heh! Tally on! Aft and walk away with her!
Handsome to the cathead, now; O tally on the fall!
Stop, seize and fish, and easy on the davit-guy.
Up, well up the fluke of her, and inboard haul!

Well, all fare you well, for the Channel wind's took hold of us,
Choking down our voices as we snatch the gaskets free.
And it's blowing up for night,
And she's dropping Light for Light,
And she's snorting under bonnets for a breath of open sea.

—from "Anchor Song," by Rudyard Kipling

Old naval slang

Admiralty ham—Royal Navy canned fish

Batten your hatch—shut up

Beachcomber—ne'er-do-well

Cape Horn fever—phony illness

Cheese-parer—a cheat

Claw off—sidestep an embarrassing question or argument

Cockbilled—drunk

Cumshaw—petty graft

Dead marine—empty liquor bottle

Donkey's breakfast—straw-stuffed mattress

Dunnage—sailor's personal gear

Flog the clock—push the hands of the clock forward to end the watch
    sooner

Flying fish sailor—seaman stationed in Asiatic waters

Galley yarn—rumor

Get out your web feet—prepare for foul weather

Gone west—killed in action

Greasy luck—good fortune

Hog-yoke—sextant

Holy Joe—ship's chaplain

Irish hurricane—dead calm

Irish pennant—frayed line or garment

Jamaica discipline—unruly behavior

Keep a shot in the locker—save something for a rainy day

Knock galley west—knock a person out

Leatherneck—a marine

Limey—British sailor

Liverpool pennant—piece of string used in place of a lost button

Loaded to the guards—drunk

Old Man—captain of the ship

One and only—a sailor's best girl

On the beach—ashore without a berth

Pale ale—drinking water

Quarterdeck voice—the voice of authority

Railroad pants—uniform trousers with braid down the outside leg seam

Railroad tracks—insignia of a full lieutenant

Raising the wind—soliciting donations for a specific cause
Round-bottomed chest—sea bag
Schooner-on-the-rocks—roast beef and baked potatoes
Sea lawyer—sailor who will argue about anything
Show a leg—rise and shine
Sling it over—pass it to me
Slip his cable—die
Soldiering—loafing on the job
Son of a gun—male baby born at sea
Sou'-Spainer—seaman stationed in the Mediterranean
Sparks—wireless operator
Splice the main brace—have a drink
Strike-me-blind—rice pudding with raisins
Sundowner—unreasonably tough officer
Swallow the anchor—retire
Sweat the glass—shake the hourglass to make time on watch pass quickly
The Andrew—Royal Navy
The best girl's on the towrope—the weather is fair and the going is easy
The eagle screams—payday
Tom Sawyer traverse—a waste of time
Tops'l buster—strong gale
Trim the dish—balance the vessel so it will sail on an even keel
Turnpike sailor—panhandler ashore, a landlubber claiming to be an old
    seaman in distress
Water bewitched—weak tea
White rat—sailor who curries favor with the officers

A bibliography of sailor's slang
Sailors' Language, by W. Clark Russell, 1883
Soldier and Sailor Words and Phrases, by Edward Fraser and John Gibbons, 1925
Sea Slang, by Frank C. Bowen, 1929
Royal Navalese, by Commander John Irving, 1946
Sea Slang of the Twentieth Century, by Wilfred Granville, 1949
The Sailor's Word Book, by Admiral W.H. Smyth, 1967

Fake down the lubber's line, and be snappy about it!
Captain Godfrey was "making sail," and he was moving the men around
briskly. He made short work of the job, and his orders were marked by a
felicity of language which challenged my imagination. Said he:
    "Let go the main-hatch. Belay! Haul away on your tops'l jib! Belay!

Port your gaff-tops'l sky-scrapers! Belay! Lively, you lubbers! Take a reef
in the lee scuppers! Belay! Mr. Baxter, it's coming on to blow at about
four bells in the hog-watch; have everything taut and trim for it. Belay!"

—Mark Twain

Proper sailorizing pronunciations
Boatswain—bosun
Coxswain—coxsun
Crossjack—crojik
Forecastle—folksil
Gunwale—gunnel
Mast—mist
Patent (as in patent block)—paytent
Sail—sill
Schooner—skunner
Sheave—shiv
Tackle—taykull
Topgallant mast—t'gallant mist
Topgallant sail—t'gallant sill
Topmast staysail—topmist staysill

Expressive nautical terms
Ash breeze—oar power
Beating the booby—swinging the arms in cold weather to increase
        circulation
Bird's nest—tangled rope
Black gang—engine-room crew
Blood money—payment to an agent for the recruitment of seamen
Blowing up and down—dead calm
Bluenose—Novascotiaman
Brass hat—naval officer with rank of commander and above
Bricklayer's clerk—a sailor who acts as if he is above it all
Catch a crab—an oar when rowing is caught aback
Clearing for Guam—getting underway to nowhere
Deadeye watch—4 A.M. to 8 A.M.
Dead horse—sailor's debt for advance wages
Dockwalloper—a person who saunters around the docks, rubbernecking

Dogs running before their master—a heavy swell in advance of a hurricane

Dutch courage—fearlessness brought on by strong drink

Dying man's dinner—quickly prepared food during an emergency

Fourth-class liberty—watching the shore when confined to the ship

Fuel fever—fuel oil is in short supply

Galley news (also called galley wireless)—gossip and rumor

Gongoozler—a person who stands around on the waterfront with his hands in his pockets, watching other people work

Granny knot—failed, unseamanlike attempt at a square knot

Graveyard watch (also known as the Churchyard)—midnight to 4 A.M.

Half seas over—just short of being drunk

High-pressure hat—an officer's cap

Homeward-bound stitches—excessively long sewing stitches, taken in a hurry

Hot bunk—a bunk used successively by more than one sailor

Jackass brig—a variation on the brigantine rig

Jimmy the One—first lieutenant or executive officer

Lime juicer (also Limey)—British vessel or sailor

Metal, or iron, mike—mechanical self-steering device

Nantucket sleigh-ride—a whaleboat being towed out of control by a harpooned whale

North River jibe—uncontrolled standing jibe

Paper jack—a licensed captain seen to be incompetent

Pig boat—submarine

Rocks and Shoals—the portion of naval regulations concerning punishments for crimes

Rope-yarn Sunday—an afternoon off devoted to washing and sewing clothes

Sailor's blessing—a curse

Scuttlebutt—gossip, idle chat, rumor

Seaman's disgrace—a fouled anchor

Soldier—a sailor who dodges work

Soldier's breeze—a fair, light wind

The nautical meaning of chance

Chance—the ability to sail

Fair chance—A vessel can sail with the sheets eased.

Hard chance—A vessel is headed by strong winds or seas, or both; a tight situation.

No chance—A vessel is stymied by unfair wind or tide, or no wind.

Chance-along—fair conditions for sailing

The nautical meaning of foul

Foul—anything bad; the opposite of clear

Foul ground—The bottom is not suitable for anchoring.

Foul anchor—an anchor that has become entangled by the rode or something on the bottom that will not allow the flukes to dig in

Foul wind—headwind

Foul tide—a tidal current that is against you

Foul bottom—The bottom of a vessel has an excessive growth of weed or barnacles.

Foul hawse—The chains of two anchors have become crossed.

Different kinds of dead

Dead-beat compass—magnetic liquid compass constructed to reduce or eliminate oscillation

Dead calm—absolutely no wind

Deadeye—a round block with three holes for taking a lanyard for setting up standing rigging

Dead flat—that part of a vessel's hull without curvature

Dead freight—money earned on space in the hold reserved by a shipper but not used

Dead head—a mostly submerged spar or log floating on end

Dead horse—a cash advance for wages to be earned

Deadlight—a portlight that cannot be opened; also, a round plate fastened over an opening portlight to protect it

Dead load—the fraction of a vessel's displacement devoted to the work intended for the vessel; i.e., on a merchant vessel, the weight of the cargo, fuel, stores, and water; aka useful load

Dead man—loose rope end; Irish pennant; empty beer bottle

Dead man's fingers—coral found on the beach after a storm

Dead marine—an empty beer bottle

Dead muzzler—a headwind

Deado—dead drunk

Dead on end—an engine-powered vessel driving into a headwind

Dead peg—close-hauled tack to windward

Dead reckoning—the determination of position by advancing a known position for courses and distances

Deadrise—the rise of floor of a vessel above the horizontal

Dead rope—a rope used for hauling that doesn't run through a block

Dead sheave—a stationary sheave in a block

Dead tarpaulin—a tarp without grommets

Dead water—the water that is drawn with the vessel along the side and at the stern

Dead way; also, dead in the water—the absence of motion

Deadweight—the carrying capacity of a vessel beyond her own weight

Dead wind; also, dead on end, dead muzzler—wind blowing directly
against the course a vessel is trying to make

Deadwood—solid timbers that serve as fillers

Dead work—that part of a vessel above the waterline when loaded; i.e.,
the freeboard

Seagoing words taken from human anatomy

Arm—part of an anchor

Belly—the part of a sail that bulges out from the pressure of the wind

Bottom—underside of the hull

Breast—docking line leading at an angle of 90 degrees from the side
of a vessel

Brow—gangplank

Bum—two-masted lateen-rigged craft of the Arabian region; aka boom

Butt—end-to-end planking joint

Buttock—line representing a vertical section of a hull parallel to
the centerline

Cheek—side piece of a block

Chest—box containing cargo, usually tea

Chin—lower portion of a vessel's stem

Elbow—curve in a river or channel

Eye—loop at the end of a line

Foot—lower edge of a sail

Hand—member of the crew

Head—forward part of a vessel; also, the toilet

Heel—lowest part of the mast

Knee—angle used to connect timbers or beams

Knuckle—sharp angle or bend in a hull

Lip—coaming

Mouth—opening to a bay, harbor, river, etc.

Neck—part of an oar where the loom or shaft meets the blade

Nose—stem of a vessel

Palm—part of an anchor; also, a sailmaker's tool

Rib—frame

Shin—to climb a mast, rope, or spar

Shoulder—projection on a block or mast

Throat—the forward or inner end of a gaff; the corner of a gaff sail
between the head and the luff

Tongue—block of wood between the jaws of a gaff

Waist—central part of a vessel

The hand at sea
Hand—a unit of measure: 4 inches
Hand—a member of the crew
Lend a hand—Help me (a request).
Bear a hand—Help me (an order).
All hands!—All members of the crew assemble here.

From the log of the quahog skiff *Bugsy's Boomer*
Pamet Harbor, Cape Cod Bay, April 15, 1956. We tied her off at the town landing and while Larry and I culled the day's catch Fred went up to Snow's store with a hod full of cherrystones. By 'n' by he came back grinning from ear to ear, carrying a paper sack. "Traded Snowy a black dog for a white monkey," he said, and pulled out a six-pack of Pabst Blue Ribbon.
—E.H. Morgan

The dog, nautically speaking
Black dog for a white monkey—a fair exchange
Dog—handle on a watertight door used to wedge the door shut
Dog in a blanket—sausage in a roll
Dogsbody—a sailor of lower rank or little importance; also, hard biscuit soaked in water and sugar
Dog bolt—a bolt used with a manhole dog to hold manhole covers and inspection plates in place
Dog's ear—corner of a canvas awning
Doggo—sailor's slang for ugly

Doghouse—a shelter just forward of the cockpit

Dog iron—a bar with pointed, right-angle ends, used to hold timbers together temporarily

Dogshore—a short timber used to support a vessel temporarily during a launch

Dog stopper—a rope or chain stopper used to relieve strain on a windlass

Dog vane—a wind sock set in the rigging to indicate wind direction

Dog watch—one of two, two-hour watches between the hours of 4 P.M. (1600 hours) and 8 P.M. (2000 hours)

Dogs running before their master—a heavy swell preceding a hurricane

Manhole dog—a bar used to hold a manhole cover in place

Mooring dog—a bar fastened near a vessel's waterline to take a mooring line

Sea dog—sailor

Spotted dog—boiled currant dumpling

Thirsty dog—a sailor on his way to a saloon

The cat, nautically speaking

Cat block—a block for catting the anchor

Cat hook—a hook used for attaching the cat block to the anchor ring

Cat fall—the rope that passes through the cat block

Cat hole—an aperture in the stern of a ship for running out mooring and docking lines

Catboat—a wide, shallow boat with a single mast stepped far forward; usually gaff-rigged with a short luff and long, overhanging boom

Cathead—a heavy timber projecting outboard from the bow; used for hauling the anchor aboard

Cat the anchor—haul the anchor to the cathead

Cat-o'-nine-tails—the principal implement for flogging recalcitrant sailors

Cat schooner—a schooner with no bowsprit or headsails

Cat yawl—a two-masted craft with no bowsprit or headsails

Catspaw—a light wind that riffles an otherwise calm surface

Catwalk—a fore-and-aft bridge connecting a midship house with the forward or after part of a large ship

The higher the altitude, the stronger the language, according to Basil Lubbock

It is curious how the language of a nation and the vocabulary of an individual are affected by the air they breathe. It is a well-known fact that the stronger the air the stronger the language and the more varied and vivid the adjectives and similes.

When mountaineers swear their language far transcends that of the lowly plain dweller: and even at sea most sailing ship men will agree that the worst language is used up aloft when taking in sail, and specially is this the case when struggling in the grip of a westerly gale when the lungs are filled with ozone.

Captain: *Bad language or abuse,*
        I never, never use,
        Whatever the emergency;
        Though "Bother it" I may
        Occasionally say,
        I never use a big, big D—
  All: *What, never?*
Captain: *No, never!*
  All: *What, never?*
Captain: *Hardly ever!*
  All: *Hardly ever swears a big, big D—*
        Then give three cheers, and one cheer more,
        For the well-bred Captain of the Pinafore!
                      —from Gilbert and Sullivan's HMS *Pinafore*

The price of bad language

Article II. If any shall be heard to swear, curse, or blaspheme the name of God, the Commander is strictly enjoined to punish them for every offense by causing them to wear a wooden collar or some shameful badge, for so long a time as he shall judge proper.
            —from the *Rules for the Regulation of the Navy of the United Colonies*

The silent language of the sea, according to Filson Young

Hoists of bunting broke out at yardarms, ascended to mast heads, hovered a minute or two, and came down in rainbow curves where flagship talked to flagship. A shore signal station was speaking in white flashes that dazzled you even in the strong sunshine; and between ship and ship of the same squadron minute conversations, visible only through a strong glass, were being carried ceaselessly on by the busy tossing arms of semaphores and by the small flags that a signalman, perched on the rail of a bridge like a fly, was waving to his opposite number in the next ship. What were they all saying?

Signaling the old-fashioned way

The International Signal Code

International Code flags—twenty-six unique designs representing the letters of the alphabet; flags for letters A and B are swallowtailed, the remainder are squared-off at the fly.

International Code pennants—eleven unique designs representing the numerals 0 to 9, plus the Code and Answering pennant; all are tapered, and squared-off at the fly.

International Code triangular flags—three unique designs representing the First, Second, and Third Substitutes

Group—one or more letters and/or numerals that make up a signal

Numeral group—a group of one or more numerals

Halyard—line used to hoist a flag or group

Tackline—a length of halyard separating groups of flags

Hoist—one or more groups flying on one halyard

Superior—a flag or group flying above another

Inferior—a flag or group flying below another

At the dip—a signal half-hoisted

Close up—a signal fully hoisted

Answering pennant—used to indicate a signal from another vessel has been received; also used in a group as a decimal point

Substitutes—used to repeat one or more letters in a group

Basic flag signaling procedure

The sending vessel makes up the signal and hoists it close up.

113

The receiving vessel hoists the answering pennant at the dip to indicate the signal has been seen. Once the receiving vessel has deciphered the message—that is, understands the signal's meaning—it brings the answering pennant close up.

Admiral Lord Nelson's signal preceding the battle off Cape Trafalgar, October 21, 1805

England expects every man will do his duty!

The evolution of Nelson's famous signal, according to HMS *Victory*'s signal lieutenant

His Lordship came to me on the poop, and, after ordering certain Signals to be made, about a quarter to noon, said, "Mr. Pasco, I want to say to the fleet, 'England confides that every man will do his duty.'" He added, "You must be quick, for I have one more to add, which is for 'Close Action.'" I replied, "If your Lordship will permit me to substitute expects for confides, the Signal will soon be completed, because the word expects is in the Vocabulary [code book], and confides must be spelt." His Lordship replied in haste, and with seeming satisfaction, "That will do, Pasco, make it directly."

From the 1830 code book of the Royal Yacht Squadron

5005—Oil, salad. Have you any you can spare me?
9402—Plates. Can you spare me some dinner plates?
6218—Sealing wax. Can you lend me some?
2492—Dice. Send me a pair.
9164—Wine. My stock is out.

A short story in flag signal code, composed from the regulations of the Eastern Yacht Club, Marblehead, Massachusetts, 1914

FT—Wish to communicate with you.
Y—Come within hail.
BW—Where are you from?
QS—Hampton Roads, Virginia.
BU—Where are you bound?
NH—Bar Harbor, Maine.
GC—Will you lunch with me?
C—Yes.
GI—And bring your guests.
FW—Thank you.
GF, JA—Will meet you at the Club at noon.
GJ—Send a boat for me.
GW—At once.

Salutes

In the age of sail, guns were fired in salute as a form of greeting between two naval vessels, or between an armed merchant vessel and a naval vessel. In the territorial waters of the vessel being saluted, the saluting vessel struck her topsails in lieu of firing guns. Unarmed merchant vessels struck their topsails when saluting a naval vessel. Now that sail is no longer used on merchant vessels, the latter salute naval vessels by dipping their ensigns. This is done by dropping the ensign about halfway down the staff, then raising it again after the naval vessel dips her ensign in reply.

The universal phonetic alphabet for calling out letters

The old style, first instituted by the U.S. Navy and later adopted by other American vessels, was used for calling out the names of signal flags. The current style is used internationally for voice communications.

	Old Style (signal flags)	Current Style (voice communications)
A	Affirm	Alpha
B	Baker	Bravo
C	Cast	Charlie
D	Dog	Delta
E	Easy	Echo
F	Fox	Foxtrot
G	George	Golf
H	Hypo	Hotel
I	Int. (Interrogatory)	India
J	Jig	Juliet
K	King	Kilo (pronounced kee-low)
L	Love	Lima (pronounced lee-ma)
M	Mike	Mike
N	Negat. (Negative)	November
O	Option	Oscar
P	Prep (Preparatory)	Papa
Q	Queen	Quebec (pronounced kay-beck)
R	Roger	Romeo
S	Sail	Sierra
T	Tare	Tango
U	Unit	Uniform
V	Victor	Victor
W	William	Whiskey
X	Xray	Xray
Y	Yoke	Yankee
Z	Zed	Zulu

Thoughts on flags and burgees

It adds greatly to appearance to have flags of correct size and description. Nothing looks so lubberly as to see a canoe sailing about with a jack or an ensign at her masthead, as if she was signaling for a pilot. If a member of a canoe club, or any yacht or sailing club, one should carry a burgee, and observe the custom of always flying the burgee of the club at whose station one is lying (of course if a member of it). Burgees for a canoe are lightest and smartest of silk, but bunting will do. The size should be very carefully judged; about 12 inches is the general length for a canoe. An ensign should be on board, to be set at the mizzen when at anchor, and at the peak if carried underway, which should be done on Sundays, etc., and at regattas. In foreign waters the ensign should be carried at the peak all the time, to show one's nationality.

—from *Practical Canoeing*, by "Tiphys," 1888

Choosing a flag of the proper size for your boat

The U.S. ensign or yacht ensign at the stern staff should be approximately one inch on the fly per each overall foot of the boat. The hoist should be approximately two-thirds of the fly.

The union jack should be same size as the canton of the proper U.S. ensign for the boat.

Club burgees and private signals should be approximately one-half inch on the fly for each foot of the highest mast, measured from the waterline to the masthead.

Flying the national flag

At anchor, hoist the colors at 8 A.M.
At anchor, haul down the colors at sunset.
Hoist the colors when getting underway, whatever the time, as long as there is light.

Dressing ship

Ships and boats are sometimes "dressed" for regattas, and on national holidays and other special occasions. Flags at the masthead: the vessel is "dressed." Flags in a continuous run from the jackstaff at the forward end of the vessel, to the mastheads, and then aft to the ensign staff at the stern: the vessel is "dressed overall."

A yacht properly dressed overall displays:
The yacht ensign at the stern staff.
The union jack at the bow, or jack, staff.
The flags and pennants of the International Code on a line running from
the stem or end of the bowsprit to the masthead and aft to the stern
or taffrail.

Underway, fly the U.S. ensign

Powerboat—if equipped with a mast and gaff, from the gaff; otherwise
from the stern staff.
Sportfisherman—if a stern staff will be in the way of the action, from a
halyard rigged behind the tower.

Sailboat, low-aspect-ratio Marconi rig—from the leech of the aftermost sail, two-thirds of the way up from the clew.
Sailboat, high-aspect-ratio Marconi rig—from the stern staff.
Sailboat, gaff rig—from the peak of the aftermost gaff.
All sailboats under power alone—from the stern staff.

Underway in foreign waters, as a courtesy fly the flag of the country of jurisdiction
Powerboat with no mast—from the bow staff.
Powerboat with mast and spreaders—from the starboard spreader; if two masts, from the forward starboard spreader.
Sailboat—from the starboard spreader; if two masts, from the forward starboard spreader.
Continue to fly the U.S. ensign in the customary manner.

At anchor, fly the Jack
The Union Jack is a blue flag with 50 stars—in effect, the canton of the U.S. national flag—and is flown on a jackstaff at the bowsprit cap or stem-head when a vessel is in port. Some of the old naval traditions associated with it are:
"When the anchor goes down, the Jack goes up."
The Jack is not flown if there is hard work to be done on board.
An unwritten rule is that visitors are not wanted aboard a vessel at anchor if the Jack is not flying.
The Jack is flown at the yardarm when a pilot is wanted.
When a general court is in session, the Jack is hoisted and one gun is fired.
When an American ambassador is on board an American naval vessel in a foreign port, the Union Jack is his personal flag and is flown from the fore-truck.

from "Songs for All Seas, All Ships"
Flaunt out O sea your separate flags of nations!
Flaunt out visible as ever the various ship-signals!
But do you reserve especially for yourself and for the soul of man one flag
above all the rest,
A spiritual woven signal for all nations, emblem of man elate above death,
Token of all brave captains and all intrepid sailors and mates,
And all that went down doing their duty,
Reminiscent of them, twined from all intrepid captains young or old,
A pennant universal, subtly waving all time, o'er all brave sailors,
All seas, all ships.   —Walt Whitman

Signaling by sound, the boatswain's call or pipe
The boatswain's pipe is a flute-like whistle with a distinctive sound and
shape. It serves as the symbol of the boatswain's authority to pass orders
from the captain and is used by him to call the crew to attention before an
order is given; in some cases, the sounding of the pipe represents the order
itself. The captain or the officer of the deck orders the boatswain to sound
the pipe; then the pipe is sounded to the cadence and pitch appropriate
to the order. For example, the last order at night on a naval vessel is "Pipe
Down," which is passed by the boatswain to the crew to extinguish the
lights, turn in, and maintain silence on the berthing decks.
Call to attention—a long, straight whistle
Call away a boat—same as the call to attention, followed by a verbal order,
    such as: "Away gig!" "Away dinghy!" "Away cutter!" "Away
    lifeboat!" etc.
Call to meals—three long, rolling whistles
Heave away or pull—a series of moderately short, straight whistles
Belay—two short, quick chirps, followed by a moderately short, rolling
    whistle
Pipe the side—a prolonged, straight whistle
Make colors, or make sunset—two short, quick chirps, followed by a
    long, rolling whistle
Pipe down—one long, straight whistle, followed by a long, rolling whistle
The boatswain's pipe is made of silver, or nickel-silver, and worn on a sil-
    ver chain around the neck of the boatswain. The origin of the pipe
    was in the admiral's whistle, which usually was of gold and was worn
    around the neck as a symbol of office. The parts of the pipe are:
Buoy—the bowl
Gun—the reed
Keel—the flange
Shackle—the ring

Engineers' sound signals
On American steam vessels, the movements of the engines were directed
    from the bridge by "bells and jingles," as follows:
One bell, when engines are at rest—Ahead slow.
Jingle bell, when going ahead slow—Full speed ahead.
One bell, when under full speed ahead—Slow down.
One bell, when going ahead slow—Stop.

Two bells, when engines are at rest—Astern slow.
Jingle bell, when going astern slow—Full speed astern.
One bell, when going astern full or half—Stop.
Four quick bells, when going ahead full—Astern full speed.

A whistle or horn signal code for one vessel towing another

I am turning to starboard—1 short blast
I am turning to port—2 short blasts
Go ahead—2 long blasts
Stop—1 long, 2 short
All fast—2 long, 1 short
Haul away—2 short, 1 long
Let go—2 long, 5 short
Pay out more line—1 short, 2 long
Avast hauling—3 short
I am letting go (emergency)—5 short, 5 short, 5 short
　　　Note: A short blast should not exceed two seconds; a long blast should be six seconds or longer.

And then, of course, there are voice signals or commands; here, for getting underway from a pier

Stand by your lines—Get ready to handle the mooring lines.
Single up—Take in all lines, leaving a single standing part at each station.
Ease [name of line]—Pay out the line to relieve most of the tension.
Slack off [name of line]—Pay out the line to relieve the tension.
Check [name of line]—Put tension on the line, letting it slip as necessary
　　　to relieve extreme tension.
Take a strain on [name of line]—Put the line under tension.
Hold [name of line]—Take sufficient turns so the line will not slip.
Take in the slack on [name of line]—Heave in the line but do not put a
　　　strain on it.
Let go [name of line]—Deck crew: slack off smartly so linehandlers on
　　　pier can cast off.
Cast off [name of line]—Linehandlers on pier: remove the line from the
　　　cleat or bollard.
Take in [name of line]—Retrieve the line that has been cast off.

Free at last

I find the great thing in this world is not so much where we stand, as in what direction we are moving—we must sail sometimes with the wind and sometimes against it—but we must sail, and not drift, nor lie at anchor.
—Oliver Wendell Holmes

Preparations for getting underway

In a sailboat
Ensure the sheets are ready to run free, winch handles are at hand, and
halyards and downhauls are rigged for immediate use.

In a motorboat, or an auxiliary sailboat
Sound the fuel tank.
Check that the cooling water is circulating unimpeded.
Determine the position of the helm, and that it turns freely.
Make sure that nothing is foul of the propeller, and that the slack is out of
the stern line so it cannot foul the propeller.

In any boat of any type with a compass
Make sure no loose ferrous metal objects, such as a knife or an iron pot,
are near the compass.

The sound of the windlass pawls always thrills me—it's the sound of getting underway, maybe to far places, adventure, what the whole thing is about.
—R.D. "Pete" Culler

"Getting Underway"

Danish capstan chanty

Solo: *Come, all ye jolly sailors bold,*
Chorus: *Heave and go, my Nancy O!*
Solo: *Listen till my tale is told,*
Chorus: *Heave and go, my Nancy O!*

Solo: *The king trusts to his sailors bold,*
And we shall find them as of old—
For father, mother, sisters, wives,
We're ready now to risk our lives.
For Danish girls, with eyes so blue,
We'll do all that sailors can do.
And Dannebrog upon our masts,
Shall float as long as this world lasts;
And now for our brave captain, we,
Will give three cheers right heartily.

Solo: *Then up mates, up, and blaze away,*
Chorus: *Heave and go, my Nancy O!*
Solo: *Listen till my tale is told,*
Chorus: *Heave and go, my Nancy O!*

As the sails rose to the wind, and the ship began to move, there broke from all the boats three resounding cheers, which those on board took up, and echoed back, and which were echoed and re-echoed. My heart burst out when I heard the sound and beheld the waving of the hats and handkerchiefs....
—from *David Copperfield*, by Charles Dickens

To the Liverpool Docks we'll bid adieu;
To Suke, and Sally, and Poll too;
The anchor's weighed, the sails unfurled;
We are bound to cross the watery world.
Hurrah! we're outward bound!
Hurrah! we're outward bound!
—old capstan chanty

Outward bound

…and then one morning I shall wake to the song and tramp of the sailors, the clink of the capstan, and the rattle of the anchor-chain coming merrily in. We shall break out the jib and the foresail, the white houses on the harbour side will glide slowly past us as she gathers steering-way, and the voyage will have begun! As she forges towards the headland she will clothe herself with canvas; and then, once outside, the sounding slap of great green seas as she heels to the wind, pointing South!

—from The *Wind in the Willows,* by Kenneth Grahame

"A Life"

by George Edward Woodberry

I heard my ancient sea-blood say,
        And wise in youth it counselled me—
"When women lure, when men betray,
        Break topsails for the open sea."

I crowded sail on spar and mast,
        And half the world I left behind;
But in my breast I held it fast,
        That truth in men I still should find.

I set my life on swords of three,
        My back against my castle wall;
Now should I cry, "A moi, amis!"
        It is three ghosts would come at call.

Alone upon the "Far Away,"
        And nothing human sails with me;
My bare poles dip, through sun and spray,
        The dim marge of God's outer sea.

Cutting loose

Men who would soon be sitting down to supper in their own homes
strained at great capstans on the dockside, warping us out into the
stream. In this way, without bands, without crowds and without cheering, watched by a score of unemotional laborers standing in the soft rain,
we set off on our fifteen-thousand-mile voyage.   —Eric Newby

Escape

The breeze that carries you away from the sweltering city with its din and
commotion both cools the brow and clears the mind. No clamoring tele-
phones can reach you now, no compelling salesman can corner you and
pin your reluctant mind to his proposition. There are no appointments to
keep save your anchorage by sundown, and you are on your way with a
freshening breeze and lifted sheet.   —W.E. Warrington

Happiness

For the first time not on paper and in dreams, I had the little ship alone
in my hands in a night of velvet dark below and stars above, pushing
steadily along into unknown waters. I was extremely happy.
                                          —Arthur Ransome

*While the land called "Stay!" we sailed, waving farewell to the last
fluttering handkerchief in the last dooryard of land's end.*
                                          —Rockwell Kent

We were once more upon the ocean, where sky and water meet.

—Richard Henry Dana, Jr.

"When"

by Thomas Fleming Day

When western winds are blowing soft
Across the Island Sound;
When every sail that draws aloft
Is swollen true and round;
When yellow shores along the lee
Slope upward to the sky;
When opal bright the land and sea
In changeful contact lie;
When idle yachts at anchor swim
Above a phantom shape;
When spires of canvas dot the rim
Which curves from cape to cape;
When sea-weed strewn the ebbing tide
Pours eastward to the main;
When clumsy coasters side by side
Tack in and out again—
When such a day is mine to live,
What has the world beyond to give?

The four most important qualifications for long-distance voyaging, according to L. Francis Herreshoff

1. A real knowledge of seamanship
2. A willingness to give up nearly all the comforts of home, and like it
3. A love of the sea so strong that you will be happy for a month at a time out of sight of land
4. Last but not least, plenty of time and an independent income

The three most important principles for long-distance cruising, according to L. Francis Herreshoff

1. Lay out your course so you will always be in fair winds and fair weather.
2. Use a vessel which is easy on her gear and crew, and drives economically under power.
3. Leave behind everything that is not necessary, for these things take up space and absorb power.

The difference between racing and cruising, according to Vanderdecken
Racing implies those who revel amidst huge spars, enormous spread of
canvas, and piles of lead, wherewith to enable this straining craft to stand
up to her canvas; whilst cruising denotes the quiet, comfort-loving rover of
the sea, who loves sailing for sailing sake, is possessed of peculiar notions
as to speed, and is singularly economical in the matter of setting canvas.

The first rule for coastal cruising: Start early, finish early.

—anon.

The second and third rules
Hope for the best.
Prepare for the worst.

The three Cs of coastal sailing
Chart
Compass
Confidence

Simple freedom, according to Vincent Gilpin
When you gather the necessities of life on a small sailboat and cast loose
with a roving commission, you enter into a new and wonderful freedom,
unknown on shore. You slip away from the everyday world into the space
and silence of the wide waters; you move without gasoline; you sleep
without hotels; you choose your distance from other men.

The greatest joy
Does one actually enjoy these long passages? Rather a difficult question
to answer. Definitely I would not undertake a long passage for its sake
alone, but as the only possible means of reaching a new and desirable
cruising ground they are well worth while. To my mind the greatest joy in
yachting is to cruise along some lovely coast, finding one's way into all
sorts of out-of-the-way coves and rivers. A pleasant day's sail of four to
five hours, and then, perhaps, a beat up some narrow, winding river. Handling one's ship in narrow waters, preferably where one has never been
before, is the finest sport in the world.   —R.D. Graham

And in a pub that's off the Strand, and handy to the bar,
With pipe in mouth and mug in hand sat Jobson of the Star
"Hullo!" says he. "Come, take a pew, and tell me where you've been.
It seems to me that lately you have vanished from the scene."
To Caracas and Guayaquil, to Lhasa and Pekin,

To Brahmaputra and Brazil, to Bagdad and Benin.
I've sailed the Black Sea and the White, the Yellow and the Red,
The Sula and the Celebes, the Bering and the Dead.
I've climbed on Chimborazo, and I've wandered in Peru;
I've camped on Kinchinjunga, and I've crossed the great Karroo.
I've drifted on the Hoang-ho, the Nile and Amazon;
I've swum the Tiber and the Po... " thus I was going on,
When Jobson yawned above his beer, and rumbled: "Is that so?...
It's been so damned exciting here, too bad you had to go.
We've had the devil of a slump; the market's gone to pot;
You should have stuck around, you chump, you've missed an awful lot."
—from "Jobson of the *Star*," by Robert Service

Successful passagemaking, according to Claud Worth
I attribute the success of our long passages mainly to the observance of two simple rules. First, if desirous of making a *passage* (as distinguished from a cruise) never waste a fair wind. Second, steer an outside course unless there is some special reason to the contrary.

The true peace of God begins at any spot 1,000 miles from the nearest land.
—Joseph Conrad

Early shorthanded ocean passages
First two-man Atlantic crossing, west to east—ketch *Charter Oak* (43
    feet), 1857, C.R. Webb, skipper
First two-man Atlantic crossing, west to east, yacht under 30 feet—
    square-rigged iron lifeboat *Red, White, and Blue* (26 feet), 1866,
    William Hudson and Frank E. Fitch
First two-man Atlantic crossing, east to west—converted lifeboat *City of
    Ragusa* (20 feet), 1870, John C. Buckley and Nicholas Primoraz
First singlehanded across an ocean (the Atlantic), west to east—dory
    Centennial (20 feet), 1876, Alfred Johnson
First man-and-woman Atlantic crossing, west to east—whaler *New Bed-
    ford* (20 feet), 1877, Mr. and Mrs. Thomas Crapo
First singlehanded around the world—sloop (later converted to yawl)
    Spray (32 feet, waterline), 1895–98, east to west, Joshua Slocum
First two-man rounding of Cape Horn, west to east—sloop *Pandora* (37
    feet), 1911, G.D. Blythe and Peter Arapakis
First two-man circumnavigation of the globe, east to west—ketch *Svaap*
    (32 feet), 1928–31, William A. Robinson, skipper
First singlehanded rounding of Cape Horn—cutter *Mary Jane* (36 feet),
    1933, east to west, Al Hansen

Great cruising accounts

Alone in the Caribbean, by Frederic A. Fenger, 1917. A 17-foot sailing
canoe around and about the Lesser Antilles.

Around the World Single-Handed, by Harry Pidgeon, 1933. From
California and back in a homebuilt boat.

Between Wind and Water, by Gerald Warner Brace, 1966. The coast of
Maine.

The Boy, Me and the Cat, by Henry M. Plummer. From Massachusetts to
Florida and back in a catboat, 1912–13.

The Cruise of the Nona, by Hilaire Belloc, 1925. The cruising story as
Literature.

The Cruise of the Snark, by Jack London, 1911. Across the Pacific from
San Francisco in a schooner with serious problems.

Desperate Voyage, by John Caldwell, 1949. Solo from Panama to Australia to rejoin his fiancée; the voyage as Love Story.

Down Channel, by R.T. McMullen, 1893. Around the British Isles with a
tough old buzzard.

Gipsy Moth *Circles the World,* by Sir Francis Chichester, 1968. The first
one-stop circumnavigation of the globe.

Half-Safe, by Ben Carlin, 1955. Around the world by land and sea in a
small war-surplus amphibious landing craft.

Ice Bird, by David Lewis, 1975. The first singlehanded voyage to Antarctica.

The Long Way, by Bernard Moitessier, 1973. A round-the-world solo racer
discovers the dream isn't winning the race but continuing the dream.

The Magic of the Swatchways, by Maurice Griffiths, 1932. In and around
the coast and estuaries of East Anglia.

N by E, by Rockwell Kent, 1930. From Nova Scotia to Greenland and
shipwreck; the cruising story as Art, by an artist.

Princess–*New York,* by Joe Richards, 1956. Down the U.S. east coast in a
Friendship sloop.

Racundra's *First Cruise,* by Arthur Ransome, 1928. The Baltic in a
30-foot ketch.

Rough Passage, by Robert D. Graham, 1936. Across the Atlantic from
England and back in a 30-foot cutter.

The Saga of Cimba, by Richard Maury, 1939. A voyage to the South Seas
in a 25-foot schooner by a sea writer's writer.

Sailing Alone Around the World, by Joshua Slocum, 1900. The book that set
the standard for the genre by the first singlehander around the globe.

The Southseaman, by Weston Martyr, 1926. The birth and death of a 45-
foot schooner by an epic yarn spinner.

Tinkerbelle, by Robert Manry, 1966. Across the Atlantic in a 13½-foot
     converted daysailer; Everyman goes voyaging.

The Voyage Alone in the Yawl Rob Roy, by John MacGregor, 1867. Across
     the English Channel in a 21-foot canoe yawl.

Yacht Cruising, by Claud Worth, 1910. Around and among the British Isles.

Think small

*"**D**o you know, I've never been in a boat in all my life?"*
"What?" cried the Rat, openmouthed: "Never been in a—you never—well,
I—what have you been doing, then?"
                    —Kenneth Grahame, *The Wind in the Willows*

To all whose ambition it is to become good yachtsmen, I would by all means
recommend them to commence their career in a small craft. —Vanderdecken

The pleasures of small craft, according to R.D. "Pete" Culler
Many folks nowadays say small craft don't offer a real challenge. To take
some nice, classic small craft, with properly cut and sheeted spritsail,
around some toy sandspit in what appear to be adverse conditions—
there is a favorable eddy if you know where to find it and she works won-
derfully in moderate going with only the tip of the board—takes as much
experience as driving some hard-pressed schooner around some tide-
ridden cape, and you don't get so wet!

Small-boat sailors have to know a lot, says Jack London
The small-boat sailor is the real sailor. He knows—he must know—how to
make the wind carry his craft from one given point to another given point.
He must know about tides and rips and eddies, bar and channel markings,
and day and night signals; he must be wise in weather-lore; and he must be
sympathetically familiar with the peculiar qualities of his boat which dif-
ferentiate it from every other boat that was ever built and rigged.

A few Nevers for small sailing craft
Never let go of the tiller.
Never jump around in the boat.
Never sit on the lee gunwale.
Never climb the mast.
Never allow clothes or lines to trail overboard.
Never cleat the mainsheet.
Never allow the sheets to become fouled.
Never trust a squall.
Never forget your life preserver.
Never swim away from the boat following a capsize.

Why small boats are safe in the open sea, according to Claud Worth
Though a large vessel is usually more comfortable than a small one, size
has little to do with safety in open water.

A little vessel yields to every movement of the sea—herein lies her
safety. The huge unyielding bulk of a great ship exposes her to the full
force of every blow.

**Minimum equipment for an open cruising dinghy beyond that required
by law**
Radar reflector
Pair of oars and oarlocks, plus spare of each
Paddle
Anchors—Danforth-type for mud and sand; fisherman or grapnel for
    rocky bottoms
Anchor rode—6 feet of chain, at least 100 feet of rope
Inflatable boat rollers
Fenders
Compasses—one mounted away from ferrous metal; one handheld
Sea anchor, 18-inch or 24-inch drogue, with swivel
Bailers or buckets, tied to boat
Bilge pump
Safety harness and lifeline for each person on board
Water containers
Flashlights and spare batteries
Whistle
Rigger's knife with marlinspike and shackle key

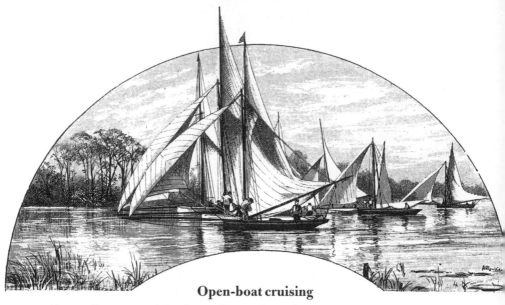

Open-boat cruising

Long-distance cruising in small open boats is not as uncommon as one would think. Many transoceanic passages have been made in the past, and no doubt many more will be made in the future.

Knowing what sail combinations to use and when to reef are critical to going offshore in an open boat. Always keep in mind that anticipating the need for a sail change, and carrying it out before it is necessary, is preferable to reacting when it is too late. In other words, if you see a squall approaching, reduce sail long before it becomes a threat. In general:
When wind speeds reach Beaufort Force 4 (11–16 knots), reef the main
 or change to the working jib.
Force 5 (17–21 knots), carry a reefed main and working jib.
Force 6 (22–27 knots), carry a reefed main only; or double-reef the main
 and carry the working jib.
Force 7 (28–33 knots), double-reefed main only, or if sailing off the wind,
 working jib only.
Force 8 (34–40 knots), sailing under control may be impossible; heave-to
 under storm trysail, or lie to a sea anchor.
The above are guidelines only. Specific weather and sea conditions, as
 well as the characteristics of your boat, should dictate your actions.
The safest options are to be conservative and cautious no matter the conditions.

It is always time to reef when you think it is.

—Thomas Fleming Day

Three signals that it is time to reef
Excessive heel

Excessive weather helm

Constant need to luff to keep her under control

Reef before you start
If it appears to be blowing heavily outside, tuck in a reef or two before getting underway from a sheltered harbor. It is easier to shake out an unnecessary reef than it is to tuck in a reef when pressed by heavy weather outside.

Two methods of shortening down
Take in large sails and replace them with smaller ones.

Reef the sails currently set.

In either case, for these evolutions to be successful, the boat must be slowed down or even stopped.

To simplify reefing in reduced visibility
In a sail with more than one row of reef points, make up each row with line of a different material—for example, one of laid nylon, another of laid spun Dacron, and another of yacht braid. You will then be able to distinguish one row of reef points from another by feel alone.

When underway, always have the tack lashing and reef pendant rove, ready to use.

A quick, scandalous reef
In an unexpected squall, the sail area of a gaff-rigged craft can be reduced quickly by scandalizing the mainsail—that is, by dropping the peak and leaving the throat hoisted. Also, when running directly downwind in a gaff-rigged craft, the danger of broaching can be reduced by dropping the peak.

Slowing the boat for a sail change
Ease the sheets and steer off the wind, somewhat on a close reach, depending on the handling characteristics of the boat.

Stopping the boat for a sail change
Heave-to, generally by backing the jib, sheeting in the main, and lashing the tiller to leeward. The boat will fall off and on the wind, drifting slowly to leeward. Different boats will respond differently to this maneuver; adjust the components as necessary.

When sailing a small boat in a seaway
Position all weight, including crew and passengers, as close to the center
of the boat, and as low down, as possible.
Reduce sail area to lower the angle of heel.
Do not allow anyone to move about, or stand on the deck, or sit on the
gunwale.

Sailing a small boat in a strong beam sea
If at all possible, avoid doing it.
Reduce sail to prevent excessive heeling.
To reduce pressure in a puff, do not luff up; rather, ease the sheet and
bear off.
In heavy going, zigzag, or quarter, the seas.

When running off downwind under sail
Haul in on the jibsheet to flatten the sail. If the vessel starts to broach, the
wind pressure on the flat jib will drive her head off.
Use the topping lift to raise the end of the boom to keep it clear of the
water when the vessel rolls.
Sheet in as necessary to prevent the boom from bearing against the
shrouds; otherwise, the boom will become chafed and the shrouds
will become weakened.

Running before a heavy sea in a small sailing boat
Reduce sail.
Take up on the topping lift to keep the boom from striking the waves.
Haul up the centerboard, or take it at least halfway up.
If the boat is running too fast, throw a drag on a long line overboard; a
drogue if you have one, or an oar, a thwart, a floorboard, or even a
seat cushion.
Concentrate on steering to prevent a broach.

Two common mistakes when sailing in a seaway
1. Carrying too much sail—the sails must be kept luffing to prevent the
boat from being overburdened.
2. Carrying too little sail—the boat doesn't have sufficient drive to keep
moving.

What to do if caught in a sudden squall in a small boat, according to L. Francis Herreshoff

Drop the jib first, and furl or tie it down.

If you are on your boat, take charge; on someone else's, obey orders.

Keep cool and try not to work so fast as to get out of control.

Anchor if you can.

In a real jam, in a small open boat, in rough weather, on a lee shore

Let go the anchor and try to ride it out.

If the ground tackle gives way, do not hesitate:

Set the sails, or man the oars if it's a rowboat, and drive boldly for the
   shore, head on, in the hopes of being carried high and dry.

Do not allow the boat to come broadside to the waves.

Keep in mind that at this point the fate of the boat is no longer relevant;
   the safety of the crew is.

Small-boat-sailing don'ts

Don't try to learn to sail in different boats. Learn in one first, then try others.

Don't try to learn to sail in a large boat and/or one with a complicated rig.

Don't try to learn in anything but the best weather.

Don't be afraid of the opinions of others.

Don't be afraid to fear foul weather.

Don't be afraid to refuse to go sailing if you think the conditions are not
   favorable.

Don't be afraid to assert your authority if you are the skipper. You're in
   charge, after all.

Don't be afraid to be afraid.

Don't go sailing with someone who is nervous, hysterical, overbearing,
   capricious, or a know-it-all.

Don't take any passengers until you have mastered the art of sailing.
Don't take any passengers unless you have a lifesaving device for each.
Don't go sailing unless you know how to swim.
Don't get underway without the proper gear and safety equipment.
Don't skylark while underway.
Don't allow anyone to sit on the mainsheet or any line that might have to
     be used at any moment.
Don't cleat the mainsheet.
Don't showboat in heavy weather; reduce sail as appropriate.
Don't try to ride the waves in the wake of a powerboat.
Don't get underway in the face of a storm, gale, or squall.
Don't forget that you cannot judge the force of the wind or the size of
     waves from the shore.
Don't sail in a fog without a compass.
Don't sail too close to obstructions, sandbars, buoys, ledges, etc.
Don't forget to keep an eye out for sudden gusts of wind, especially
     alongshore.
Don't fail to keep everything shipshape and orderly.
Don't sail with water in the bilge; the free-surface effect can destabilize
     the boat.
Don't pinch pennies on maintenance, especially on your running rigging.
Don't sail in a leaky boat.
Don't sail at night without lights.
Don't assume that the other fellow knows the rules of the road.
Don't try to sail too close to the wind.
Don't run downwind in a seaway if possible.
Don't sit on the lee side when sailing on the wind.
Don't climb the mast when underway.
Don't lash the helm under any circumstances.
Don't leave a lowered sail unfurled.
Don't overload the boat.
Don't sail in strange waters without a chart.
Don't try to tack into a large wave; wait for it to pass.
Don't jibe in heavy weather.
Don't panic if the boat capsizes.
Don't let go of the helm when underway.
Don't let sails or lines trail in the water.
Don't trust a squall that you cannot see through.
Don't sail in a beam wind and sea if you can avoid it.
Don't "drink and drive."
Don't lose your head.

A few rules on small-boat sailing laid down in 1894 by the Earl of Pembroke and Montgomery

As soon as your sails are set and properly trimmed, coil away the ends of all your halliards, topping lift, etc., in the bottom of the boat, capsizing the coil after you have made it so that the part of the rope that has to go up first becomes uppermost, and so will not get foul when the halyards are let go.

See that all your blocks are clear.

See that boathooks, oars, and crutches are all ready for use if required.

Never make fast your sheets in any way that can possibly jam.

Always see that your mainsheet is clear, and that it cannot get foul of anything in running out. The most favored lady passenger should not be allowed to put her feet on it.

When you have passengers on board in dangerous, squally weather, try to get them to sit down in the bottom of the boat.

Always carry an anchor or grapple and a line attached to it, and see that both are ready for instant use.

Always carry a knife. A sheath-knife is best: there is no difficulty about opening it when fingers are cold, and it will not shut on them when you are using it.

Always carry a pocket compass in case of fog.

Always carry oilskins and a sou'wester.

Always carry some spare rope, particularly odds and ends; you may always want it for something.

When you are exploring and have ladies on board, do not forget to take a landing board.

Always carry some water and biscuits when you may be out many hours.

Always have the centerboard down in coming alongside. The boat will answer her helm better and steer more accurately.

If it is ever necessary to leave your boat unattended, take great care that she can neither damage herself nor get adrift when the tide rises.

Keep out of the way of steamers and big ships when you can, even when by the rule of the road it is their business to keep out of yours.

Finally, never "moon" or think about such things as politics, philosophy, or people, when boat sailing.

Sailing on the sea proves that motion disturbs the body.
—Hippocrates

The symptoms of seasickness, according to Charles Dickens

A stout wooden wedge driven in at my right temple and out at my left, a floating deposit of lukewarm oil in my throat, and a compression of the bridge of my nose in a blunt pair of pincers.

…and according to Harriet Beecher Stowe

That disgust of existence, which, in half an hour of sailing, begins to come upon you; that strange, mysterious ineffable sensation which steals slowly and inexplicably upon you; which makes every heaving billow, every white-capped wave, the ship, the people, the sight, taste, sound, and smell of every thing a matter of inexpressible loathing!

Seasickness aboard an English cutter

In the middle of the day, when we were regaling at lunch, who should heave up his awful figure, with head enveloped in red night-cap, but Willkie, pale, hollow-cheeked, his quivering lips blue and parched, and his chin unshaven. We received him with hearty shout, but the sight of the meat and the porter and our jolly uproarious air so shook his nerves that he dropped down again in despair. —B.R. Haydon

The good in being sick at sea, according to Charles Dickens

I lay there, all the day long, quite coolly and contentedly; with no sense of weariness, with no desire to get up, or get better, or take the air; with no curiosity, or care, or regret, of any sort or degree, saving that I think I can remember, in this universal indifference, having a kind of lazy joy—of fiendish delight, if anything so lethargic can be dignified with the title—in the fact of my wife being too ill to talk to me.

One of the best temporary cures for pride and affectation is seasickness; a man who wants to vomit never puts on airs.
—Josh Billings

How holy people look when they are seasick.
—Samuel Butler

from "The Captain's Song"
by W.S. Gilbert

Captain: *I am the Captain of the* Pinafore;
    All: *And a right good captain, too!*
Captain: *You're very, very good,*
    And be it understood,
    I command a right good crew,
    All: *We're very, very good,*
    And be it understood,
    He commands a right good crew.
Captain: *Though related to a peer,*
    I can hand, reef, and steer,
    And ship a selvagee;
    I am never known to quail
    At the fury of a gale,
    And I'm never, never sick at sea!
    All: *What, never?*
Captain: *No, never!*
    All: *What, never?*
Captain: *Hardly ever!*
    All: *He's hardly ever sick at sea!*
    Then give three cheers, and one cheer more,
    For the hardy Captain of the Pinafore!

"Channel Passage"
by Rupert Brooke

The damned ship lurched and slithered. Quiet and quick
    My cold gorge rose; the long sea rolled; I knew
I must think hard of something, or be sick;
    And could think hard of only one thing—you!
You, you alone could hold my fancy ever!
    And with you memories come, sharp pain, and dole.
Now there's a choice—heartache or tortured liver!
    A sea-sick body, or a you-sick soul.

Do I forget you? Retchings hoist and tie me,
    Old meat, good meals, brown gobbets, up I throw.
Do I remember? Acrid return and slimy,
    The slobs and slobber of a last year's woe.
And still the sick ship rolls. 'Tis hard, I tell ye,
    To choose 'twixt love and nausea, heart and belly.

Dealing with seasickness

Before getting underway and while at sea: avoid heavy meals,
      particularly fried food, and alcohol.

Eat soda crackers or saltines.

Drink plenty of water; ginger ale or ginger beer is excellent.

Remain on deck in the fresh air.

Resist the temptation to lie down in your bunk.

If you must lie down, find a lee on deck.

Don't go near the galley.

Keep your eyes on the horizon.

Position yourself amidships, where motion is least.

Anticipate the vessel's motion.
Keep warm on cold days and cool on hot days.
Keep occupied.
Don't smoke; get upwind from those who do, especially if they smoke green cigars.

Four surefire ways to bring on seasickness when underway in foul weather
Read a book, especially one with fine print.
Remain below decks.
Use binoculars for extended periods.
Have a sausage bomb for lunch.

...with a beer chaser.
—Fred Brooks

We all like to see people sea-sick when we are not ourselves.
—Mark Twain

Save yourself, save others

It is best for the mariner, if he can manage it, not to think too deeply during times of stress.
—Ralph Stock

Be prepared!
Never expect anything to go as planned.
Keep emergency gear close at hand.
Know where all spares are stowed—make a list and post it.
Maintain a "culch" box—odds-and-ends for quick repairs.
Carry gear for damage control—wooden plugs of various sizes, hose
    clamps, sheet lead for emergency patches, pieces of leather and
    inner tube, several buckets, plenty of rope and marline, duct tape,
    seizing wire, etc.
Make up a "panic" bag in the event you have to take to the life raft; check
the contents periodically.

The very first actions to be taken in an emergency
Fire—man the fire extinguishers; maneuver the vessel so the fire is on the
    leeward side.
Collision—man the pumps.
Abandon ship—distribute the lifesaving devices and make sure everyone
    puts them on.
Man overboard—throw a lifesaving device; point at the person in the
    water and keep pointing at him for the benefit of the navigator.

Most desirable qualities of a lifeboat
Able to be launched quickly and easily
Resistant to capsizing
Self-righting in the event of a capsize
Speed and power against a heavy sea
Able to be run ashore without upsetting or damage
Provision for quick discharge of water taken aboard
Strong
Room for a large number of passengers
More than one method of propulsion

Required lifeboat equipment, turn of the twentieth century
Lifeline the entire length of the boat, each side, with a seine float in
    each bight
Painter
Full complement of oars, plus two spares
No fewer than four oarlocks, plus two spares
One steering oar, with oarlock or becket; or one rudder, with yoke
    and steering lanyards
Boathook
Bucket with lanyard
Two plugs for each drain hole, attached with lanyards or chains
At least two life preservers, or wooden life floats

**The above applied to lifeboats in general. Additional equipment
was required for classes of vessels depending on size. For example,
an oceangoing vessel of 150 gross tons and above had to carry
much more lifeboat gear, including:**
Lugsail
Mast, yard, and rigging
Boat compass
Lantern and one gallon of oil
Box of matches in waterproof packet
Beaker of water with at least 15 gallons capacity
Twenty-five pounds of hard bread in a sealed container
Six night distress signals
Waterproof ditty bag with sailor's palm and needles, sail twine, marline,
    marlinspike, hatchet, smoker's flint and steel, and a small bottle of
    turpentine for priming the lantern wick

The ship leaks faster than the pumps can free her
Find out where the leak is; thrum an old sail very thickly, and have stout ropes attached to each leech; make it up, take it under the bowsprit, and get the ropes on their respective sides; heave the ship to; when her headway eases, drop the sail overboard; after it has sunk beneath the keel, break the stops, haul aft on the ropes attached to each clew; when the body of the sail is over the leak, haul well taut all the ropes attached to the leeches and the head, which will prevent the sail from going aft when going ahead; make sail, and continue pumping.
                                        —from *The Kedge Anchor*, by William N. Brady, 1876

I want to make it clear to all of you that I shall never give the order "abandon ship." The only way you can leave the ship is if she sinks beneath your feet.
                                        —Admiral Earl Mountbatten, to the crew of HMS *Kelley,* 1940

If you must take to the life raft
Set off a visual distress signal—smoke bomb by day, flare by night.
Send a distress signal if a radiotelephone is on board.
Dress warmly, with foulweather gear and boots over sweaters, long
        underwear, heavy socks, etc.; above all, a lifejacket—PUT IT ON AND
        KEEP IT ON.
Take extra clothes, including more than one hat if possible—the wider
        the brim, the better.
Don't forget food, water, can openers, matches, knives, fishing gear, charts,
        compass, paper and pencils, flashlights, flares, first-aid kit, etc.
Take the radiotelephone with you if you have one.
The last things to think about are the vessel's papers, but collect them if
        you have time. Leave the love letters for last.

Two time-honored cardinal rules for abandoning ship
Women and children first
Passengers before the crew

International distress calls
CQD, the first international distress code, was composed of the general call CQ, followed by D for distress. Wireless operators used the mnemonic *Come Quickly, Danger.*

SOS was chosen to replace CQD because it was easy to send and read in Morse Code (three dots, three dashes, three dots). Wireless operators used the mnemonic *Save Our Souls*, or *Save Our Ship*.

Calling for help by radiotelephone, according to the *U.S. Coast Pilot*
Radiotelephone distress communications include the following actions:

The radiotelephone alarm signal (if available): The signal consists of two audio tones, of different pitch, transmitted alternately; its purpose is to attract the attention of persons on radio watch or to actuate automatic alarm devices. It may only be used to announce that a distress call or message is about to follow.

The distress call, consisting of:
• the distress signal MAYDAY (spoken three times);
• the words THIS IS (spoken once);
• the call sign or name of the vessel in distress (spoken three times).

The distress message follows immediately and consists of:
• the distress signal MAYDAY;
• the call sign and name of the vessel in distress;
• particulars of its position (latitude and longitude, or true bearing and distance from a known geographical position);
• the nature of the distress;
• the kind of assistance desired;
• the number of persons aboard and the condition of any injured;
• present seaworthiness of the vessel;
• description of the vessel (length; type; cabin; masts; power; color of hull, superstructure, trim; etc.);
• any other information that might facilitate the rescue, such as display of a surface-to-air identification signal or a radar reflector;
• your listening frequency and schedule;
• THIS IS (call sign and name of vessel in distress). OVER.

To remove survivors from a sinking vessel
Approach the sinking vessel from leeward, come alongside, fend off, and prepare to push away in an emergency.

Be aware of wreckage in the water, especially anything that can foul the propeller, and be wary of loose rigging and falling objects from the sinking vessel.

If it is unsafe for the survivors to drop directly into the boat, have them jump into the water first and then pull them aboard. Be sure they don life preservers before jumping and, if possible, have a lifeline attached, which will make pulling them alongside that much easier.

A few principles of lifeboat survival
Keep a level head.
Accept the leadership of the senior survivor.
Wear your life jacket.
See to the buoyancy and stability of your craft.
Do what has to be done.
Prepare for the worst weather.
Think through every maneuver.
Inventory, share, and husband resources.
Stay warm.
Exercise if possible, but avoid overexertion.
Get plenty of rest.
Keep the boat neat and clean.
Trust your mates.
Maintain a sense of humor.
Never give up.

The establishment of lifesaving services
United States (Massachusetts Humane Society)—1789
Great Britain (Royal National Lifeboat Institution)—1824
Belgium—1838
Denmark—1848
Sweden—1856
France—1865
Turkey—1868
Russia—1872
Italy—1879
Spain—1880
Germany—1885

Houses of charity

The Massachusetts Humane Society, the first lifesaving service in the United States, erected huts—known as charity, refuge, or Humane houses—at strategic locations along the coast to shelter shipwrecked sailors cast ashore on uninhabited beaches. Each of these huts was eight feet square by seven feet high, with a sliding door on the south side, a sliding shutter on the west, and a 15-foot flagpole on the east side at the top. Inside was a bench upon which to sit or lie and a pile of straw to keep the shipwrecked mariner warm while he prayed for help to arrive. Some houses also contained a lantern filled with sperm oil, a small stove, dry firewood, kindling chips, matches, a hatchet, a can of hardtack, and a jug of fresh water. Later, when the U.S. Life-Saving Service took over from the Humane Society, many of the charity houses became Halfway Houses, so-called because they were situated halfway between the main stations.

You have to go out
And that's a fact.
Nothin' says
You have to come back.
> —informal code of the old U.S. Life-Saving Service,
> successor to the Massachusetts Humane Society

The principal tools of the lifesaving station

Flare gun
Beach cart containing, among other equipment, a Lyle line-throwing gun,
    charges, faking box, ropes, lines, and the breeches-buoy apparatus
Lifeboat and cart for hauling it, plus oars, steering oar, thole pins,
    boathooks, collapsible canvas buckets, life jackets, and a sea anchor
Horse for hauling the cart

"The Life-Saver"

(Dedicated to the Men in the United States Life-Saving Service)
by Joseph C. Lincoln

When the Lord breathes his wrath above the bosom of the waters,
    When the rollers are a-poundin' on the shore,
When the mariner's a-thinkin' of his wife and sons and daughters,
    And the little home he'll, maybe, see no more;
When the bars are white and yeasty and the shoals are all a-frothin',
    When the wild no'theaster's cuttin' like a knife;
Through the seethin' roar and screech he's patrollin' on the beach,—
    The Gov'ment's hired man fer savin' life.

He's strugglin' with the gusts that strike and bruise him like a hammer,
    He's fightin' sand that stings like swarmin' bees,
He's list'nin' through the whirlwind and the thunder and the clamor—
    A-list'nin' fer the signal from the seas;
He's breakin' ribs and muscles launchin' life-boats in the surges,
    He's drippin' wet and chilled in every bone,
He's bringin' men from death back ter flesh and blood and breath,
    And he never stops ter think about his own.

He's a-pullin' at an oar that is freezin' to his fingers,
    He's a-clingin' in the riggin' of a wreck,
He knows destruction's nearer every minute that he lingers,
    But it don't appear ter worry him a speck:
He's draggin' draggled corpses from the clutches of the combers—
    The kind of job a common chap would shirk—
But he takes 'em from the wave and he fits 'em fer the grave,
    And he thinks it's all included in his work.

He is rigger, rower, swimmer, sailor, doctor, undertaker,
    And he's good at every one of 'em the same:
And he risks his life fer others in the quicksand and the breaker,
    And a thousand wives and mothers bless his name.
He's an angel dressed in oilskins, he's a saint in a "sou'wester."
    He's as plucky as they make, or ever can;
He's a hero born and bred, but it hasn't swelled his head,
    And he's jest the U. S. Gov'ment's hired man.

Annals of U.S. lifesaving

1785—The Massachusetts Humane Society, the first organization for the welfare of shipwrecked sailors, was established.

1789—The first Massachusetts Humane Society House of Refuge for shipwrecked sailors was built on Lovell's Island, Boston Harbor.

1807—The first lifeboat expressly for lifesaving was built on Nantucket Island, Massachusetts.

1807—The first lifeboat station expressly for housing a surfboat was built in Cohasset, Massachusetts.

1847—The U.S. Congress appropriated funds for the first time for rendering assistance to shipwrecked sailors.

1849—The Lifesaving Benevolent Association of New York was established.

1854—The first lifesaving stations were established on the Great Lakes.

1871—The U.S. Congress appropriated funds for the first full-time surfmen, to be supervised by the Revenue-Marine Bureau.

1878—The U.S. Congress established the U.S. Life-Saving Service.

1881—The first floating station of the U.S. Life-Saving Service was established in Louisville, Kentucky.

1899—The first motor lifeboat was launched.

1905—the U.S. Life-Saving Service undertook the mechanization of the lifeboat fleet.

1915—The Revenue-Cutter Service and the Life-Saving Service were merged into a new armed service, the United States Coast Guard.

A very heavy chambermaid

"The captain swam ashore. So did the chambermaid; she was insured for a large sum and loaded with pig iron."

> —from a nineteenth-century newspaper account of a shipwreck

Wind and sails were made for each other

—anon.

A sailing vessel, in relation to the wind

In stays—The vessel is headed directly into the wind, with steerageway.

In irons—The vessel is headed directly into the wind, without steerageway.

Aback—The wind is blowing against the forward surface of the sail.

Back and fill—The helmsperson maneuvers in confined waters by alternately allowing the sails to go aback and to go full.

Backing down—The wind against the forward surface of the sails is pushing the vessel backward; in other words, the vessel has sternway.

Luffing—The sails are not completely filled with wind.

Close-hauled, or on the wind—The vessel is sailing as close to the wind as possible.

Full-and-bye—The vessel is sailing almost close-hauled, with all sails filled and pulling strongly.

Sailing free—The vessel is between full-and-bye and beam reaching.

Reaching—The wind is blowing more or less on the vessel's beam.

Beam reaching—The wind is directly on the vessel's beam.

Broad reaching—The wind is blowing on the vessel's quarter.

Running free—The wind is blowing nearly from astern.

Running—The wind is blowing from astern.

By the lee—The vessel is running, but with the wind blowing from the same quarter as the boom is lying.

Wind, in relation to the sailing vessel

Windward—the direction from which the wind blows

Leeward—the direction toward which the wind blows

Headwind—blowing against the vessel's course

Following wind—blowing with the vessel's course

A sailing vessel tacking into the wind is said to be close-hauled; it is beating to windward, or working to windward. If the wind is on the starboard side—that is, the windward side of the vessel is the starboard side—the vessel is said to be on the starboard tack. If the wind is on the port side, the vessel is said to be on the port tack.

Winds, in a nutshell

Winds are named for the direction from which they blow. A north wind, therefore, blows out of the north toward the south.

In the Northern Hemisphere, a veering wind shifts from left to right, or clockwise, or with the sun. It would therefore shift from east to west by the way of southeast, south, and southwest.

In the Southern Hemisphere, a veering wind shifts the opposite way; that is, from right to left, or counterclockwise, or against the sun.

In the Northern Hemisphere, a backing wind shifts from right to left, or counterclockwise, or against the sun. It would therefore shift from east to west by the way of northeast, north, and northwest.

In the Southern Hemisphere, a backing wind shifts the opposite way; that is, from left to right, or clockwise, or with the sun.

Generally, the wind shifts direction by veering. A backing wind is an indication of unsettled weather; it will eventually come back to its original direction as promised in the old sea couplet:

When the wind shifts against the sun,
Trust it not, for back it will run.

Wind, a glossary

Apparent wind—true wind in combination with the wind induced by the movement of the vessel

Ash breeze—very light wind, requiring the use of oars

Backing wind—wind moving from the right to the left, or against the sun

Baffling wind—a wind that shifts randomly

Becalm—block the wind to another vessel by passing to windward of it

Becalmed—caught without wind

Black squall—a sudden strong wind that comes with a dark line on the
surface of the sea

Blow—a gale of wind

Breeze—a strong wind

Breeze-up—wind increasing in strength quickly

Calm—stillness of the air, smoothness of the sea

Capful, also puff—a puff that comes and goes quickly

Cat's-paw—discrete passing breeze that ripples the surface of the water
as if it were scratched by the claws of a cat

Chill—a puff that comes with a passing cloud that briefly obscures the sun

Clock calm—no wind, with such silence that the tick of a clock can be heard

Contrary wind, also headwind, dead-on-ender, nose-ender, muzzler—
a wind blowing against a vessel's intended course

Dead calm, also roaring calm, flat-ass calm, up-and-down breeze,
Paddy's hurricane, Irish hurricane—no wind, no cat's-paws,
not even the hint of a breeze

Double-reef breeze—strong wind, requiring two reefs in the sails

Fair wind—one that allows a vessel to proceed without tacking

Fog breeze—strong wind in foggy weather

Foul wind—one that forces a vessel to tack continually

Gasoline breeze—very light wind, requiring auxiliary power

Glass calm—no wind, causing the sea to look like a sheet of
glass

Great guns—a heavy wind

Hauling wind—the wind direction moving more ahead

Lane of wind—a narrow wind with calm on either
side

Living gale—a severe storm

Paltry wind—light and intermittent wind, and
not much of it

Piping up—wind strength increasing suddenly and quickly

Quarter wind—one that blows on a
vessel's quarter

Scant wind—not much more
than just enough to
induce steerageway

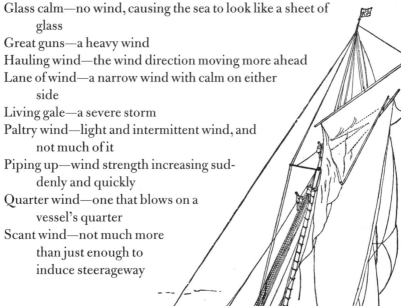

Fred. S. Coggens.

Slant—a favorable wind

Soldier's wind—steady wind from a direction that allows a vessel to
maintain her course without tacking

True wind—the wind as it is, without taking into consideration the
movement of the vessel

Veering wind—wind moving from the left to the right, or with the sun

White squall—a sudden wind so strong that it turns the surface of the sea
to white froth

Whole-sail wind—enough wind for a vessel to carry all her canvas

Windbound—trapped at anchor or in port without a favorable wind for
getting underway

To determine true wind

Look for indicators on the shore, such as flags, wind vanes, or smoke
from a chimney; or on moored or anchored vessels, such as telltales and
pennants.

To determine apparent wind

Look at a telltale or pennant *on your own vessel*.
—or—
Take off your hat and face into the wind; when you can hear the wind
equally in both ears, your nose is pointing toward the apparent wind.

The Beaufort Scale

Beaufort number	State of air	Velocity (in knots)
0	Calm	0–1
1	Light airs	1–3
2	Slight breeze	4–6
3	Gentle breeze	7–10
4	Moderate breeze	11–16
5	Fresh breeze	17–21
6	Strong breeze	22–27
7	Moderate gale	28–33
8	Fresh gale	34–40
9	Strong gale	41–47
10	Whole gale	48–55
11	Storm	56–65
12	Hurricane	above 65

Judging wind speed

Less than 1 knot—Smoke rises vertically.

1–3 knots—Smoke drifts.

4–6 knots—Wind is felt on face.

7–10 knots—Light flag extends from pole.

11–16 knots—Wind raises dust, cinders, loose paper, etc.

17–21 knots—Flag waves and snaps briskly.

22–27 knots—Wind whistles in rigging.

28–33 knots—Walking against the wind is difficult.

34–40 knots—Wind impedes progress.

The major wind belts

The northern trade winds, blowing from the northeast in the Northern
Hemisphere, from about 30 degrees north latitude to the equator

The southern trade winds, blowing from the southeast in the Southern
Hemisphere, from about 30 degrees south latitude to the equator

The prevailing southwesterlies in the middle latitudes of the Northern
Hemisphere

The prevailing northwesterlies in the middle latitudes of the Southern
Hemisphere

The polar easterlies, blowing from the east in the polar regions

One source of the wind

King Erik of Sweden was in his time held second to none in the magical
art; and he was so familiar with the evil spirits whom he worshipped, that
what way soever he turned his cap, the wind would presently blow that
way. For this he was called Windycap.   —Olaus Magnus

Winds around the world

Mistral—cold, dry northwest wind in the Gulf of Lyon, the Tyrrhenian
Sea, and the Adriatic

Sirocco—dry southerly or southeasterly wind from Africa's Sahara,
blowing across the Mediterranean

Tramontana, or Gli Secchi—cold, dangerous wind blowing down
the Adriatic

Levanter—prevailing summer easterly or northeasterly on the North
African coast of the Mediterranean

Harmattan—hot easterly wind, filled with dust, blowing off the west
coast of Africa

Solano—southeasterly wind, charged with dust, blowing from Africa
into Spain

Norte—northerly gale in the Gulf of Mexico

Pampero—southwesterly gales blowing out of the Argentine pampas into the South Atlantic

Papagayo—strong northeasterly wind with fine, clear weather on the west coast of Central America

Tehuantepecer—violent northerly wind in the Gulf of Tehuantepec, Central America

Willi Waw—strong wind gusts blowing down steep mountainsides, particularly in the Strait of Magellan and off Gibraltar

Coastal breezes

During the day—sea breeze, caused by air becoming heated over the land and rising, thus drawing cool air in from the sea

At night—land breeze, caused by air becoming cooled over the land and falling, resulting in an outflow of air toward the sea

O for a soft and gentle wind!
I hear a fair one cry;
But give to me the snoring breeze
And white waves heaving high.
—Allan Cunningham

Expect wind if any of these exist

Clouds with bright edges

Rainbows

Unusually clear atmosphere

From "The Rime of the Ancient Mariner"

by Samuel Taylor Coleridge

But soon there breathed a wind on me,
Nor sound nor motion made:
Its path was not upon the sea,
In ripple or in shade.

It raised my hair, it fanned my cheek
Like a meadow-gale of spring—
It mingled strangely with my fears,
Yet it felt like a welcoming.

Swiftly, swiftly flew the ship,
Yet she sailed softly too:
Sweetly, sweetly blew the breeze—
On me alone it blew.

Bessie Miller of Stromness, in the early eighteenth century, had a way with the wind, according to Sir Walter Scott

Her fee was extremely moderate, being exactly sixpence, for which, as she explained herself, she boiled the kettle and gave the bark the advantage of her prayers, for she disclaimed all unlawful arts. The wind thus petitioned for was sure, she said, to arrive, though occasionally the mariner had to wait some time for it.

One way to summon the wind, according to Henry Fielding

The kitten at last recovered, to the great joy of the good captain: but to the great disappointment of some of the sailors, who asserted that the drowning of a cat was the very surest way of raising a favourable wind.

Five ways to raise a wind, least effective to most effective

Stick the point of a knife into the mast.
Throw a penny overboard.
Say the word "pig."
Say the words "black pig."
Throw a penny overboard and at the same time say the words "black pig."

Then hang onto your hat!
      —Fred Brooks

What you are bound to get is a little of everything, according to Mark Twain

Probable northeast to southwest winds, varying to the northward and westward and eastward and points between. High and low barometer swapping around from place to place, probable areas of rain, snow, hail, and drought, proceeded or preceded by earthquakes with thunder and lightning.

On the northeast coast of the U.S.

North winds send hail,
South winds bring rain.
East winds we bewail,
West winds blow amain.
Northeast is too cold,
Southeast not too warm.
Northwest is too bold,
Southwest blows no harm.
      —anon.

A head wind, according to Charles Dickens
Imagine a human face upon the vessel's prow, with fifteen thousand Samsons in one bent upon driving her back, and hitting her exactly between the eyes whenever she attempts to advance an inch. Imagine the ship herself, with every pulse and artery of her huge body swoln [sic] and bursting under this mal-treatment, sworn to go on or die.

A headwind, according to Henry Fielding
The captain now grew outrageous, and declaring open war with the wind, took a resolution rather more bold than wise of sailing in defiance of it and in its teeth. He declared he would let go his anchor no more, but would beat the sea while he had either yard or sail left.

A pennon whimpers—the breeze has found us—
A headsail jumps through the thinning haze.
The whole hull follows, till—broad around us—
The clean-swept ocean says: "Go your ways!"
—Rudyard Kipling

Enjoy yourself
What can be more magnificent than a strong gale of a clear winter's day— the ship springing forward under reefed topsails, and nothing to be seen but the white foamy tops of the waves. There is nothing that elevates the spirits so much as this, it is like riding a fiery horse, he goes at his own speed, but he carries you where you guide.
—John M. Forbes

Sailcloth and rope

*M*en *in a ship are always looking up, and men ashore generally
looking down.*   —John Masefield

A shipboard conversation, according to Eric Newby
"Beautiful, isn't she? said the Sailmaker, coming up at this moment to
look aloft at his sails.

"Yes, very," I answered, reluctant to spoil the moment by an
unseemly display of sentiment.

"Dammit, why not say so then?" he exploded blimpishly, and then
added more softly: "Sails, loveliest things ever made."

And so I sing of man-made things,
    That fascinate, inspire me.
Yes, fabrics that can live and breathe—
    These tops'ls, rising from the sea!
              —Joseph Chase Allen

.

**In the selection of canvas for making a suit of sails, a yachtsman can-
not be too particular, says Vanderdecken**
Whether good or bad material be put in them, the cost of making will all
be the same; but badly woven canvas will not last in form or work any
length of time, whereas a first-rate material when well cut and made up, if
it receives fairplay in the handling, will work until the last rag leaves the
bolt ropes; therefore the worst economy a yachtsman can exercise is in
clipping down and paring the expenditure under the head of sails.

How much sail area is enough?

Too little can be frustrating.

Too much can be overwhelming.

The ideal is the amount the boat can stand up to and the crew can
reasonably handle in all conditions.

Sail area rules of thumb, cruising boats

Sail area in square feet = square of the waterline length.
> —or—

100 square feet of sail for every ton of displacement.

To measure the area of a triangular sail

Drop a vertical line from any corner to the opposite side.

The length of the opposite side multiplied by half the vertical equals sail area.

To measure the area of a gaff sail

Divide the sail into two triangles.

Determine the area of each triangle using the method above.

The sum of the areas of the two triangles equals the area of the sail.

Components of canvas

Warp—the threads running lengthwise

Weft—the threads running crosswise

Selvage—the finished edge

Material for sailcloth down the ages

earliest—rush, reed, grass, and animal skins

Ancient Greece—hemp

Middle Ages—flax

mid-nineteenth century—cotton canvas

mid-twentieth century—manmade fibers

The first sail made of manmade fiber used in a yacht race was a genoa
made of rayon on the J-boat *Ranger* in 1937. The first nylon sails were
introduced in the mid-1940s; the first Dacron in the early 1950s. The first
big success for Dacron sails in yacht racing was at the 1954 Star World
Championships, where the only competitor with such sails took first place.

Polyester sailcloth around the world

Dacron—United States

Terylene—Great Britain

Tergal—France

Tetron—Japan

The major parts of a sail
Cloths—the panels of fabric
Seams—the sewn joints of the cloths
Boltrope—the rope reinforcement around the edges of the entire sail

Sail covers
Cotton sails—covers of cotton canvas
Dacron or synthetic sails—covers of Dacron, or other synthetics,
     or cotton canvas
Do not use Dacron sail covers with cotton sails, as Dacron traps
     condensation and will cause the cotton to rot.

Sailors versus tailors
Sailors sit and sew very differently from tailors; instead of doubling up
their legs under them they stretch them out straight before them as they
sit upon the deck. Their thimble is also peculiar, not being worn on the
top of the finger, but upon the ball of the thumb, to which it is fastened by
a leather strap, buckled around the wrist. I was surprised at the expedition and neatness with which they sewed with their coarse needles and
long threads.   —Robert Whyte, passenger on an immigrant ship, 1847

The tools of the sailmaker
Bench
Needles, and cases to hold them
Palms, of two types—one for seaming, the other for roping. The roping
     palm had an extra layer of leather at the thumb guard so the twine
     could be drawn up tightly without cutting the user's thumb.
Beeswax—for lubrication and to hold the lay of the twine, and to keep
     moisture out of the twine of the finished sail
Bench hook—to hold the canvas taut while seaming
Fids and spikes—to open the lay of boltropes
Stabbers—to open holes in the cloth for eyelets, cringles, and other fittings
Seam rubber—to smooth the seam and work the twine into the surface of
     the sail to reduce chafe
Rigging knives and sharpening stones
Scissors
Seam gauges
Tape measure

Old-style composition for waxing twine used in sailmaking
4 pounds beeswax
5 pounds tallow
1 pound turpentine
 All were heated together in a double boiler, stirred thoroughly, and used after it had cooled.

An old recipe for tanning natural-fiber sails (cotton or flax) to prevent rot
Heat 5 gallons raw linseed oil and 1¼ pounds beeswax in a large copper kettle.
When it reaches the boiling point, gradually add 20 pounds red ochre and 10 pounds light brown ochre. (These proportions produce a rich, red-brown color; for a redder tone, add more red ochre and less light brown; for a browner tone, add less red ochre and more light brown.)
Allow to boil for 5 minutes, stirring all the time; then shut off the heat.
When cool, add 10 gallons kerosene.
Spread the sail—it must be dry before you begin—on a clean surface.
Drive the mixture thoroughly into the weave of the sailcloth with a stiff brush on both sides of the sail.
Hang the sail in a well-ventilated shed to dry for about two weeks, then lay it in the sun for a day or two, turning it occasionally.

Old-style recipes for maintaining cotton or flax sails
Waterproofing—Add 1 ounce yellow soap and 1 ounce beeswax to 1 quart boiled linseed oil; boil together to the consistency of wet paint; apply to canvas with a brush.
Preventing mildew—Steep canvas for eight or ten hours in a solution of 1 pound finely powdered alum and 2 ounces finely powdered sugar of lead in fresh water; allow the canvas to dry slowly.
Bleaching—Mix together 1 barrel salt water, 3 pounds chloride of lime, 3 pounds soda-ash, 2 pounds whiting, and 3 pounds salt; use solution to scrub the sail on both sides with a broom; spread the sail to dry.

Sails are like clothes, says Thomas Fleming Day
Take the same care of your sails as you do of your best suit of clothes. When you put your clothes away you don't roll them up in a tight ball and leave them in a damp place for days at a time.

To test sail canvas for deterioration
Bore a sample with a fid. If the threads are in poor condition, they will break easily.

To protect sails and cushions in storage from vermin
Rats and mice love to chew up stored canvas products during winter layup. They do this not because they are hungry but because they are looking for material for their nests. Distract them with a stack of newspapers left out in the open near the sails and cushions; they will usually take the paper because it is easier to shred.

The elemental differences between a fore-and-aft sail and a square sail
The leech and the luff of a fore-and-aft sail are always the same, no matter the tack.
The leech of a square sail becomes the luff, and vice versa, when the vessel changes tacks.

Principal sails of a square-rigger, bottom to top
Course
Lower topsail
Upper topsail
Topgallant
Royal
Skysail
Moonsail, or moonraker (rare)
Starsail, or stargazer (fanciful)
Heavensail, or heaven-disturber (more fanciful)
Angel's footstool (even more fanciful)
    The topmost sail on a ship, no matter which one it was, was often nicknamed the Curse o' God, as it required such a climb to reach it.

He picked up the ball of twine and put it to his nose and drew in the smell of boats, caulking smell, rope-locker smell.   —John Hersey

There is no rope cult at sea
As I looked at the rope I further considered how strange it was that rope had never been worshiped. Men have worshiped the wall, and the post, and the sun, and the house. They have worshiped their food and their drink. They have, you may say, ceremonially worshiped their clothes; they have worshiped their headgear especially, crowns, mitres, ta-ra-ras; and they have worshiped the music which they have created. But I have never heard of any one worshiping a rope.   —Hilaire Belloc

Ropemaking in the classical manner

Ropes are a combination of several Threads of Hemp, twisted together by means of a Wheel in the Rope-Walk. These Threads are called Rope-Yarns, and the Size of the Rope in Diameter, will be according to the Number of Yarns contained in it.

A Proportion of Yarns (covered with Tar) are first twisted together. This is called a Strand; three, or more of which being twisted together, form the Rope; and according to the number of these Strands, it is said to be either Hawser-laid, Shroud-laid, or Cable-laid.

A Hawser-laid rope is composed of three single Strands, each containing an equal Quantity of Yarns, and is laid right-handed, or what is termed with the Sun.

A Shroud-laid rope consists of four Strands of an equal Number of Yarns, and is also laid with the Sun.

A Cable-laid rope is divided into nine Strands of an equal Number of Yarns: these nine Strands being again laid into three, by twisting three of the small Strands into one. It is laid left-handed or against the Sun.

—from Darcy Lever's *The Young Sea Officer's Sheet Anchor,* 1819

The major natural fibers used to make rope

Hemp, made from the fiber of the hemp plant, mostly from Russia and America. Brown in color, moderately coarse in texture, with great strength. In the late nineteenth century, the best rope for yachting purposes was made of hemp and was graded as follows: "clean" (also known as "staple"), made from hemp fibers stripped from plants that had not yet gone to seed; "half clean," made from rejected "clean" fiber; "outshot," made from fibers stripped from the plant after it had gone to seed.

Manila, made from abaca, the stalk of the wild banana, mostly from the Philippines. Light brown in color, moderately light in texture, strong, but not as strong as hemp.

Sisal, made from a Javanese (Indonesian) plant resembling cactus. Light in color, coarse, moderately strong.

Coir, made from coconut-husk fiber from the palm tree. Brown with a reddish cast, coarse in texture, strong, very buoyant and resistant to waterlogging, but only one-quarter the strength of manila.

Hide, made from rawhide. Stronger than hemp, but subject to becoming swollen when wet.

Cotton, made from the fibers of the cotton plant. White or off-white in color, fine in texture, not strong.

Linen, made from the fibers of the flax plant. Tannish-gray in color, limp and flexible, very strong.

Hemp is a dusky, dark fellow, a sort of Indian; but Manilla is as a golden-haired Circassian to behold.   —Herman Melville, *Moby-Dick*

Small cordage, aka small stuff

Small cordage, or "stuff," was known generically by the number of threads it contained ("18-thread stuff," "15-thread stuff") or by a specific name, such as:

Spun-yarn—rough, cheap stuff, loosely laid up, left-hand lay, of two, three, or four strands; used for seizings and service where neatness wasn't required

Marline—two-strand stuff, left-hand lay

Houseline—three-strand stuff, left-hand lay

Roundline—three-strand stuff, right-hand lay

Twine—small stuff made from the finest hemp

Seizing-stuff—used for seizings and service where high strength and extreme neatness were required. It was made by ropemaking machinery and was three-strand, right-hand lay, with two, three, or four threads to the strand. The greater the number of threads, the higher the quality of the stuff.

Ratline-stuff—similar to seizing-stuff, but larger. It was three-strand, right-hand lay, with four, five, six, seven, or even eight threads to the strand.

Rope-yarn—made from remnants of old cordage, known as "junk," untwisted and tarred; used for temporary seizings and other quick, temporary work

Fox—two rope-yarns twisted together by hand, or single yarns twisted against their natural lay, and rubbed smooth; used for light seizings

Modern rope construction

Stranded, aka twisted, or laid—made up of yarns twisted in one direction, strands (usually three) twisted the other

Single braid—yarns twisted into strands, which are braided

Double braid—a braided core inside a braided cover

Parallel-fiber core—a core of bundled unidirectional fibers with a braided cover

Characteristics of synthetic ropes

Nylon—strongest of the common synthetics, with a great amount of elasticity. Easy to handle. Resistant to alkalines but susceptible to acids and paint solvents. Reasonably resistant to abrasion and ultraviolet light. Ideal for mooring and towing lines, and anchor warps, because of its ability to absorb shock. Poor choice for halyards and standing rigging, because of its stretchiness.

Polyester, aka Dacron, Terylene—strong, but not quite as strong as nylon. Substantially less elastic than nylon. Reasonably resistant to abrasion and ultraviolet light. Resistant to acids but susceptible to alkalines and paint solvents. Because of its low-stretch characteristics, it is suitable for sheets, halyards, and other running rigging, especially if it has been prestretched. Can be given texture, such as the "feel" of cotton line, which makes it excellent for lines that are frequently handled.

Polypropylene—weaker than nylon and polyester, and more susceptible to chafe and abrasion. Very light and buoyant. Little elasticity.

Will deteriorate quickly in sunlight unless manufactured with ultraviolet inhibitors. Resistant to most acids and alkalis, but susceptible to paint solvents. Tends to be hard on the hands. Good for heaving lines, standing rigging, water-ski towropes, lanyards on life buoys, and mooring lines if protected from chafe. Less expensive than nylon or polyester.

Kevlar, aka Aramid—strong, low stretch, stiff, difficult to work, expensive; used for running rigging.

High-modulus polyethylene—stronger than wire weight for weight, floats, low stretch, expensive; replacement for wire

Take this to heart
Do not be cheap with rope. If it is worn out, throw it out.

Good rope
Fibers are long and uniform.
Yarns are uniform.
Strands are smooth and symmetrical.
The finished rope looks slick and feels smooth.

Poor rope
Stray fibers stick out from the surface.
Fibers vary in size.
Individual fibers are kinked and snarled.
Yarns vary in thickness and are bunchy in places.
The lay is not uniform—too loose in some spots; too tight in others.

Old, useless rope
Looks dirty and tired.
Fibers are too limp, or too stiff.
Surface of the strands is chafed and raggedy.
Inside fibers are matted and powdery.

The two greatest enemies of natural-fiber rope
Friction
Rot

The two greatest enemies of synthetic-fiber rope
Friction
Sunlight

The protection of rope

Worming—the laying of marline tightly into the seams between the
strands in rope

Parceling—the wrapping of narrow strips of canvas around the rope with
the lay (to the right in right-laid rope and to the left in left-laid
rope). The canvas is well tarred.

Serving—the tight wrapping of marline around the rope against the lay
(to the left in right-laid rope and to the right in left-laid rope)

The purpose of all this is to protect rope from chafe. Some small ropes
are served only. Large ropes are wormed first, parceled next, and
finally served.

To tar rope

Warm Stockholm tar in a double boiler over low heat.

Apply with a stiff-bristle brush.

If the tar will not brush out properly, even after warming, thin with turpentine before applying.

Care of synthetic rope

Keep the rope free of sand, dirt, and grit.

Keep clean and smooth any surfaces on which the rope is bent or tied.

Prevent contact with rust, which will rob oxygen from the fibers and
weaken the rope's strength.

Avoid uses that result in abrasion; do not run rope over sharp edges; tape
anything—cotter pins, for example—that can cause snags.

Dirt and salt can ruin the interior fibers, so wash down with fresh water
after it has been used in salt water; do not use strong detergents or
very hot water.

Rope can be cleaned in a washing machine by putting it in a mesh bag
and using a gentle cycle; do not use harsh detergents, and do not
use a mechanical dryer—hang in coils to dry.

Store the rope out of the sun when not used for long periods.

Uncoiling and coiling rope

If rope is purchased in a coil, it should be uncoiled from the inside.

If rope is purchased on a reel, remove it by pulling it off the top, with the
reel free to rotate.

Rope should be coiled in the direction of the lay. Right-laid rope should
be coiled in a clockwise direction. Left-laid rope should be coiled
in a counterclockwise direction.

To work the kinks out of rope
Coil the rope against the lay, pull the lower end up through the center of
the coil, and then recoil it with the lay. If the rope is severely kinked,
repeat the procedure.

     —alternatively—

Stream the rope over the stern while underway until the kinks are worked
out, then wash it thoroughly with fresh water, coil properly, and allow to dry.

Knots, rigging, rigs, and ballast

A knot is a picky thing; if you don't tie it exactly right, it is an entirely different knot—or it is nothing at all. —Brion Toss

Learning from a knot

Amongst others, he taught me a fisherman's bend, which he pronounced to be the king of all knots; "and, Mr. Simple," continued he, "there is a moral in that knot. You observe, that when the parts are drawn the right way, and together, the more you pull the faster they hold, and the more impossible to untie them; but see, by hauling them apart, how a little difference, a pull the other way, immediately disunites them, and then how easy they cast off in a moment. That points out the necessity of pulling together in this world, Mr. Simple, when we wish to hold on."
—from *Peter Simple*, by Captain Frederick Marryat

Knot tying is more than tying knots

To me the simple act of tying a knot is an adventure in unlimited space. A bit of string affords a dimensional latitude that is unique among the entities. For an uncomplicated strand is a palpable object that, for all practical purposes, possesses one dimension only. If we move a single strand in a plane, interlacing it at will, actual objects of beauty and utility can result in what is practically two dimensions; and if we choose to direct our strand out of this one plane, another dimension is added which provides opportunity for an excursion that is limited only by the scope of our own imagery and the length of the ropemaker's coil. —Clifford Ashley

"Haul out to leeward," comes at last,
With a cheering from the fore and main;
"Knot your reef-points, and knot them fast!"
—from "Reefing Topsails," by Walter Mitchell

Four basic knot groups
Knots
Bends
Hitches
Splices

The elements of a good knot
Quickly and easily tied
Secure, without danger of slipping or loosening
Jam-free, yet easy to untie or cast off
Appropriate for its use

The terminology of knots
Knot—a combination of loops, some interlocking, in a rope
Bend—a knot used to fasten a rope to an object, such as a stanchion, or to
    join two ropes
Hitch—a temporary knot used to fasten a rope, usually under strain, to an
    object
Splice—the joining of two ropes by intertwining the strands
Standing part—the portion of a rope coming from a fixed point
Working part—the portion of a rope being used to form a knot
Bitter end—the end of a rope
Bight—a bend or loop in a rope
Turn—a bight around an object
Round turn—a bight going all the way around an object and back on itself

It is far better to understand rope and its care, and to thoroughly under-
stand a few useful knots (in darkness, ice, or snow) than it is to know sev-
eral hundred knots only slightly.   —Carl Lane

Elementary knots according to use
To prevent a line from running out of a block or fairlead—
    figure-of-eight knot
To join two lengths of line of equal thickness—square or reef knot

To join two lengths of line of unequal thickness—sheet or becket bend
To temporarily shorten a line—sheepshank
To join the end of a line to an object—round turn and two half hitches; clove hitch
To put a temporary eye in the end of a line—bowline

Three rope-working tools
Marlinspike for fiber rope—highly polished tool steel, averaging about 8 inches long, with a straight taper to a point and no head at the other end
Marlinspike for wire rope—same as above, except with a head or knob at the thickest end
Fid—polished hickory, ash, or, best, lignum vitae; thicker than a marlinspike and with a quicker taper and a blunter point

The various types of splices
Eye splice—for creating an eye in the end of a rope
Sailmaker's eye splice—preserves the lay of the rope when making an eye
Sailmaker's splice—for splicing together two ropes of unequal size
Short splice—a quickly made splice for ropes of moderate size; increases the diameter of the rope at the splice
Long splice—the strongest splice; maintains the diameter of the rope
Mariner's splice—a long splice in a cable-laid rope
Chain splice—for splicing rope into a chain
Back splice—for finishing off the end of a rope (the strands being crowned and then short-spliced back into the lay of the rope)
Cut splice—for creating an eye in the middle of a rope

In splicing, practice makes perfect, and in the doing you will learn more than from reading any ten books on the subject.   —Hervey Garrett Smith

Yes, we did a heap o' riggin'
In those rampin' boomin' days,
When the wooden ships were buildin'
On their quaint old greasy ways;
Crafts of every sort an' fashion,
Big an' little, lithe an' tall,
Had their birthplace by the harbor,
An' we rigged 'em one and all.

Our riggin' was for sailors,
Tough an' hardy Bluenose dogs,
With their hands as hard as leather,
An' their boots thick heavy clogs,
They were nuthin' much like angels,
But they'd learned their business right,
An' they trusted to our riggin'
When the sea was roarin' white.

           —from "Old Ship Riggers," by H.A. Cody

Rigging, in a nutshell

The Rigging of a Ship consists of a quantity of Ropes, or Cordage, of various Dimensions, for the support of the Masts and Yards. Those which are fixed and stationary, such as Shrouds, Stays, and Back-stays, are termed Standing Rigging; but those which reeve through Blocks, or Sheave-Holes, are denominated Running Rigging; such as Halliards, Braces, Clew-lines, Buntlines, &c. &c. These are occasionally hauled upon, or let go, for the purpose of working the Ship.

      —from *The Young Sea Officer's Sheet Anchor*, by Darcy Lever Esq., 1819

Rig her with the best materials

There is nothing pertaining to a yacht that the yachtsman should be more particular about than the materials composing his running and standing rigging, for upon them very often his life and the lives of his crew depend;—niggardly economy has to my own knowledge been frequently exercised in this particular branch, and in all cases failure ensued. It is the supremest folly in the world to imagine that a hull can be brought to perfection, launched, and indifferently sparred, and worse rigged, and that success may be anticipated.   —Vanderdecken

The two principal reasons for running a line through a block

To change the direction of the pull
To increase the power of the pull

A block-and-tackle lexicon

Block—a device used to change the direction of pull of a rope
Made block—one made up of several pieces of wood or iron fastened
    together with rivets or bolts

Mortised block—one made of a single piece of wood, mortised

Shell—the outside part, of either metal or wood

Swallow—the space between the shell and the sheave through which the rope passes

Breech—the space opposite the swallow

Strap—the metal, wire, or rope wrap around the outside of the block; holds the hook or the eye to the block

Score—the cut made around the outside of the block to take the strap

Sheave—the revolving, grooved wheel on which the rope lies

Pin—the axle on which the sheave turns

Single block—one sheave

Double block—two sheaves

Treble block—three sheaves

Internal-bound block—a metal strop inside the shell

External-bound block—a metal strop outside the shell

Fiddle block—two sheaves, one above the other in the same shell

Snatch block—fitted with a hinged clamp at the side to permit rope to be slipped over the sheave

Patent block—one in which the sheave pin is surrounded by ball bearings or a roller bushing

Tackle—blocks and rope arranged to multiply power

Fall—the rope portion of a tackle

Standing part—the part of the fall attached to a block

Hauling part—the part of the fall that is hauled upon

Reeve—to pass a rope through a block

Two-block—to bring two blocks of a tackle together

Overhaul—to separate two blocks of a tackle

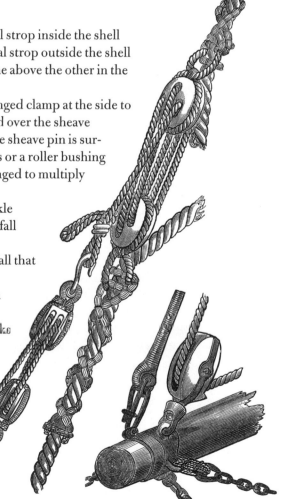

To determine the amount of weight a tackle will lift
First determine the amount of weight one part of the rope will lift; this is
     generally available from the manufacturer.
Multiply this by the number of parts at the movable block.
Subtract one quarter from this to account for resistance.
     For example: A tackle is made up of rope rated at 1,000 pounds and
a two-part movable block. Then, 1,000 times 2 (parts) equals 2,000,
minus one quarter equals 1,500 pounds—the amount of weight the tackle can safely lift.

A major principle when considering the advantage of a block and tackle
What is gained in power is lost in speed, and vice versa.

Blocks without sheaves
Deadeye—a circular piece of wood with three holes in it and a groove
     around the outer edge for a shroud or stay to lie in; a lanyard is rove
     through the holes to set up the shroud or stay.
Bull's-eye—a circular piece of wood with a single hole in it and a groove
     around the outer edge; as with the deadeye, a lanyard is rove
     through the hole.

Wood for blocks, deadeyes, and bull's-eyes, in order of preference
Lignum vitae
Elm
Locust
Hickory
Walnut
According to Arthur Dauphinee, blockmaker of Lunenburg, Nova
Scotia, teak makes poor deadeyes and shell blocks.
     Look for well seasoned stock that is close grained and without
checks. Soak the block shell or deadeye in hot raw linseed oil until it is
saturated, about two to three hours, wipe off the excess, and allow to
harden for a week before use.

Big ropes and small blocks to ya!
               —a sailor's curse, anon.

Joseph Conrad on the fore-and-aft rig

The fore-and-aft rig in its simplicity and the beauty of its aspect under every angle of vision is, I believe, unapproachable. A schooner, yawl, or cutter in charge of a capable man seems to handle herself as if endowed with the power of reasoning and the gift of swift execution.

No matter how fetching the theoretical arguments in favor of a gadgety rig may be, the fact is that a complicated and highly mechanized sailing rig is inherently dangerous in heavy weather. —Howard I. Chapelle

With the smallest rig you will get just as much fun as with the most expensive. —Edwin W. Kendrick

A single sail does not necessarily denote simplicity in handling. —Carl Lane

The una boat gets its name

In Britain, the generic name for a catboat—a small craft with a single sail—is una boat, which comes from a catboat named *Una* bought in America from boatbuilder and yacht designer Robert Fish by the Marquis of Conyngham in 1853 and shipped to England, where she was brought to Cowes.

Pros and cons of the popular cruising-yacht rigs

Sloop

One mast, at least two sails (main and jib).

Pro—Only two primary sails to handle; mast stepped relatively far forward, allowing more open space in the cabin (assuming the mast is stepped on the keel); rigging relatively simple.

Con—Forward-stepped mast concentrates weight toward bow, sometimes causing the hull to plunge into steep seas; heaving-to without a split foretriangle can be problematical in some conditions; relatively large size of the mainsail can cause difficulty in handling, especially when reefing.

Cutter

One mast, at least three sails (main, forestaysail, jib).

Pro—Good balance between the headsails and the mainsail; more possible sail combinations than with the sloop; heaving-to relatively easy.

Con—Relatively large mainsail can be difficult to handle; position of the mast when stepped on the keel breaks up the open space in the cabin; more rigging required than on the sloop.

Yawl and Ketch

Yawl: two masts, at least three sails (main, jib, mizzen), the after mast stepped behind the rudderpost.

Ketch: two masts, at least three sails (main, jib, mizzen), the after mast stepped forward of the rudderpost.

Pro—Large after-sail triangle broken up into a smaller main and small mizzen; more reduced-sail combinations possible; mainmast stepped farther forward than on the cutter, preserving open space below.

Con—Windward ability not as good as the cutter's, nor is it as fast, size for size; more spars and rigging required than for the sloop and cutter.

Schooner

Two or more masts, at least three sails (main, fore, jib), the forward mast shorter than the after one, or of equal height.

Pro—Many possible sail combinations; fast off the wind; handsome.

Con—Largish mainsail; complex rigging; can be difficult to handle with a shorthanded crew.

Oh! the yawl, the shippy little yawl,
She's able and stable—
She has no faults at all;
You tack her, or back her,
She'll answer ev'ry call;
The handy little, dainty little,
three-ton yawl.

—anon.

A full-rigged ship is a royal queen,
Way-hay for Boston town, oh!
A lady at court is a barquentine,
A barque is a gal with ringlets fair,
A brig is the same with shorter hair,
A topsail schooner's a racing mare,
But, a schooner, she's a clown-o!

—old chanty

The evolution of the cargo schooner

Sixteenth or seventeenth century—The fore-and-aft two-masted
schooner rig was developed in Europe.

1713—A two-masted vessel built by Captain Andrew Robinson in
Gloucester, Massachusetts, was allegedly given the name
"schooner" after a bystander allegedly said, "See how she schoons!"

1849—A three-masted schooner, the *Zachary Taylor*, was built in
Philadelphia, Pennsylvania.

1866—The largest two-master, the *Oliver Ames*, 456 tons, was built at
Berkeley, Massachusetts.

1880—The first four-master, the *W.L. White*, 995 tons, was built at Bath,
Maine.

1882—The first schooner over 1,000 tons, the *Ellicott B. Church*, a four-
master at 1,137 tons, was built at Bath, Maine.

1884—The largest three-master ever, the *Bradford C. French*, 968 tons,
was built at Kennebunk, Maine.

1888—The first five-masted schooner, the *Governor Ames,* 1,778 tons, was built at Waldoboro, Maine.

1897—The first schooner over 2,000 tons, the four-master *Frank A. Palmer,* was built at Bath, Maine.

1900—The first schooner over 2,600 tons, the five-master *William C. Carnegie,* was built at Bath, Maine.

1900—The first six-master, the *George W. Wells,* 2,970 tons, was built at Camden, Maine.

1902—The first and only seven-master, the *Thomas W. Lawson,* 5,218 tons, was built at Quincy, Massachusetts.

The accepted names of schooner masts; from the bow, aft

Two-master—fore, main
Three-master—fore, main, spanker
Four-master—fore, main, mizzen, spanker
Five-master—fore, main, mizzen, jigger, spanker
Six-master—fore, main, mizzen, jigger, driver, spanker
Seven-master—fore, main, mizzen, jigger, driver, pusher, spanker

The names of square-rigger masts

Naming the masts of the monster five-masted square-riggers of the late nineteenth and early twentieth centuries was always a problem; several sets of names were used, but none became universal:

Bow, fore, main, mizzen, after
Fore, main, mizzen, after, jigger
Bow, fore, main, after, jigger
Fore, main, mizzen, jigger, after jigger
Fore, main, mizzen, jigger, spanker
Fore, main, middle, mizzen, jigger

One wag, the captain of the *Agincourt,* simplified the matter by naming the masts 1, 2, 3, 4, and 5.

To prevent halyards from tapping the mast in an anchorage and keeping the crew awake

Pull the halyards away from the mast with bungee cord or light line looped to the shrouds

—or—

Unfasten the halyards from the heads of the sails and belay them to a pin or a cleat by the rail.

That tapping? Ah, my owner friend, that sound has driven some yachts-men crazy; others it has lulled to sleep.   —Maurice Griffiths

Care of running lines

Coil running lines to keep them neat but ready for use.

Once a running line is coiled up, turn it over so it will run clear when let go.

Put a stopper knot in the ends of halyards and sheets so they will not run out of the block or fairlead.

End-for-end running lines periodically to add length to their lives.

The two pieces of running rigging that must not be allowed to let go at sea

The main halyard

The centerboard pennant

Without them, in most circumstances, you're a cooked goose. The worse loss could be that of the centerboard pennant, as the board will be in the down position and could wrack the trunk in heavy seas, causing irreparable leaks.

The two points where a halyard gets the most wear

Where it runs over the sheave

Where it is cleated

Tuning up

When making adjustments to a boat—the rig, the ballast, whatever—that will affect performance, make only one adjustment at a time. Assess the consequences of each adjustment before going on to the next.

The art of ballasting

The whole art of ballasting consists in placing the center of gravity to correspond with the trim and shape of the vessel, so as neither to be too high nor too low; neither too far forward, nor too far aft; and to lade the ship so deep, that the surface of the water may nearly rise to the extreme breadth amidships; and thus she will be enabled to carry a good sail, incline but little, and ply well to windward.

—William Falconer, *An Universal Dictionary of the Marine,* 1769

Too much ballast is as bad as too little.

—anon.

Types of ballast

Inside—The ballast is inside the skin of the boat.

Outside—The ballast is hung from the keel, outside the skin of the boat.

Fixed—The ballast is permanently secured in place.

Shifting—The ballast can be moved according to conditions (in a small
   craft, the crew, in effect, becomes shifting ballast).

**While there are many advantages to outside ballast, at least some
should be placed inside because it can be**
Shifted to trim the hull to the lines.
Removed to lighten the boat if necessary for hauling or refloating if aground.

To these we entrust our lives
The keel is an iron casting weighing three tons. It is secured to the boat
by vertical iron bolts. On the end of these are nuts screwed upon slender
threads. It is these threads that hold that iron to the boat. God, is that all!
                                                              —Rockwell Kent

Ballasting materials
Lead
Cast iron
Fabricated steel
Reinforced concrete

We deal in lead.
   —Steve McQueen, *The Magnificent Seven*

The advantages of lead as ballast
Does not corrode.
Does not deteriorate.
Does not lose its market value as scrap.

Old-style recipe for protecting the ballast in the bilge, and the bilge itself
1 part pine tar
3 parts linseed oil

The bilge
Nine times out of ten, a foul smell below is caused by a dirty bilge.
Before launching in the spring, clean the bilge thoroughly and make sure
   the limber holes are free.
A small amount of leakage is good, because the water, pumped out from
   time to time, will help keep the bilge sweet.
If there is no leakage, pour clean water into the bilge from time to time, let
   it slosh around, then pump it out.
Dirt and rubbish in the bilge should never be out of sight, out of mind, as
   trash can clog the limber holes and the pump.

When it stinketh it is good

When a ship is staunch, that is takes in but little water into her hold, she is said to be tight. And this tightness is best known by the very smell of the water that is pumped out of her; for when it stinketh much, it is a sign that the water hath lain long in the hold of the ship; and on the contrary, when it is clear and sweet, it is a token that it comes freshly in from the sea. This stinking water therefore is always a welcome perfume to an old seaman; and he that stops his nose at it is laughed at, and held but a fresh-water man at best.   —from Boteler's *Dialogues,* 1634

How to tell whether a leak is increasing

With a hand pump, pump the bilge at regular intervals—every hour, day, week, etc., as necessary.
Count how many strokes it takes to empty the bilge.
If the number of strokes increases per interval, the leak is increasing; the difference in strokes will tell you the rate of increase.

To sweeten the bilge

Pump it dry.
Pour in a pint of non-sudsing heavy-duty cleaning detergent and enough fresh water to allow the solution to reach most corners of the bilge.
Allow the solution to slosh around for a week while the boat is underway or rolling in an open anchorage.
Pump the bilgewater into a holding tank.

Pump that bilge

Small craft at the very least should have a scoop bailer, or a portable hand pump with a hose long enough to reach over the side; preferably both.

Larger craft should have redundant systems: fixed hand pump, fixed power pump, portable hand pump, and buckets suitable for bailing. DO NOT depend on a power pump alone: you lose your power, you lose your pump. In an emergency, bail water into the head and then pump it out. In a real emergency, use the engine's cooling water pump as a bilge pump by removing the seawater intake hose from the hull fitting and running it into the bilge.

When the porpoise jumps,
Look out for your pumps.
                    —old weather saying

Who wants to be foretold the weather?

It is bad enough when it comes, without our having the misery of knowing about it beforehand. —Jerome K. Jerome

Forecasting short-term weather changes
Stand with your back to the surface wind. Look up at the clouds to see the direction of the upper-altitude wind. If the upper wind is blowing from your left, the weather will most likely deteriorate. If the upper wind is blowing from your right, the weather will most likely improve. If the upper wind is blowing directly toward or away from you, the weather will most likely stay the same.

Approaching storms, according to the National Weather Service
When the wind sets in from points between south and southeast, and the barometer falls steadily, a storm is approaching from the west or north-west, and its center will pass near or north of the observer within twelve to twenty-four hours, with wind shifting northwest by way of south and southwest. When the wind sets in from points between east and north-east, and the barometer falls steadily, a storm is approaching from the south or southwest, and its center will pass near or to the south of the observer within twelve to twenty-four hours, with wind shifting to northwest by way of north. The rapidity of the storm's approach and its intensity will be indicated by the rate and the amount of the fall in the barometer.

Signs of an approaching hurricane
Unusually long sea swell
Abnormal rise in the tide
Exceptional clearness and visibility
Rapidly falling barometer

Weather indicators

Wind
Clouds with bright edges
Rainbows
Unusually clear atmosphere

Good weather
Heavy dew at night
Mist in the morning, burned off later by the sun
Wind dying at sundown
Fish playing on the surface of the sea
Considerable phosphorescence in the water
Seabirds well out to sea

Bad weather
Afternoon wind continuing into and through the night
Heavy swell offshore
Porpoises in sheltered waters
Seabirds close inshore or resting on land
Halo around the moon; the larger the halo, the closer the bad weather.

Look to the sky for your immediate future
Red in the morning—bad weather, or at least strong winds
Gray in the morning—fine weather
Red at sunset—fine weather
Bright yellow at sunset—wind
Pale yellow at sunset—rain
Dark blue during day—wind
Light blue during day—fine weather
Soft, delicate clouds during day—fine weather
Hard-edged, oily clouds during day—wind

Of two men looking at a sunset, the scientist will say, "Tomorrow will be clear," while the philosopher observes, "What a wonderful sunset!"
—Eric Sloane

The visibility of the moon and the weather
Large, bright moon—cold
Dull moon—heat
Full moon—fair
Red moon—wind
Pale, watery moon—rain
Ring around the moon—storm (warm weather, rain; cold weather, snow).
      The wider the ring, the worse the storm. The number of stars in the
      ring equals the number of days that will pass before the storm strikes.

Sound matters, too
Sound travels better in air of higher humidity than low. A good hearing
day—far-off sounds are easily heard—suggests that wet weather is on the
way, whereas a bad hearing day suggests the onset of fair weather.

Prognosticators
It is generally supposed that they who have long been conversant with the
Ocean can foretell by certain indications, such as its roar and the notes of
the sea-fowl, when it will change from calm to storm; but probably no
such ancient mariner as we dream of exists; they know no more, at least,
than the older sailors do about this voyage of life on which we are all
embarked. Nevertheless, we love to hear the sayings of old sailors, and
their accounts of natural phenomena, which totally ignore, and are
ignored by, science.   —Henry David Thoreau

Barometric rules of thumb
In the middle latitudes, 30.50 inches of barometric pressure at sea level is
      considered high, 29.50 considered low.
Persistent decrease in barometric pressure foretells foul weather.
Sudden fall in barometric pressure (more than .04 inch per hour) fore-
      tells heavy winds.
Steady barometric pressure indicates fair weather.
A slow, persistent increase in barometric pressure, especially when accom-
      panied by rising temperatures, foretells a stabilization in the weather.
A rapid rise in barometric pressure foretells unsettled weather.
A distant storm is indicated by a local drop in barometric pressure while
      local weather remains unchanged.

Watching the barometer
Ignore the labels on the face of the usual barometer indicating "Stormy,"
"Rain," "Change," "Fair," "Very Dry." The number or label to which the

barometer needle is pointing has little to do with weather forecasting. What you are interested in is the rate and direction of change in barometer readings.

General conditions leading to fog
A large temperature spread between cold air and warm water
Warm, humid air flowing over a colder surface (water or land)
Warm rain falling through the cold air preceding a warm front
At sunset—clear sky, light wind, humid air

Radiation fog
On a clear, calm night, the land radiates heat and becomes cooler, cooling the air just above the surface. Fog forms when the air is cooled to its dew point. Radiation fog is shallow and densest near the surface, and it is seldom found more than ten miles out to sea.

Advection fog
Warm, moist air blows over a colder surface and is cooled below its dew point. This is the fog commonly found at sea; it tends to be dense and long-lasting.

Foggy breath
In the warm weather months, if you can see your breath before sunset, expect fog shortly.

If you see fog about to set in
Immediately take bearings on identifiable objects that are also shown on
    the chart before they are lost from view.
Send a lookout forward.
Prepare to cut your speed.
Prepare to sound the fog-signaling device at the proper intervals.

Speed in fog is not a matter of guesswork. It should be moderate.
—Felix Riesenberg

Principal principles of navigation in fog
Keep your eyes open.
Keep your ears open.
Keep your dead-reckoning plot.
Keep your head.

We heard her a mile to west'ard—the liner that cut us through—
As crushing the fog at a twenty-jog she drove with her double screw.
We heard her a mile to west'ard as she bellowed to clear her path,
The grum, grim grunt of her whistle, a leviathan's growl of wrath.
We could tell she was aimed to smash us, so we clashed at our little bell,
But the sound was shredded by screaming wind and we simply rung
*   our knell.*
And the feeble breath, that screamed at Death through our horn,
*   was beaten back,*
And we knew that doom rode up the sea toward the shell of our
*   tossing smack.*   —from "As Beseemeth Men," by Holman F. Day

Mariner's weather sayings
Barometer high—heave short and away,
Barometer low—let the mudhook stay;
Barometer shifting—reef tackles prepare,
Barometer steady—set sails without fear.

Long foretold, long last
Short notice, soon past.

A rainbow in the morning
It is a sailor's warning;
But a rainbow at night
It is a sailor's delight.

Red in the east I like the least,
Red in the west I like the best.

When the mist takes to the open sea,
Fair weather, shipmate, it will be;
But when the mist rolls o'er the land,
The rain comes pouring off the sand.

North—stormy—stormy and bold,
East—steady—frost and cold;
South—rain—with troubled sea,
West—squalls—and helm's a-lee.

When the lofty hills the mist doth bear,
Let the mariner then for storms prepare.

When rise begins after low,
Squalls expect, and a clear blow.

The hollow winds begin to blow,
The clouds look black, the glass is low;
Last night the sun went pale to bed,
The moon in halo's hid her head.
Look out, my lads, a wicked gale,
With heavy rain, will soon assail.

When the rain comes before the wind,
Look out, and well your topsails mind;
But when the wind comes before the rain,
Then hoist your topsails up again.

Sound traveling far and wide
A stormy day will betide.

Seagull, seagull, get out on t'sand,
We'll ne'er have good weather with thee on t'land.

The farther the sight
The nearer the rain.

Count the stars in the halo

Out on the river there was a peaceful, motionless silence. The sky was streaky with clouds in the north and was open everywhere else. There were stars and a half-moon surrounded by a weak, misty halo. The proprietor stepped out of his office.

"How many stars in the halo?"

We counted three.

"It'll snow in three days," he said, and waved good-bye.

Three days later, just as he had promised, it snowed.

—from "Saturday Afternoon on the Eastern River," by P.H. Spectre

Sailors sail on their stomachs

"A Nautical Ballad"
by Charles Edward Carryl

A capital ship for an ocean trip
    Was the Walloping Window-blind—
No gale that blew dismayed her crew
    Or troubled the captain's mind.
The man at the wheel was taught to feel
    Contempt for the wildest blow,
And it often appeared, when the weather had cleared,
    That he'd been in his bunk below.

The boatswain's mate was very sedate,
    Yet fond of amusement, too;
And he played hop-scotch with the starboard watch,
    While the captain tickled the crew.
And the gunner we had was apparently mad,
    For he sat on the after-rail,
And fired salutes with the captain's boots,
    In the teeth of the booming gale.

The captain sat in a commodore's hat
    And dined, in a royal way,
On toasted pigs and pickles and figs
    And gummery bread, each day.

But the cook was Dutch, and behaved as such;
    For the food that he gave the crew
Was a number of tons of hot-cross buns,
    Chopped up with sugar and glue.

And we all felt ill as mariners will,
    On a diet that's cheap and rude;
And we shivered and shook as we dipped the cook
    In a tub of his gluesome food.
Then nautical pride we laid aside,
    And we cast the vessel ashore
On the Gulliby Isles, where the Poohpooh smiles,
    And the Anagazanders roar.

Composed of sand was that favored land,
    And trimmed with cinnamon straws;
And pink and blue was the pleasing hue
    Of the Tickletoeteaser's claws.
And we sat on the edge of a sandy ledge
    And shot at the whistling bee;
And the Binnacle-bats wore water-proof hats
    As they danced in the sounding sea.

On rubagub bark, from dawn to dark,
    We fed, till we all had grown
Uncommonly shrunk,—when a Chinese junk
    Came by from the torriby zone.
She was stubby and square, but we didn't much care,
    And we cheerily put to sea;
And we left the crew of the junk to chew
    The bark of the rubagub tree.

Food for the circumnavigator

At a Cruising Club dinner in the 1920s, Harry Pidgeon, the second person to sail around the world alone, spoke at length on his experiences at sea, then solicited questions from the audience. "What did you eat, Harry?" someone asked. Pidgeon looked a bit confused, then smiled quizzically and said, "Grub."

Food for the common sailor

Boiled salt meat—meat that has been soaked overnight in fresh water, rinsed in fresh water, then simmered for three hours; generally served with dumplings and vegetables

Brews—hard biscuit soaked overnight, then stewed with salt pork and salt cod

Bully beef—salt beef from which all the fat and substance has been boiled away

Burgoo, sometimes called skillygalee—oatmeal cooked in the water in which salt meat had been boiled for a previous meal, seasoned with salt and butter, sweetened with sugar; thought to be an antidote to seasickness and stomach cramps

Crackerhash—hardtack, pounded to pieces and mixed with pork or beef scraps, then baked

Dandyfunk, aka dunderfunk, aka dundyfunk—hard biscuit, broken up and pounded, mixed with beef fat, molasses, sometimes ground ginger, and water, and baked brown in a pan

Dogsbody—hard biscuit soaked in water and sugar until melted into a pulp

Fanny Adams—tinned meat, named after a seven-year-old girl who was murdered and then dismembered in 1820. Among sailors, rumor had it that her remains had been canned by unscrupulous ships' provisioners.

Irish stew—meat, potatoes, onions, salt, pepper, flour, and water

Liverpool pantile, aka hardtack, aka sea biscuit—biscuit especially notable for its hardness

Lobscouse, aka 'scouse—stew made of small pieces of salt meat, broken biscuit, potatoes, onions, and whatever spices are available, all boiled together and seasoned with pepper

Midshipman's muffin—hardtack soaked in water, then baked in the oven

Plum duff—pudding made from flour and raisins

Poor John—salted, dried fish, usually of the cheaper species, such as cod and hake. Sailors preferred salt beef or pork and considered fish a poor substitute, hence the name.

Schooner-on-the-rocks—roast beef and potatoes

Sea pie—layered meat or fish and vegetables, with a crust on top and bottom and between the layers. Each layer was known as a deck, so a two-decker had two layers and a three-decker had three layers.

Skillygalee, aka 'skilly (see Burgoo, above)

Slumgullion—any dish considered to be beyond contempt

Strike-me-blind—boiled rice and raisins, soaked in blackstrap molasses

On shore, dinner at the best is but a prosaic and commonplace entertainment, but on ship-board it becomes the acme of the day's pleasures, the theme of hourly thoughts, and, I am bound to say, the stimulant to ghastly and gruesome nightmares. —E.J. Banfield

Hardtack

Sea biscuit, or common ship's bread, is made from wheaten flour (retaining some of the bran), water, and common salt. The materials are kneaded together, either by manual labor—that is, by the hands and feet of the workmen—or by introducing the materials into a long trough or box, with a central shaft to which a series of knives are attached, and made to revolve rapidly by machinery. The mass of dough so obtained is then kneaded and thinned out into a sheet the proper thickness of the bread, by being passed and repassed between heavy rollers. This sheet is placed below a roller with knife-edge shapes, is readily cut into hexagonal or round shapes; the cuts are not complete but are indentations, and the slab remains in one piece. These slabs are placed in an oven for about 12 minutes and are then placed in a warm room for 2 to 3 days to dry thoroughly. The more modern ovens are fitted for continuous baking, the bread being drawn through in sheets on endless chains. These ovens have a capacity of 2,000 pounds of bread a day.   —*Chambers Encyclopedia,* 1881

To maintain butter for several weeks without refrigeration

Press fresh salted butter into jars.
Put a thick layer of dry salt on top.
Store covered in a cool place.

    To use, wash away the salt with fresh water, remove the amount required, and cover the remaining butter with a new layer of dry salt.

To preserve bacon indefinitely

Put a layer of dry salt in the bottom of a food-grade container.
Alternate layers of dry salt and strips of bacon.
Cover the container.

    To use, remove bacon as needed; brush off excess salt; gently wash if necessary.

To salt down beef

Select boneless beef with not too much fat on it.
Cut into five- or six-pound pieces.
In a large food-grade tub or jar, make a brine of water with enough salt in
    it to float a potato; add an ounce of saltpeter for every four gallons.
Immerse the beef in the brine, with a weighted object on top to keep the
    beef from rising to the surface.

Cover the tub or jar.
The beef will keep indefinitely, and the brine can be used over again.

A little beef with the salt
Some salt beef was so heavily pickled that it had to be soaked in fresh
water for at least twenty-four hours before it was usable. The worst had to
be put in a metal cage and towed astern for hours to get rid of the majority
of the salt, and then it still had to be steeped in fresh water.

Irish horse
Salt beef that was tougher than usual—which was tough indeed—was
known to sailors as "Irish horse." The name came from the belief that the
Irish, being poor, worked their horses harder than usual, and therefore
the meat from them would be stringier.

Ode to an Irish Horse
Salt horse, salt horse, what brought you here?
   You've carried turf for many a year.
From Dublin quay to Ballyack
   You've carried turf upon your back.
                    —from an eighteenth-century sea song

Seagoing culinary slang, early twentieth century
Admiralty ham—canned meat
Afters—dessert
Albany beef—sturgeon caught in the Hudson River, boiled
Atlantic ranger—herring
Baby's head—meat pudding
Bag meal—box lunch
Bangers—canned sausages
Bargemen—maggots in the biscuits
Bilge cod—any meal of fish
Black meat—bacon
Bombay duck; also dock pheasant—smoked herring
Cheesy-eggy-hammy-topsides—omelette
Chicken fruit; also farmyard nuggets; also cackleberries—eggs
Chinese wedding cake—rice pudding
Covered wagon—pie
Cowboy's breakfast—bacon and baked beans
Dalmatian pudding; also spotted dog—boiled currant dumpling

Deep sea beef—haddock; also St. Peter's fish
Egg on a raft—poached egg on toast
Figgy duff—suet pudding
Fisherman's sauce—salt water, vinegar, mustard, and beaten eggs
Fishes' eyes—tapioca pudding
Floaters in the snow; also zeppelins in a fog—
    sausages and mashed potatoes
Full house—mixed grill
Hard fish—salt or dried fish
Hollow meat—rabbit or chicken
Horse cock—bologna
Irish mail—sack of potatoes
Make-and-mend pudding—
    baked jam roll
Nuts and bolts—stew
Nuts and bolts with awning—meat pie
Oosh-me-gosh—sliced beef and vegetables
Poison-on-armorplate—
    biscuits dipped in beef tea
Red lead—canned herrings in tomato sauce
Resurrection pie—any meal of leftovers
Sharks; also whales—canned sardines
Soap and flannel—cheese and bread
Soft tack—bread, cake, muffin
Spudoosh—stew heavy on potatoes
Squashed fly—biscuit with currants
Torpedo—sausage
Twice laid—leftovers

God sends meat but the Devil sends cooks.
                —Thomas Deloney, 1600

Disagreeable food? Flog the cook!

As the crew set down to dinner they found their peas soup was not
boiled, the peas as hard as when put in the coppers. The complaint of
this kind to me being daily from the crew, I ordered all hands to be called
and punished the cook with one dozen lashes on his bare back and his
mate half dozen for the neglect.
        —Captain Alexander P. Griggs, privateer *Harpy* of Baltimore, 1814

This morning our Steward was brought to the geers and whipped, for making an extravagant use of flour in the puddings, and for several other misdemeanors.   —from *Journal of a Voyage,* by Benjamin Franklin

Nicknames for the sea cook
Slushy
Slush
Old Slush
Grub-spoiler
Kitchen physic
Doctor

Note on the refrigerator, Browns Head Light, Vinalhaven Island, Maine, 1988
Heaven is where the police are British, the cooks French, the mechanics German, the lovers Italian, and all is organized by the Swiss.

Hell is where the cooks are British, the mechanics French, the lovers Swiss, and all is organized by the Italians.

They may do without compass, or do without charts,
Trust to tides and the stars when they seek foreign parts;
They may do without ladies—unless they've good looks—
But where are the yachts that can do without cooks?
                                        —anon.

Let's hear it for clam chowder
Mrs. Hussey... said—"Clam or Cod?"

"What's that about Cods, ma'am?" said I, with much politeness.

"Clam or Cod?" she repeated.

"A clam for supper? a cold clam; is THAT what you mean, Mrs. Hussey?" says I, "but that's a rather cold and clammy reception in the winter time, ain't it, Mrs. Hussey?"....

Mrs. Hussey hurried towards an open door leading to the kitchen, and bawling out "clam for two," disappeared.

"Queequeg," said I, "do you think that we can make out a supper for us both on one clam?"

However, a warm savory steam from the kitchen served to belie the apparently cheerless prospect before us. But when that smoking chowder came in, the mystery was delightfully explained. Oh, sweet friends! hearken to me. It was made of small juicy clams, scarcely bigger than hazel nuts, mixed with pounded ship biscuit, and salted pork cut up into little flakes; the whole enriched with butter, and plentifully seasoned with pepper and salt.   —from *Moby-Dick,* by Herman Melville

...and for fish chowder

1 lb. haddock or cod
4 cups raw diced white potatoes
1 sliced onion
1 qt. milk
½ pt. cream
1½-inch cube salt pork, diced
¼ lb. butter
1 tsp. salt
½ tsp. coarse-ground back pepper

Wash fish in cold water; simmer in two cups water for twenty minutes. Strain, and save water. Break fish into small chunks.

In a kettle, brown the pork, then remove and save the scraps. Sauté the onion in the pork fat.

Boil the potatoes for five minutes; add with its water to pork fat and onions in the kettle. Add the fish and the water in which it was simmered and simmer for ten minutes. Add the pork scraps, butter, salt, and pepper.

Scald the milk and add it to the chowder. Stir in the cream. Heat the chowder, below the boiling point, for a few minutes.

Allow to cool, then refrigerate overnight.

Serve piping hot—never allow chowder to boil!—in heated bowls, topped with hard soda crackers.

L. Francis Herreshoff, yacht designer and gastronome, on eating
Take my advice—eat your potatoes with their jackets on; eat your whole apple, skin, core, and all; chew everything well. Don't forget the prunes.

Lots of men love beans; I love 'em too, but they do have their drawbacks on a small boat.   —Eugene V. Connett III

From the "Rules for the Regulation of the Navy of the United Colonies"
There shall be allowed to each man serving on board ships in the service of the thirteen United Colonies, a daily proportion of provisions, according as is expressed in the following table, viz.
Sunday, 1 lb bread, 1 lb beef, 1 lb potatoes or turnips.
Monday, 1 lb bread, 1 lb pork, ½ pint peas, and 4 oz cheese.
Tuesday, 1 lb bread, 1 lb beef, 1 lb potatoes or turnips, and pudding.
Wednesday, 1 lb bread, 2 oz butter, 4 oz cheese, and ½ pint of rice.

Thursday, 1 lb bread, 1 lb pork, and ½ pint of peas.
Friday, 1 lb bread, 1 lb beef, 1 lb potatoes or turnips, and pudding.
Saturday, 1 lb bread, 1 lb pork, ½ pint peas, and 4 oz cheese.

Half pint of rum per man every day, and discretionary allowance on extra duty, and in time of engagement.

A pint and half of vinegar for six men per week.

Meanwhile, one hundred years earlier

This day our noble Captain feasted the officers of his small squadron with four dishes of meat, viz. four excellent hens and a piece of pork boiled in a dish; a gigget of excellent mutton and turnips; a piece of beef of eight ribs, well seasoned and roasted; and a couple of very fat green geese; last of all a great Cheshire cheese; a rare feast at shore.

His liquors were answerable, viz.:

Canary, sherry, Rhenish, claret, white wine, cider, ale, beer, all of the best sort; and punch like ditch-water; with which we conclude the day and week in drinking to the "King and all that we love, while the wind blows fair."   —Henry Teonge, naval chaplain, 1675

Seaman's bill of fare recommended by Britain's Merchant Shipping Victualling Scale Committee, 1892

Sunday
Breakfast—dry hash, soft bread
Dinner—sea-pie and plum duff
Supper—cold beef and pickles

Monday
Breakfast—Irish stew
Dinner—pea soup, pork, calavances [legumes]
Supper—dry hash

Tuesday
Breakfast—rice and molasses
Dinner—salt beef, potatoes, plum duff
Supper—cold meat and pickles

Wednesday
Breakfast—porridge and molasses
Dinner—sea pie
Supper—potato stew

Thursday
Breakfast—Irish stew
Dinner—pea soup, pork, calavances
Supper—dry hash

Friday
Breakfast—dry hash
Dinner—preserved meat or salt fish and potatoes
Supper—twice laid of fish

Saturday
Breakfast—porridge and molasses
Dinner—salt beef, rice, and molasses
Supper—cold meat and pickles

In addition, daily
Breakfast—coffee, biscuit, butter, marmalade
Dinner—biscuits and switchell
Supper—tea, biscuits, butter, marmalade

Scale of Provisions, sanctioned by the U.S. government, allowed seamen on board the American square-rigged ship *A. J. Fuller*, 1897

Sunday
1 pound bread, 1½ pounds beef, ½ pound flour

Monday
1 pound bread, 1¼ pounds pork, 1⅛ pints peas

Tuesday
1 pound bread, 1½ pounds beef, ½ pound flour

Wednesday
1 pound bread, 1¼ pounds pork, 1⅛ pints peas

Thursday
1 pound bread, 1½ pounds beef, ½ pound flour

Friday
1 pound bread, 1¼ pounds pork, 1⅛ pints peas

Saturday
1 pound bread, 1½ pounds beef

In addition, seamen were provided each day with ⅛ ounce tea, ½ ounce coffee, 2 ounces sugar, 3 quarts water, and an issue of lime and lemon juice and sugar.

"Our fare on the *Fuller*," wrote Felix Riesenberg, "was of the regular deep water variety, made palatable by the fact that we were living the open air life of a lot of human gorillas. Cockroaches were not mentioned in the Scale of Provisions. Our tea was never without these disgusting vermin and none of us was ever able to tell what gave it the peculiar flavor we came to relish—the twigs and leaves floating about in the brown liquor, or the roaches lying drowned in the bottom of the can."

Provisions carried aboard a typical transatlantic passenger steamer, 1890s

Beef, 20,000 pounds
Pork, 500 pounds
Mutton, 3,500 pounds
Lamb, 450 pounds
Veal, 500 pounds
Sausage, 200 pounds
Liver, 230 pounds
Corned beef, 2,900 pounds
Salt pork, 2,200 pounds
Bacon, 479 pounds
Ham, 500 pounds
Tongues, 8 dozen
Sweetbreads, 200 pounds
Fish, assorted, 2,100 pounds
Oysters, 5,000
Clams, 5,000
Soft-shell crabs, 500
Green turtle, 200 pounds
Turkeys, 50
Geese, 50
Fowls, 248
Chickens, 150
Squabs, 300
Snipe, 500
Quail, 500
Ducklings, 216
Wild game, 108 pair
and all the trimmings

First-class menu, transatlantic passenger steamer, 1890s

Soups
Turtle and Spring

Fish
Scotch Salmon and Sauce Hollandaise

Entrees
Blanquettes de Poulet aux Champignons
Fillets de Boeuf a la Bordelaise
Cailles sur Canapes

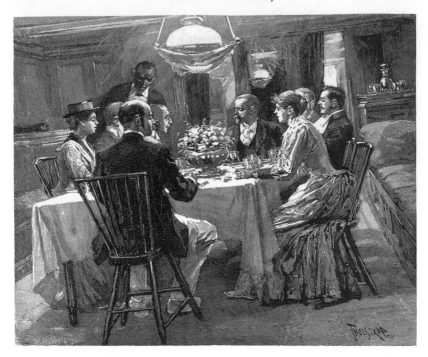

Joints
Saddle of Mutton and Jelly
Beef and Yorkshire Pudding
York Ham and Champagne Sauce

Poultry
Roast Turkey and Truffles
Spring Ducklings

Vegetables
Pommes de Terre Duchesse
Asparagus. Potatoes. Parsnips.

Sweets
International Pudding
Rhubarb with Custard
Strawberry Jam. Tartlets. Sandwich.

Pastry
Genoese Pastry. Marlborough Pudding. Gooseberry Souffles. Lemon Cream.

Dessert
Seville Oranges. Black Hamburg Grapes. English Walnuts. Madeira Nutes.
     Cantaloupes. Cafe Noir.

Second-class menu, transatlantic passenger steamer, 1890s
Soup—Julienne
Fish—Boiled Rock Fish, Butter Sauce
Meats—Haricot of Mutton; Roast Beef, Baked Potatoes; Boiled Mutton,
    Caper Sauce; Mashed Turnips; Potatoes
Dessert—Rice Pudding; Apple Tart; Small Pastry; Biscuit and Cheese

Steerage-passenger menu, transatlantic passenger steamer, 1890s,
from a contemporary description
At breakfast we usually had oatmeal porridge and molasses, with coffee in
plenty, and rolls and butter. This was varied by hash instead of porridge
on some days, or perhaps an Irish stew; but fresh baked rolls and butter
were always in abundance. There was always soup at dinner, and some
boiled beef, pork, or fish, with potatoes and bread. Supper did not
amount to much, but there was plenty of plain, good stuff to eat. Roast
beef and plum duff were served at Sunday's dinner.

Tastes differ, according to Captain A.J. Kenealy
Tastes differ so widely that it is hard to advise a man as to his cuisine
when afloat. What would suit an old sea dog "right down to the ground"
might not be palatable to the nautical epicure with a taste for humming-
bird livers on toast, or other such dainty kickshaws. Personally, I can
enjoy a good square meal of sardines and hardtack, wash it down with a
cup of coffee and wind up with a pipe of plug tobacco, and conclude that
I have feasted like a prince.

"Little Billee"
by William Makepeace Thackeray

There were three sailors of Bristol City,
    Who took a boat and went to sea;
But first with beef, and captain's biscuits,
    And pickled pork, they loaded she.

There was gorging Jack, and guzzling Jimmy,
    And the youngest he was little Billee:
Now, when they got as far as the Equator,
    They'd nothing left but one split pea.

Says gorging Jack to guzzling Jimmy,
 "I am extremely hungaree."
To gorging Jack says guzzling Jimmy,
 "We've nothing left: us must eat we."

Says gorging Jack to guzzling Jimmy,
 "With one another we shouldn't agree:
There's little Bill, he's young and tender,
 We're old and tough: so let's eat he.

"O Billy! we're going to kill and eat you,
 So undo the button of your chemie."
When Bill received this information
 He used his pocket-handkerchie.

"First let me say my catechism
 Which my poor mammy taught to me."
"Make haste, make haste!" says guzzling Jimmy,
 While Jack pulled out his snickersnee.

So Billy went up to the main-topgallant mast,
 And down he fell on his bended knee:
He scarce had come to the Twelfth Commandment,
 When up he jumps, "There's land I see!

"Jerusalem and Madagascar,
 And North and South Amerikee;
There's the British flag a-riding at anchor,
 With the Admiral Napier, K.C.B."

So when they got aboard of the Admiral's,
 He hanged fat Jack, and flogged Jimmee;
But as for little Bill he made him
 The Captain of a Seventy-three.

"The Captain's charge is to command all."

—Captain John Smith

The qualities of command
Knowledge
Experience
Balance
Understanding
Decisiveness
and, most of all,
Coolness
     In other words, when all about are losing their heads, the captain must keep his.

The one real crime at sea is the crime of indecision.
—John Irving

To command is to serve, nothing more and nothing less.
—André Malraux

No man is fit to command another that cannot command himself.
—William Penn

"The Old Man'll get us through," they said to one another. "The Old Man ain't afraid of Hell."
—from *The Secret Life of Walter Mitty,* by James Thurber

"The Captain Stood on the Carronade"

by Captain Frederick Marryat

The captain stood on the carronade—"First lieutenant," says he,
"Send all my merry men aft here, for they must list to me:
I haven't the gift of the gab, my sons—because I'm bred to the sea;
That ship there is a Frenchman, who means to fight with we.
Odds bobs, hammer and tongs, long as I've been to sea,
I've fought 'gainst every odds—but I've gain'd the victory!

"That ship there is a Frenchman, and if we don't take she,
'Tis a thousand bullets to one, that she will capture we;
I haven't the gift of the gab, my boys; so each man to his gun;
If she's not mine in half an hour, I'll flog each mother's son.
Odds bobs, hammer and tongs, long as I've been to sea,
I've fought 'gainst every odds—and I've gain'd the victory!"

We fought for twenty minutes, when the Frenchman had enough;
"I little thought," said he, "that you were of such stuff."
The captain took the Frenchman's sword, a low bow made to he;
"I haven't the gift of the gab, monsieur, but polite I wish to be.
Odds bobs, hammer and tongs, long as I've been to sea,
I've fought 'gainst every odds—and I've gain'd the victory!"

Our captain sent for all of us: "My merry men," said he,
"I haven't the gift of the gab, my lads, but yet I thankful be:
You've done your duty handsomely, each man stood to his gun;
If you hadn't, you villains, as sure as day, I'd have flogg'd each mother's son.
Odds bobs, hammer and tongs, long as I'm at sea,
I'll fight 'gainst every odds—and I'll gain the victory!"

U.S. naval officers must be gentlemen, says John Paul Jones
It is by no means enough that an officer of the navy should be a capable mariner.... He should be as well a gentleman of liberal education, refined manners, punctilious courtesy, and the nicest sense of personal honor.

Coast guard officers, too, says Alexander Hamilton
They will always keep in mind that their countrymen are freemen, and, as such, are impatient of everything that bears the least mark of domineering spirit. They will, therefore, refrain, with the most guarded circumspection, from whatever has the semblance of haughtiness, rudeness, or insult.

And Royal Navy officers, says Admiral Lord Nelson to a newly appointed midshipman

As you from this day start in the world as a man, I trust that your future conduct in life will prove you to be both an Officer and a Gentleman. Recollect that you must be a Seaman to be an Officer, and also, that you cannot be a good Officer without being a Gentleman.

How the U.S. Navy works

If the Commanding Officer has strong views on certain matters which may appear to be at some variance with doctrine or with past practices, then by all means do it his way. — *Watch Officer's Guide*

"Master and owner of the *Racundra*"

Does any man need a prouder title or description? In moments of humiliation, those are the words that I shall whisper to myself. I ask no others on my grave. —Arthur Ransome

The glamour of the ship captain, according to William McFee

In the imagination and opinion of the general public, the captain of a ship retains a certain glamour which has not yet gathered around the figure of the conductor of a train or the pilot of an airliner.

How to be a good skipper, according to Thomas Fleming Day

If you are to command, show yourself a leader, not by talk, but by action. Always be first in everything that requires skill or courage. Thus you will win your crew's respect, and if they respect you they will obey you. Never send a man to do a task you fear to do yourself. If there is any danger, lead, and your men will follow.... Don't put all the hard work on the crew; do your share of it; also the dirty jobs. If you are working watch and watch, be sure to be the first on deck when your watch is called, and don't leave it, unless you are sure that the yacht is in safe hands and that your care and skill is not needed.

"My Boat"
children's song lyrics by Edna Cobb Dutcher

I watched the big boat sail out to the sea,
One fine day in September.
She'll voyage they say,
Two months and a day,
And come sailing home in November.

My father commands, the sailors obey;
No captain ever was grander;
And when I am grown,
A vessel I'll own,
And stand on the bridge as commander.

The perfect crew, according to H.W. Tilman
All must be cheerful, equable temper, long-suffering, patient in adversity, tolerant of the whims and uncouth manners or habits of others, neat and cleanly, adaptable, unselfish, loyal—in fact, possessed of most of the qualities in which the majority of men, including myself, are notably deficient.

Your shipmate must be compatible, and to be such he must have the following qualifications, according to Charles M. Blackford
1. He must like, or not mind, the way you live aboard your boat.
2. He must be willing to eat the things you eat.
3. He must like to cruise in the same fashion you do (of course all this applies to a she or an it).

Once you get them eliminated through the above there is another thing to take into consideration:
a. Does he know as much (or more) about sailing as you?
b. Does he know a little and thinks he knows all the answers?
c. Is he plum green and knows it?

The "a" type is the ideal but extremely elusive, the "c" kind are my second choice because they generally will do what you tell them, but the "b's" have to be approached with caution and trepidation.

Dealing with the yacht crew, late nineteenth century, according to Dixon Kemp

There must be no shirking; whatever a man is set to do, he must do thoroughly, and with a will; if he does not do this he should be unshipped without compunction, as one lazy, slovenly, or half-hearted hand on board will spoil three good ones.

Oh, to be selected for the crew of an ocean-racing yacht!

The ideal crew member is a rare creature indeed. He has the coolness, courage, and derring-do of James Bond; the inventiveness and mechanical skills of Tom Swift; the agility and strength of an Olympic decathlon winner; and the winning ways and affableness of a graduate *summa cum laude* of the Dale Carnegie Institute of charm. He has a fund of new stories, is a good listener, and is as neat in his cabin habits as Mr. Clean.

—William Snaith

According to L. Francis Herreshoff, there are four common peculiar personalities at sea—gluttons, exhibitionists, imitators, and perfectionists

On gluttons: "By golly, this man's stomach is going to make the cruise singlehanded."

On exhibitionists: "They get their thrill from causing astonishment, so they wire and electrify the whole cabin until it no longer resembles a yacht but looks like some boy scouts' clubroom."

On imitators: "A queer lot and you should help them if you can, for they are quite unhappy. If they should see some yacht set a purple balloon jib it may be a whole week of torture before they can imitate it."

On perfectionists: "Sometimes I sympathize with them at first, but in the end you will find them the most troublesome of all, for nothing will quite suit them."

Beware the sloven, says Dixon Kemp

A man may be tolerated in a racing yacht in spite of his moral delinquencies and faults of temper, because he is a very smart seaman, but a sloven should be given a very wide berth, as he will not only be offensive to the rest of the crew, but in all probability not a good seaman.

The threatened consequences of slovenliness

I'll have your blood for breakfast

—or—

Your intestines for a necktie

—or—

Your guts for garters.

A paid hand can be a damned annoyance, according to Francis B. Cooke
Even if you are fortunate enough to secure the services of a decent man,
you will soon find him an intolerable nuisance. When you are on board
his presence will be a restriction on your conversation, to say nothing of
occupying the fo'c'sle, which is about the only place you have in a small
yacht where you can stow your suitcases out of the way.

*Give me the little boat with the light anchors, and you can have the
paid hands.*   —William Atkin

Why teamwork is essential at sea
Once upon a time, two men went sailing. One was in the bow; one was in
the stern. The man in the bow objected to the way the man in the stern
was steering the boat. Angry words were passed.

"You take care of your end," the man in the stern finally said, "and
I'll take of mine."

"Fine," the man in the bow said. "I'll be anchoring my end."

If you need a crew, marry it.
                    —Conor O'Brien

Advice to amateur crews and guests, according to L.F. Callingham
Be slow in telling the Skipper or Owner how a thing should be done; if
you are wrong you will look foolish, if you are right the gratitude due to
you may not be forthcoming.

Don't ask silly questions, but remember the old Chinese proverb,
"It is better to keep your mouth shut and be thought a fool than to open it
and remove all possible doubt."

Don't always want to be going ashore; you are presumed to have
come for a yachting cruise, not for a walking tour.

When at sea don't make a habit of continual swearing; reserve it for
special occasions.

Lose the beer, lose your hat, lose your bearings, but don't lose your
temper.

*When a yacht fails to make her port to windward, in nine cases out of ten
it is the crew that fails rather than the vessel.*   —Claud Worth

A sailor in his distinctive costume,
as observed by Chaucer in The Canterbury Tales
A shipman was ther, wonynge fer by weste;
For aught I woot, he was of Dertemouthe.
He rood upon a rounce, as he kouthe,
In a gowne of faldyng to the knee.
A daggere hangynge on a laas hadde he
Aboute his nekke, under his arm adoun.

Literally translated, this is:
There was a Shipman, from far in the West;
For all I know, he came from Dartmouth.
He rode a nag as well as he knew how,
In a gown of frieze to the knee.
He had a dagger hanging on a lace
Around his neck and under his arm.

A good uniform must work its way with the women, sooner or later.
—Charles Dickens

The mid-nineteenth-century merchant sailor's garb, according to Richard Henry Dana, Jr.

A sailor has a peculiar cut to his clothes, and a way of wearing them which a green hand can never get. The trousers, tight around the hips, and thence hanging long and loose round the feet, a superabundance of checked shirt, a low-crowned, well-varnished black hat, worn on the back of the head, with half a fathom of black ribbon hanging over the left eye, and a slip-tie to the black silk neckerchief, with sundry other minutiae, are signs, the want of which betrays the beginner at once.

The archetypal sailorman's sailor suit, generally known in the old days as the "Square Rig"

Jumper—A waist-length over-the-head shirt made of a type of light canvas known as "duck." The typical flap collar was originally designed to protect the back of the jumper from the grease or tar the sailor used to hold his ponytail in place.

Bell-bottom trousers—Made of duck, with a buttoned flap on the front. The legs were belled from the knee down to simplify rolling up when washing the decks. Bell-bottoms could also be used as an emergency life preserver by knotting the legs and thus trapping air for buoyancy.

Hat—In the mid-nineteenth century, the typical hat was of canvas stiffened and made waterproof with tar. Known as a tarpaulin, it suggests the origin of the word "tar" for a sailor. The white cotton sailor's cap first came into use in the late nineteenth century.

Pea coat—A jacket made from pilot cloth (p-cloth, pea cloth), a coarse blue-colored wool twill napped on one side.

Two elements borrowed from Britain's Royal Navy for the traditional uniform of enlisted men in the twentieth-century U.S. Navy

The three white stripes around the collar of the jumper represent Horatio Nelson's great victories at the Nile, Copenhagen, and Trafalgar.

The black silk neckerchief is a symbol of mourning for the death of Nelson at the Battle of Trafalgar.

Sartorial advice from Captain A.J. Kenealy

The adventurous voyager must use his own discretion as to his wardrobe. The marine "dude" is in evidence in our midst, and who am I that I should condemn a man for trying to look his prettiest both ashore and afloat? Don't forget to buy a good suit of oilers [oilskins], and don't fail to slip them on when it rains.

Oilskins were literally that

Oilskins were made with unbleached white cotton cloth. After the garment was made—pants, jacket, long coat, hat, or apron—it was soaked in boiled linseed oil and then hung to dry. Afterward, the outside was given two top coats of oil, the second producing a glossy surface. Light-yellow oilskins were made with light-colored oil; black oilskins were coated with a blackish oil.

Old-style recipe for waterproofing seagoing clothes

Dissolve ½ pound shredded paraffin wax in one gallon warm kerosene in a large pot.

Dip the oilskins in the mixture, squeeze out the excess fluid, and hang to dry either outdoors or in a well-ventilated space.

When dry, brush on two thin coats of a mixture of one part kerosene and one part yacht varnish. Pay special attention to the seams.

He clashed on my notions of a yachtsman—no cool white ducks or neat blue serge; and where was the snowy-crowned yachting cap, that precious charm that so easily converts a landsman into a dashing mariner?
—from *The Riddle of the Sands,* by Erskine Childers

In case you were wondering what to wear

Specifications for the full-dress mess jacket of the Eastern Yacht Club, Marblehead, Massachusetts, 1914

Of blue undress worsted, single-breasted, front edges to just meet, with rolling collar made with a long roll, pointed lapels, buttonhole on left lapel three and three-quarters inches from upper end. Lapels faced with grosgrain silk. The opening of the lapel to be the same length as an evening full dress coat, cut square corners in front; length to crotch. One-piece back five inches wide at the bottom, with side slashes at the second seam, with a five-inch opening. Bound all around edges and side slashes, from below the lapel, with one inch wide black silk braid with tracing of one-ligne black silk soutaches. One device on either front corner, trefoil, one and one-quarter inches total length. Braided navy style, side slashes with soutache trefoil at upper end, seven-eighths of an inch total length. One-ligne black silk soutache on edges of collar only. One buttonhole on either side of jacket under braid, suitable for links. No pockets on outside. Two inside pockets. Closed cuffs. Designation of rank on sleeves as prescribed for service dress, except to be of black silk braid one-quarter of an inch wide, with four medium-size Club buttons, the first to be

placed seven-eighths of an inch from lower end of cuff; the others at equal distances of three-quarters of an inch. Device on the collar embroidered in gold bullion, same as described for cap device for members, but reduced to three-quarters of an inch in length.

Waistcoat blue or white with four small gilt buttons.

Black tie to be worn.

Clothes Chafe
Don't hang clothes in a locker for a long period of time during an ocean passage. The constant motion of the vessel can cause the cloth to become severely chafed—in extreme cases, ruined.

Felt-lined seaboots
Rubber seaboots with permanent felt linings seem like a good idea, but stay away from them. Once wet at sea, they are nearly impossible to dry out.

Cotton versus wool
On an offshore passage, wool clothing is superior to cotton. Wool will keep you warm even when it is wet. Cotton, when wet, feels cold against the skin, and when it dries, residual salt makes it stiff.

Terrycloth towels
Carry a few terrycloth towels on board beyond those needed for washing
and drying. In foul weather, use a towel as a neck scarf under your foulweather jacket. It will sop up spray that gets under your sou'wester.
Change the towel as necessary.

*A helpful hint to the cruising man: I wear my clothes inside out while sail-
ing, then change them to right side out when going ashore. That way I keep
the good side clean.* —Tom McGrath

*If yachting has its pleasures, it also has its minor worries, and not the
least troublesome of these is connected with what is known domestically as
"the wash."* —Sir Edward Thorpe

Rules of the wash
No clothes are ever to be suffered in the fore rigging, or on the bowsprit,
when in harbour. Should any person wish to dry his wet clothes, permis-
sion will be granted for clothes-lines to be rove, by applying to the officer
of the watch. When at sea, every measure is to be adopted, in order to prevent the use of fresh water for washing clothes, or other improper uses.
—from *Observations and Instructions for the Use of the Commissioned,
the Junior and Other Officers of the Royal Navy,* 1804

Washing clothes at sea
Use two buckets—one for washing, one for rinsing.
Soak in salt water and liquid (not powder) laundry detergent. N.B.: Wisk
 and Joy create suds in salt water; most others do not.
Empty soaking water and wash in clean salt water.
Rinse twice in fresh water; use liquid fabric softener, if you have it, in the
 second rinse.
Wring excess water from clothes by looping around lifelines or a stan-
 chion, then twisting.
Eliminate mildew from clothes by washing in liquid detergent, then put-
 ting lemon juice and water on affected areas, then hanging out to
 bleach in the sun.
Don't rely on clothespins to secure clothes while drying. Tie securely
 with line through sleeves and legs.

Sailors are a superstitious lot

I am an optimist about things in general, but I look upon the sea as the ancients view their gods, with superstition. —E.A. Pye

Auspicious times to begin construction of a ship or a boat
On a fair day with a fair wind and a coming tide
On a Wednesday
When the moon is full, or close to reaching that state
When gulls are overhead, or porpoises are at play near shore

Inauspicious times to begin construction of a ship or a boat
On the thirteenth day of the month
On a Thursday or, worse, a Friday
On an unfair day with an unfair wind, a going tide, and heavy surf
When birds are absent
When women are present

Bad luck will follow if you
Encounter a black cat or a barefooted woman on the way to the ship.
Sail with a man who has failed to pay his washerwoman before going to sea.
Depart on a Friday, or the first Monday in April, or the second Monday in
	August, or December 31.
Launch a vessel on a Friday, or allow the keel of a new vessel to be laid on
	a Friday.
Drive a nail on a Sunday.

Allow a vessel to stick on the launching ways.

Get underway after seeing a rat leave the ship.

Paint a hatch cover blue.

Turn a hatch cover bottom up, or drop it into the hold.

Accidentally overturn a filled bucket.

Leave a bucket overturned.

Turn upside down a loaf of bread, a barrel, or a pair of shoes, and leave it that way.

Wear red mittens in a shipyard.

Watch a departing vessel out of sight.

Sight a whale, or following sharks, especially an odd number of sharks.

Sight a comet, or an eclipse of the sun or the moon.

Whistle on board.

Say the word "pig," or "black cat," or "egg," or "fox," or "hare," or "rabbit" on board.

Dream of white horses, or a ghost ship, or ghosts of any kind while underway.

Turn a vessel against the sun, or counterclockwise.

Coil a rope against the sun, or counterclockwise.

Return a pocket knife in any way other than how it was given, open or closed.

Carry on board a black bag, or an umbrella, or flowers.

Wear a new pair of trousers without putting a coin in the pocket first.

Put on trousers and boots left foot first.

Lay boots or shoes on a table.

Throw fish bones on a fire.

Carry a two-dollar bill.

Throw a hat on a bunk.

Change the name of a boat.

Encounter a swallow at sea.

Allow lawyers, clergymen, "Russian Finns," or women on board.

Strike the ship's bell by mistake.

Strike nine bells while underway.

See a phantom ship.

Lose a bucket, a mop, or a knife overboard.

Hand a flag to a sailor between the rungs of a ladder.

Hear bells other than the ship's bell at sea.

Sign aboard a ship on which a sailor recently died.

Wear the clothes of a dead man after that man had died on the same voyage.

Take over as master of a ship after her previous skipper died on the
    last voyage.

Allow the shadow of one sailor to cross that of another on deck.

Invoke the name of the Devil, or of Davy Jones.

Sight a derelict ship or a floating wreck.

Lose a St. Christopher medal at sea.

Carry a corpse on board for any length of time.

Carry black walnuts on board, or anything made of black-walnut wood.

Burn pieces of a wreck that occurred with the loss of life.

Play a harmonica during bad weather.

Intentionally cause harm to an albatross, a spider, or a seagull.

This passage, about the region off Cape Horn, provided the inspiration for Coleridge's "The Rime of the Ancient Mariner"

We all observed that we had not had the sight of one fish of any kind since we were come to the southward of the Straits of Le Maire, nor one sea-bird, except a disconsolate black albatross, who accompanied us for several days, hovering about us as if he had lost himself, till Hatley, my second captain, imagining from his colour that it might be some ill-omen, after some fruitless attempts, at length shot the albatross, not doubting, perhaps, that we should have a fair wind after it. [There would be no fair wind, only foul—and bad luck.]

    —from *Voyage Around the World,* by George Shelvocke, 1726

"God save thee, ancient Mariner!
From the fiends, that plague thee thus!—
Why look'st thou so?"—With my cross-bow
I shot the Albatross.

    —from "The Rime of the Ancient Mariner," by Samuel Taylor Coleridge

How to fool bad luck

Some seafaring men are very superstitious of going to sea at certain days, and commonly those hold it good to begin the voyage on Sundays; and therefore to seem to have begun the voyage that day (though they be not ready to go) they will weigh, or (as the term is) trip the anchor, and go a little way, and so come to anchor again: this they call breaking ground.

—from the *Seaman's Dictionary*, by Sir Henry Mainwaring

Seagoing good-luck charms

Rabbit's foot
Lock of hair from a loved one
A piece of lodestone (magnetic rock)
Image of an anchor, or a lighthouse
A found coin, especially one with the image of an anchor, or a lighthouse
A St. Christopher medal
A Christian cross
The image of an eye carved or painted on the bow
A horseshoe nailed to the mast or bowsprit; it must be positioned upright
　　like the letter "U" so it will "hold" the luck.
The horn of a narwhal, or unicorn
A necklace of shark's teeth

Good luck will follow if you

Have a priest or minister bless the keel of a ship under construction, and
　　sprinkle holy water on the ship's timbers.
Affix a gold coin to the keel, or embed one in it.
Align the building stocks in a north-south direction.
Keep pigs and chickens away from the shipyard.
Encounter a bare-breasted woman just before boarding ship.
Bake bread on Good Friday.
Carry a broom on board that has been used in a church.
Have a child on board.
Get underway on a Sunday.
See dolphins or porpoises following the ship, especially if playing in the
　　bow wave.
Throw back the first-caught fish.
Step on board with the right foot first.
See a mermaid.

Carry a lump of coal collected from the high-tide line.
Go shipmates with a sailor wearing a gold earring.
See a dove at sea.
Carry on board the bell of a famous ship, especially one that had great
     good luck herself.
See St. Elmo's Fire, especially if double lights.

Names for St. Elmo's Fire, the strange light in the rigging caused by the atmospheric discharge of electricity

St. Elmo's Stars
Helena
Castor and Pollux
Corpo Sancto
Corpusant
Cormazant
Capra Saltante
Corbie's Aunt
Davy Jones
Jack Harry
Sailor Devil
St. Nicholas
St. Hermes

"Look aloft!" cried Starbuck. "The corpusants! the corpusants!"

All the yard-arms were tipped with a pallid fire; and touched at each tri-pointed lightning-rod-end with three tapering white flames, each of the three tall masts was silently burning in that sulphurous air, like three gigantic wax tapers before an altar.   —from *Moby-Dick*, by Herman Melville

Sometimes I'd divide
And burn in many places; on the topmast,
The yards and bowsprit, would I flame
distinctly, then meet and join.
                    —from *The Tempest*, by William Shakespeare

Superstitions about St. Elmo's Fire

One light—impending storm
Two lights—storm center has passed
Three lights—impending gale or hurricane
Descending light in the rigging—bad omen; worsening weather ahead
Ascending light in the rigging—good omen; improving weather ahead
Light shining on a sailor's face—warning of death within twenty-four hours

Superstitions about Mother Carey's chickens

Mother Carey's chickens are storm petrels. The name is thought to derive from *Mater Cara* (Mother Dear), the Mother of God—in French, the birds are called *les oiseaux de Notre Dame*—and that the Holy Mother, protectress of sailors, sends the stormy petrel as a herald of a coming storm.

Mother Carey's chickens are thought to be the receptacles of the souls of departed seamen, so a sailor who kills one kills one of his own. A sailor who does so will suffer the same fate as any murderer—i.e., the penalty is a life for a life.

Consequences

Carrying a wren's feather at sea will prevent shipwreck.

Whistling the tune "San Antonio" or "Saint Nicholas" will induce these patron saints of the mariner to end a headwind.

Whistling any other tune in any other circumstance will produce extremely bad luck.

The vision of a naked woman during a storm will cause the seas to subside. (This is one reason why so many figureheads feature women with bare breasts.)

If stolen wood is mortised into the keel of a ship under construction, she will sail faster at night.

If sparks fly when the first blow is struck to fashion the keel of a wooden ship, she will be wrecked on her maiden voyage.

A silver coin placed in the mainmast step will ensure a lucky voyage; gold will not.

It is a bad omen for a ship if a passerby refuses a sip of wine from the sponsor during the launching celebration.

Tossing sand or stones in the air will produce a storm.

Sticking a knife in a mast will produce a gale.

Whistling will bring strong winds.

If you sleep on deck in the light of the moon, it will make you moonstruck, or crazy.

The devil can be beaten out of a ship by climbing the rigging at sunset and beating the sheaves and pins of the blocks.

The state of the tide affects the gender of babies: rising tide, a boy; falling tide, a girl.

Babies baptized with water from an incoming tide will never drown.

A boy born on Christmas Day will become a captain.

A sailor who was born with his face covered by the caul—the inner mem-

brane enclosing the fetus—cannot possibly drown, no matter the
circumstance.

A vessel carrying a caul is unsinkable.

If you throw bread overboard during a storm, it will calm the sea.

A drowned man can be found by floating a loaf of bread with a lighted
candle on the water; the loaf will drift to the spot where the body
lies and stop.

If a glass is struck accidentally and caused to ring, the ringing must be
stopped immediately or a sailor will drown.

An eggshell must be crushed immediately after being emptied; if not, a
witch will use it as a boat, head out to sea, and brew storms to tor-
ment sailors.

Seeing a rainbow is an indication of good weather; a moonbow, disaster.

Cutting the shape of a cross in the mainsail can bring on wind; so, too, the
throwing of money overboard. There's an old story about an American skipper who, by throwing a half dollar over, brought on a gale
of wind. "Wind's cheap here, mister," he said to his mate. "I should
have asked for change."

A sure way to erase the accidental breaking of a taboo at sea
Spit to leeward.

A sure way to ruin the moment
Spit to windward.

The terrors of the deep
As late as the sixteenth century, there were superstitions and fancifica-
tions about the unknown seas that struck terror into the hearts of seamen.
Among the regions of horror were:

Frigor Inhabitabilis—the empty wastes of the northernmost and southernmost oceans

Perusta—the burning zone, where flames leap into the sky

Oceanus quem nemo vidit hominum propter zonam torridam—a boiling
sea that must be crossed by ships headed south of the equator

Brumae, Mare Tenebrosum—tracts of ocean with weed that swallow
ships; human-faced, batwinged demons; octopuses large enough to
swallow an elephant; sea serpents

Antipodes—home of the Troglodytes, the Anthropophagi, the Gara-
mantes, and the scaly dragons

The sea monsters rave for food

The sea-monsters that are nurtured in the midst of the seas are very many
in number and of exceeding size. And not often do they come up out of
the brine, but by reason of their heaviness they keep the bottom of the sea
below. And they rave for food with unceasing frenzy, being always hun-
gered and never abating the gluttony of their terrible maw: for what food
shall be sufficient to fill the void of their belly or enough to satisfy and
give a respite to their insatiable jaws?   —Oppian, second century A.D.

"The Sea-Deeps"

by Thomas Miller

Deeper than the narwhal sinketh,
Deeper than the sea-horse drinketh,
There are miles and miles of sea,
Where darkness reigns eternally.
Nor length of line, nor sounding lead,
Have ever reached the deep sea-bed;
Nor aught again beheld the light,
Which touched that land of endless night.
Above, a ship might strike and ground,
Below, no bottom could be found,
Though, o'er the rocks the white waves hiss,
Unfathomed lay the dark abyss.
Depths measureless—rocks that were hurled
From the foundations of the world.
Deeper than plummet e'er can go
Lie those grim endless depths below,
Which neither wind nor wave come near,
For all is dark and silent there.
Perchance, huge monsters feed and sleep
Below that black and soundless deep;
Monsters of such weight and size,
That they have no power to rise:
The mighty kraken, which they say,
Will heave upon that awful day,
When the last trumpet's startling sound
Shall pierce the inmost depths profound;
And many a league of ocean part,
While his huge bulk he doth uprear,
And like an island vast appear.
Such monstrous things, they say, now sleep
Within the caverns of the deep.

He looked about to see that there were no listeners, and said, in a very
earnest voice, that the king of the fish was the sea-serpent. —John Masefield

Report from the cutter-yacht *Leda* in the Sound of Sleat, Isle of Skye, Scotland, August 20, 1872

As we were watching the creature, it began to approach us rapidly, causing a great agitation in the sea. Nearly the whole of the body, if not all of it,

had now disappeared, and the head advanced at a great rate in the midst of a shower of fine spray, which was evidently raised in some way by the quick movement of the animal—it did not appear how—and not by spouting. F. was alarmed and retreated to the cabin, crying out that the creature was coming down on us. When within about a hundred yards of us it sank and moved away in the direction of Skye, just under the surface of the water, for we could trace its course by the waves it raised on the still sea to the distance of a mile or more.

—Rev. John Macrae and Rev. David Twopeny

Report from the Earl of Crawford's yacht *Valhalla*, South Atlantic Ocean off the coast of Brazil, December 7, 1905

I was on the poop of the *Valhalla* with Mr. Nicoll, when he drew my attention to an object in the sea about 100 yards from the yacht; he said: "Is that the fin of a great fish?"

I looked and immediately saw a large fin or frill sticking out of the water, dark seaweed-brown in colour, somewhat crinkled at the edge. It was apparently about 6 feet in length and projected from 18 inches to 2 feet from the water.

I got my field-glasses on to it (a powerful pair of Goerz Trieder), and almost as soon as I had them on the frill, a great head and neck rose out of the water in front of the frill; the neck did not touch the frill in the water, but came out of the water in front of it, at a distance of certainly not less than 18 inches, probably more. The neck appeared to be about the thickness of a slight man's body.... The head had a very turtle-like appearance, as had also the eye.   —E.G.B. Meade-Waldo

Report from the rowing dory *English Rose III*, Atlantic Ocean, July 25, 1966

I was shocked to full wakefulness by a swishing noise to starboard. I looked out into the water and suddenly saw the writhing, twisting shape of a great sea creature. It was outlined by the phosphorescence in the sea as if a string of neon lights were hanging from it. It was an enormous size, some thirty-five or more feet long.... Chay [Blyth] and I had seen whales and sharks, dolphins and porpoises, flying fishes—all sorts of sea creatures—but this monster in the night was none of these. I reluctantly had to believe that there was only one thing it could have been—a sea serpent.

—John Ridgway

"That's not a sea serpent! It's a ..."
(a few of the various explanations)
Basking shark
Leatherback sea turtle
Whale
Giant squid or cuttlefish
School of fish
Gang of dolphins
Hallucination
...or perhaps it's a mermaid.

Hey, Captain, take a look at this!
This morning one of our companie looking over boord saw a mermaid,
and calling up some of the companie to see her, one more came up and by
that time shee was come close to the ships side, looking earnestly on the
men. A little after a sea came and overturned her. From the navill upward
her backe and breasts were like a womans, as they say that saw her, but
her body as big as one of us. Her skin very white, and long haire hanging
downe behinde of colour blacke. In her going downe they saw her tayle,
which was like the tayle of a porposse, and speckled like a macrell. Their
names that saw her were Thomas Hilles and Robert Rayner.
—Henry Hudson, June 15, 1608

One Sunday morn when we set sail,
    And our ship not far from the land,
We there did espy a fair pretty maid,
        With a comb and a glass in her hand, her hand, her hand,
        With a comb and a glass in her hand.
—from an old sea song

**Report from a party of ladies and gentlemen on a sailing excursion in
the English Channel off Exmouth, Devon, England, August 13, 1812**
The head [of the mermaid], from the crown to the chin, forms rather a
long oval, and the face seems to resemble that of the seal, though, at the
same time, it is far more agreeable, possessing a peculiar softness.... The
upper and back part of the head appeared to be furnished with something
like hair, and the fore part of the body with something like down, between
a very light fawn and very pale pink colour, which at a distance had the
appearance of flesh, and may have given rise to the idea, that the body of
the mermaid is, externally, like that of the human being.... From the waist

it gradually tapered so as to form a tail, which had the appearance of being covered with strong broad polished scales, which occasionally reflected the rays of the sun in a very beautiful manner. —J. Toupin

She had a voice of silver and lips of coral red,
She climbed the dolphin-striker and kissed the figure-head.
—Crosbie Garstin

Marriage among the mermaids

He said, "Your servant, Captain Sullivan, Sir, I'm a Merman.
   This, Sir, is my lawful wife, the queen of all the Mermaids,
   The sovereign of coral rocks, and these, good Captain, her maids."
"A mermaid!" squall'd the Captain; "I have heard of such an odd fish,—
   A kind of—sort of—as it were, half woman and half cod-fish;
   My lad, your nonsense won't do here,—you've not a fool to talk to;
   And, if you don't sheer off, my buck, I'll show you where you'll walk to."
"To prove, Sir," quoth the Merman, "that we do not mean to gammon,
   Look at my tail," by Jove, he did, and found it was a salmon.
—from "Irish Mermaids," anon.

What you call it affects what it is

Superstitions about the names of vessels
Seven letters in a name will ensure good luck, as will three of the letter "A."
Bad luck is certain if you launch a vessel without a name and then name
    her after she is afloat.
- Other portents of bad luck:
A name that begins with "A"
A vessel named after a snake or reptile
A vessel named after one that has sunk *(Titanic, Andrea Doria, Edmund
    Fitzgerald,* etc.), or after a storm *(Hurricane, Gale, Cyclone,* etc.),
    or a fearsome creature of the deep *(Kraken, Octopus, Serpent,* etc.),
    or a cataclysm *(Quake, Eruption, Big Bang,* etc.), or an evil charac-
    ter *(Judas, Brutus, Pilate,* etc.)
Don't give a vessel a high-and-mighty name *(Sovereign of the Seas, Auda-
    cious, Winged Victory)* if she is not of the highest quality, as the gods
    of the sea might be angered.

When choosing a name, keep in mind that it should be
Easy to remember
Easy to spell
Easy to pronounce
Easy to understand
Easy on the ears

*Whatever name one chooses, it may soon be invested with properties one
didn't mean it to have; it may lack qualities one had hoped for. Yet, one is
impressed by names like* Bloodhound *and* Northern Light, *which seem to
evoke the long, lean ocean-racing yawls they were attached to. There is a
martial ring of discipline and strength to* Resolution *and* Despatch, *and
an inescapable romance in* Malay, Bandit, *and* Finisterre.

—Anthony Bailey

Now, what a ship was christened, so let her stay, I says.

—Long John Silver

On renaming the boat

Don't do it (bad luck will likely follow if you do), but if you must:
Go heavy on the appeasement end of things.
Confess your sins, and beg the gods and goddesses of the sea for forgiveness.
Never perform the ceremony on a Friday.
Never, ever, rename the craft *Black Pig* or *Friday the 13th*.
Circle the boat twice, against the sun, or counterclockwise, to awaken the
    demons; then with the sun, or clockwise, to drive the demons away.
    If the boat is on land, circle her on foot: barefoot preferably; if not,
    wear sandals. If the boat is afloat, circle her by rowboat; oars or pad-
    dle only, as the gods and goddesses referred to above are offended
    by outboard motors.
Burn the old nameboard and scatter the ashes on the sea.
Wash away the old name—figuratively speaking—by splashing the bow of
    the boat with a pail of fresh water.
Break a bottle of the most expensive wine or single-malt Scotch over the
    bow (the gods and goddesses of the sea are not impressed by cheap
    hooch).
Whisper the new name so as not to alert the demons.
Promise the gods and goddesses of the sea that you will sin no more.

Earliest known ship name

Praise of Two Lands, an Egyptian vessel of the time of Sneferu, circa
2600 B.C.

Some names of Viking ships, from the Norse sagas

Fjord Elk
Ocean-Riding Bison
Surf Dragon

Unusual ship names of the past

Falcon in the Fetterlock, English warship, mid-sixteenth century
Three Ostrich Feathers, English ship, mid-sixteenth century
Bull, Bear, and Horse, English ship, early seventeenth century
Mousenest, English fireship, mid-seventeenth century
Blade of Wheat, English ship, late seventeenth century
Who's Afraid, British privateer, late eighteenth century
Sturdy Beggar, Salem privateer, late eighteenth century
Mouse of the Mountain, Hudson River steamboat, early nineteenth century
Grumbler and Growler, Salem privateer, early nineteenth century
Precious Ridicule, New Orleans schooner, early nineteenth century
Free Love, Mississippi barge, early nineteenth century
Catch Me Who Can, Baltimore privateer, early nineteenth century
The Twenty-Sixth Day of October 1812, British schooner, early
          nineteenth century
Go-Ask-Her, Newfoundland schooner, mid-nineteenth century
Brown Smith Jones, Maryland police boat, late nineteenth century
Essence of Peppermint, Nova Scotia schooner, late nineteenth century
Bugsy's Boomer, Cape Cod quahog skiff, mid-twentieth century

Most of the great nineteenth- and twentieth-century steamship lines followed a pattern when naming their ships

Cunard Line—Almost all ended in "ia," as *Servia, Gallia, Umbria,*
          Cephalonia, Etruria, etc.
White Star Line—All ended in "ic," as *Celtic, Germanic, Britannic, Adri-*
          atic, Republic, Titanic, etc.
Royal Mail Steam Packet Company—Most were named after rivers, as
          Thames, Trent, Dee, Medway, Moselle, Tagus, etc.
Inman Line—Almost all were named after cities, as *City of Richmond,*
          City of Chester, City of Berlin, City of Chicago, etc.
Anchor Line—Almost all were named after geographic regions, as *Asia,*
          Armenia, Assyria, Australia, Britannia, Caledonia, etc.
Allan Line—Almost all ended in "ian," as *Caspian, Carthaginian, Nova*
          Scotian, Parisian, Sarmatian, etc.
Canadian Pacific Line—The largest had "Empress" in their names, as
          Empress of Britain, Empress of Australia, Empress of Canada,
          Empress of Russia, etc.
Prince Line—All were named after princes, as *Moorish Prince, Arabian*
          Prince, Siamese Prince, etc.
Bibby Line—All were named after English counties (shires), as *Der-*
          byshire, Staffordshire, Shropshire, etc.

A few unusual World War II Liberty Ship names

Big Foot Wallace
Button Gwinnett
Bernardo O'Higgins
Johnny Appleseed
Hawkins Fudske
William Williams
Pio Pico
Joseph-Augustin Chevalier
F. T. Frelinghuysen
Nachman Syrkin
Andreas Honcharenko
Mello Franco
Stage Door Canteen
Bon Air Seam

Ship name prefixes

The prefix for ships of the U.S. Navy in commission is USS, which stands for United States Ship.

U.S. Navy ships not in commission are referred to by name only.

Civilian-manned ships of the Military Sealift Command are officially "in service," not "in commission," and their prefix is USNS, or United States Naval Ship.

U.S. Coast Guard ships, regardless of type, are referred to as cutters, and therefore their prefix is USCGC, or U.S. Coast Guard Cutter.

Merchant ships generally carry the prefix SS, which stands for steamship, or MS, for motorship.

Fishing vessels generally use the prefix FV.

Prefixes used by foreign navies

HMS, Her Majesty's Ship, Britain; also, His Majesty's Ship, Saudi Arabia
HMAS, Her Majesty's Australian Ship, Australia
HMCS, Her Majesty's Canadian Ship, Canada
HMNZS, Her Majesty's New Zealand Ship, New Zealand
BRP, Barka ng Republika ng Pilipinas, Philippines
INS, Indian Naval Ship, India; also Israeli Naval Ship, Israel

The ten most-popular boat names, according to Boat/U.S.

1993—*Serenity, Obsession, Osprey, Fantasea, Liquid Asset, Therapy, Seaduction, Happy Hours, Solitude, Wet Dream.*

2002—*Liberty, Victory, Aquaholic, Bite Me, Endless Summer, Seahorse, Footloose, Silver Lining, Miss Behavin, Moondance.*

Some nineteenth-century clipper-ship names:
Game-Cock
Stag-Hound
Westward Ho!
Romance of the Seas
Witch of the Wave
Chariot of Fame
Red Jacket
Witchcraft
Belle of the West
Champion of the Seas
Herald of the Morning

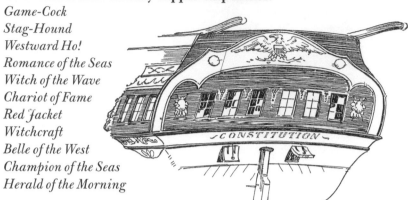

A few nicknames for famous ships

"Great Harry"—*Henri Grâce à Dieu,* English warship, 1514, because
she was the largest and most powerful of her time

"Golden Devil"—*Sovereign of the Seas,* English warship, 1637, so called
by the Dutch because she was both fearsome and covered with gild-
ed decorations

"Old Ironsides"—U.S. frigate *Constitution,* 1797, because she could
stand up to the heaviest cannon fire

"Three-Fingered Jack"—*Anglia,* English steamboat, 1866, because she
had three smokestacks

"The Glass Hack"—*Tashmoo,* Lake Erie excursion steamer, 1899,
because she had many glass windows

"Cattle Only"—Cunard liner *Catalonia,* late nineteenth century,
because she carried thousands of immigrants across the Atlantic
in steerage class

"The Covered Wagon"—U.S. aircraft carrier *Langley,* 1921, because she
had been converted to a carrier by building a flight deck over the
hull of a collier

"Maloler the Roller"—Pacific passenger ship *Malola* of the Matson Line,
1927, because she was uncomfortable in a seaway

Old Ironsides gets her name:

"Several shots now entered our hull. One of the largest the enemy could
command struck us, but the plank was so hard it fell out and sank in the
waters. This was afterwards noticed and the cry arose: 'Huzza! Her sides
are made of iron! See where the shots fell out!'"

—Moses Smith, sponger of gun no. 1 aboard the *Constitution*
during her battle with HMS *Guerrière*

Expressive nicknames for various U.S. Coast Guard cutters, past and present

Acushnet—"Crushnuts"
Barataria—"Bacteria"
Boutwell—"Bad Smell"
Campbell—"Soup Can"
Cape Hatteras—"Cape Hazardous"
Cape Henlopen—"Cape Chickenlopen"
Chincoteague—"Chickenfeed"
Coos Bay—"Booze Bay"
Cowslip—"Cow's Lip"
Cuttyhunk—"Hunk of Junk"
Dallas—"Dullest"
Eagle—"Dirty Bird"
Evergreen—"Never Clean"
Firebush—"Firewood"
Hollyhock—"Hockey-Puck"
Iris—"I-Rust"
Jefferson Island—"Jefferson Starship"
Knight Island—"Nightmare Island"
Legare—"Leg Hair"
Mallow—"Marsh Mallow"
Mellon—"Smellin'"
Modoc—"Mud Duck"
Morgenthau—"Morgenscow"
Morro Bay—"Moron Bay"
Naushon—"Nauseous"
Onondaga—"Rolling O"
Planetree—"Lame Tree"
Point Martin—"Point Martini"
Pontchartrain—"Raunchy Paunchy"
Red Oak—"Red Joke"
Redwood—"Deadwood"
Rockaway—"Rustaway"
Sagebrush—"Scrub Brush"
Sebago—"Seabag"
Steadfast—"Dead Last"
Tahoma—"Always Homa"
Vigorous—"Vig the Pig"
White Heath—"White Heat"
Winnebago—"Wind Bag"
                    —according to their crews

The Coast Guard cutter
But the men that sail the ocean
In a wormy, rotten craft,
When the sea ahead is mountains
With a hell-blown gale abaft;
When the mainmast cracks and topples,
And she's lurching in the trough,
Them's the guys that greets the cutter
With the smiles that won't come off.

—Arthur Somers Roche

Annals of the U.S. Coast Guard

1789—Lighthouse Establishment was founded.

1791—First revenue cutter, the *Massachusetts,* was launched.

1791—Hopley Yeaton of New Hampshire, commander of the revenue cutter *Scammel,* became first seagoing commissioned officer of the United States.

1799—Revenue cutter ensign, now the Coast Guard ensign, authorized.

1830—First regulations covering uniforms went into effect.

1842—Alexander V. Fraser became first Commandant of the Revenue-Cutter Service.

1843—Revenue-Marine became a bureau in the U.S. Treasury Department.

1845—Lighthouse Establishment put under administrative control of Revenue-Marine.

1861—Revenue cutter *Harriet Lane* fired first naval shot of Civil War.

1876—First Revenue-Cutter Service officer's training school established.

1896—Revenue-Cutter Service given authority to regulate yachting regattas on navigable waters.

1910—Officer's training school of Revenue-Cutter Service moved to New London, Connecticut.

1915—Revenue-Cutter Service and Life-Saving Service merged to form a new armed service, the United States Coast Guard.

1916—First aviation unit of the U.S. Coast Guard authorized.

1917—U.S. Coast Guard came under the control of the U.S. Navy during World War I.

1932—U.S. Coast Guard assigned responsibility for enforcing the International Whaling Convention for the United States.

1932—U.S. Coast Guard Academy moved to its current site in New London, Connecticut.

1939—Lighthouse Service amalgamated with U.S. Coast Guard.

1941—U.S. Coast Guard Reserve established.

1941—U.S. Coast Guard came under the control of the U.S. Navy during World War II.

1942—U.S. Coast Guard assumed responsibility for port security in the United States.

1942—SPARS, the women's branch of the U.S. Coast Guard, established.

1946—Former German sail-training bark *Horst Wessel* commissioned as the USCGC *Eagle.*

1946—Bureau of Marine Inspection and Navigation of the Commerce Department was transferred to the U.S. Coast Guard.

1965—All U.S. Navy icebreakers turned over to the U.S. Coast Guard.

1965—First U.S. Coast Guard cutters sent to Vietnam.

1967—U.S. Coast Guard transferred from Treasury Department to new Department of Transportation.

1980—First women graduated from U.S. Coast Guard Academy.

2003—U.S. Coast Guard transferred from Department of Transportation to new Department of Homeland Security.

Annals of the U.S. Lighthouse Service

1716—The first lighthouse, Boston Light, was established.

1719—The first fog signal was installed at Boston Light.

1756—The first navigation buoys were laid in the Delaware River.

1764—The first lighthouse to be financed by a public lottery, Sandy Hook Light, was built.

1789—The U.S. Congress took over jurisdiction of lighthouses and aids to navigation.

1792—Administrative control of all lighthouses was vested in the Commissioner of the Revenue.

1792—Cape Henry Light, Virginia, was the first to be built by the U.S. government.

1802—Control of all lighthouses was vested in the Secretary of the Treasury.

1813—Jurisdiction over lighthouses was returned to the Commissioner of the Revenue.

1820—The first fog bell was installed at West Quoddy Head Light.

1820—The first lightship was anchored at the entrance to the Elizabeth River, Virginia.

1831—The first lighthouse constructed on other than dry land was built at South Pass, Louisiana.

1841—The first Fresnel lens in the United States was installed in the Navesink Light, New Jersey.

1845—The Lighthouse Establishment was put under the administrative control of the U.S. Revenue-Marine.

1850—The first iron pile light structure was built on Minot's Ledge, Massachusetts.

1850—The U.S. Congress authorized the lateral system of buoyage in navigable waters.

1852—The U.S. Congress created the Lighthouse Board to oversee all U.S. lighthouses on the seacoasts and Great Lakes.

1852—The first bell buoy was put in service.

1857—The first steam fog whistle was installed at the Beavertail Light, Rhode Island.

1874—The Lighthouse Board was given jurisdiction over aids to navigation on the Mississippi, Missouri, and Ohio Rivers.

1876—The Courteney whistle buoy was put in service.

1881—The first lighted buoy, fueled by oil, was put in service.

1888—The first electric light was put in service (it was unsuccessful).

1891—The St. George Reef Light, California, was the most expensive light to be built to date.

1895—Scotch Cap Light was the first outside light to be built in Alaska.

1901—The first radio equipment used in the Lighthouse Service was installed in the Nantucket Lightship.

1910—The first lighted buoy powered by acetylene gas was put in service.

1910—Lighthouse jurisdiction was passed by Congress to the newly established Bureau of Lighthouses in the Department of Commerce and Labor.

1910—The first radio beacon was installed at the approaches to New York Harbor.

1921—The first radio fog signal stations were established.

1939—The Lighthouse Service was amalgamated with the U.S. Coast Guard.

1964—Nuclear energy was used for the first time to power a lighthouse, Baltimore Light in Maryland.

Lighthouses get a political ally

It was midnight and our captain was fast asleep. But Capt. Kennedy jumping upon deck, and seeing the danger, ordered the ship to wear round, all sails standing. An operation dangerous to the masts, but it carried us clear, and we escaped shipwreck, for we were running right upon the rocks on which the lighthouse was erected. This deliverance impressed me strongly with the utility of lighthouses, and made me resolve to encourage the building of more of them in America, if I should live to return there.

—Benjamin Franklin, on escaping shipwreck on the Scilly Isles

The three principal conditions that must be met when constructing a lighthouse

It must be situated on a geologically sound site.

It must be high enough for the full display of its light.

It must be constructed with a strength and solidity that will stand up to the worst wind and wave conditions to be expected, ever.

The terrors of lighthouse construction, in this case the Skerryvore, off the west coast of Scotland in the late 1830s

For miles around nothing could be seen but white foaming breakers, and nothing heard but howling winds and lashing waves.... Our slumbers were at times fearfully interrupted by the sudden pouring of the sea over the roof, the rocking of the house on its pillars, and the spurting of water through the seams of the doors and windows.... On two occasions in particular, those sensations were so vivid as to cause almost every one to spring out of bed; and some of the men fled from the barrack by a temporary gangway to the more stable, but less comfortable, shelter afforded by the bare walls of the lighthouse tower, then unfinished, where they spent the remainder of the night in darkness, wet, and cold.

—Robert Stevenson, Chief Engineer

For years the surge has tossed its kelp and wrack about my door;

I've heard the sea-wind sing its song in whispers 'round the place,
And fought it when it flung the sand, like needles, in my face.
I've seen the sun-rays turn the roof ter blist'rin', tarry coal;
I've seen the ice-drift clog the bay from foamin' shoal ter shoal;
I've faced this winter's snow and sleet, I've felt the summer's shower,
But every night I've lit the lamp up yonder in the tower.

—from "The Light-Keeper," by Joseph C. Lincoln

The progress of lighthouse lights

earliest—open wood or coal fire

sixteenth century—tallow candle

1763—oil lamp with an open flame intensified with a simple reflector

1780—oil lamp with cylindrical wick, glass chimney, and simple reflector

early nineteenth century—catoptric system in use

1823—Fresnel's dioptric system in use
mid-nineteenth century—catoptric and dioptric systems combined
mid-nineteenth century—introduction of kerosene fuel
1858—first use of electric arc lamp
early twentieth century—incandescent electric light bulbs in use

The two principal methods of increasing the brilliancy of the lamps in lighthouses
Catoptric system—Reflectors collect the light and throw it in the desired
    direction.
Dioptric system—Glass prisms are arranged around the light to refract
    the light beams from the lamp into parallel beams in the desired
    direction.

Keeping the light spiffy, nineteenth century
The reflectors were burnished with rouge (trioxide of iron), applied with
a soft chamois skin. They were polished with a dry, soft chamois skin,
without rouge.

    The lenses and mirrors were cleaned with a linen cloth moistened
with spirit of wine; dried with a soft, dry linen rubber; and rubbed down
with the finest chamois skin obtainable.

Light characteristics of lighthouses and other aids to navigation

F.—fixed; a continuous, steady light

Fl.—flashing; single flashes at regular intervals, the duration of light
being less than that of dark

Fl.(2)—two flashes

Fl.(2+1)—two flashes, then one

Q. or Qk. Fl.—quick flashing; no fewer than 60 flashes per minute

E.Int.—equal interval; on and off for equal period

I.S.O.—isophase; same as equal interval

Occ.—occulting; light, then equal intervals of dark, the duration of light
being longer than that of dark

Morse (A)—Morse code "A"; short flash followed by long flash

The light-frame of the thousand lenses

One star came out over the cliffs, the waters turned to lead colour, and St.
Cecilia's Light shot out across the sea in eight long pencils that wheeled
slowly from right to left, melted into one beam of solid light laid down
directly in front of the tower, dissolved again into eight, and passed away.
The light-frame of the thousand lenses circled on its rollers, and the com-
pressed-air engine that drove it hummed like a bluebottle under a glass.
The hand of the indicator on the wall pulsed from mark to mark. Eight
pulse-beats time one half-revolution of the Light; neither more nor less.

—Rudyard Kipling

Time and tide wait for no man

—Geoffrey Chaucer

Ship's bells
The ship's clock strikes in a half-hour sequence based on the four-hour
 ship's watch system.
The end of the first half hour is marked by 1 bell.
The end of the first hour is 2 bells.
The end of the first 1½ hours is 3 bells, etc.
The end of a four-hour watch is marked by 8 bells.
Eight bells are struck six times in a 24-hour period: at 12 noon, 4 P.M.,
 8 P.M., 12 midnight, 4 A.M., and 8 A.M.

The sea day and date
In the old days, navigators considered the day and date to commence at
noon, and to end and commence again the following noon. The sea day and
date, as they were known, began twelve hours before the civil day and date.

Today, navigators consider the sea day and date and the civil day
and date to be the same—both end and commence at midnight, 2400 and
0000 hours.

Keeping track of time
Time zone—a 15-degree interval between two meridians, one of twenty-
 four divisions of the earth
Greenwich Mean Time—the solar time at 0 degrees longitude, the
 Greenwich Meridian
Zone Time—the time in a given zone

The difference between a chronometer and a watch
A chronometer is a timepiece whose error, if it has any, is both known
and nearly constant. A watch is a timepiece whose error is either unknown
or erratic.

A timepiece that gains a minute a day, every day, is a chronometer. A
timepiece that gains a minute in one day, a minute and a half in another,
and loses fifteen seconds the next is a watch.

*The ship's clock in the bar says half past eleven. Half past eleven is open-
ing time. The hands of the clock have stayed still at half past eleven for fifty
years. It is always opening time in the Sailor's Arms.*
—from *Under Milk Wood*, by Dylan Thomas

Care of a chronometer with a mechanical movement
Wind the piece at the same time each day.
Turn the winding key gently.
Stow the piece as close to the center of motion in the vessel and as far
    away as possible from sources of vibration.
Keep the temperature of the piece as uniform as possible.
To avoid inducing magnetism into the works, never stow the piece near
    ferrous metals or any magnetic device.
When transporting the piece, clamp it so it will not swing in the gimbals.
Except when transporting, ensure that the piece swings freely in the
    gimbals.

Making time fly
During the days of sail, time was measured with a half-hour sandglass. The
midshipmen or ship's boys who were in charge of turning the glass when
the sand ran out theorized that if the glass were warmed, the neck would
expand and the sand would fall more quickly. To warm it, they would
sometimes put the glass under their coats, or wrap their fingers around the
neck of the glass. Time would therefore pass faster and their watch on deck
would end sooner. On some ships, this was known as "warming the bell."

The advance or loss of time when circumnavigating the globe
By sailing west, the vessel and the sun move in the same direction; the sun
overtakes the vessel; the vessel's day is therefore lengthened. The rate of
lengthening is one hour for every 15 degrees of longitude made.

By sailing east, the vessel and the sun move in opposite directions;
the sun advances to meet the vessel; the vessel's day is therefore shortened. The length of shortening is one hour for every 15 degrees of longitude made.

When crossing the International Date Line—roughly the 180-degree meridian—to keep the logbook in synch with the date half a world away at Greenwich

Sailing eastward, the day must be reckoned over again. If the vessel crosses the meridian on Tuesday, June 12, for example, there will be two Tuesdays, June 12, in the logbook.

Sailing westward, the day must be skipped. If the vessel crosses the meridian on a Thursday, July 8, for example, there will be no Thursday, July 8, in the logbook.

Three bells!—"Keep a bright look-out there," sung out the lieutenant.
"Ay, ay, Sir," from the four look-out men, in a volley.
Then from the weather-gangway, "All's well," rose shrill into the night air.
—Michael Scott

Dawn at sea, according to Richard Henry Dana, Jr.

There is something in the first gray streaks stretching along the eastern horizon and throwing an indistinct light upon the face of the deep, which combines with the boundlessness and unknown depth of the sea around, and gives one a feeling of loneliness, of dread, and of melancholy foreboding, which nothing else in nature can. This gradually passes away as the light grows brighter, and when the sun comes up, the ordinary monotonous sea day begins.

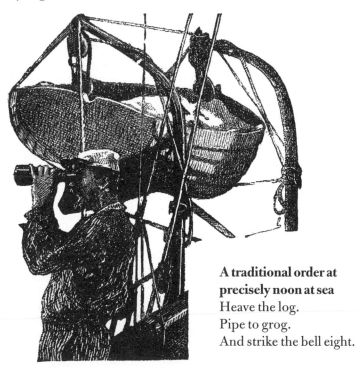

A traditional order at precisely noon at sea
Heave the log.
Pipe to grog.
And strike the bell eight.

Ship's watches

A ship's crew is normally divided into two watches, called the port and starboard watches. The captain heads the starboard watch; the first mate, the port. One watch is always on duty and the other off, except in situations when "All Hands" are required. The tradition is that the starboard watch stands the first watch outward bound; the port watch, the first homeward bound. Each watch is on duty for four hours, except from 4 to 8 P.M., which is divided into two watches of two hours each, called Dog Watches. The Dog Watches allow the watches to be changed every day so that each watch gets a turn of eight hours' rest at night. The standard watches are as follows:

First Watch—8 P.M. to midnight
Middle Watch, aka "The Churchyard"—midnight to 4 A.M.
Morning Watch, aka "The Deadeye"—4 A.M. to 8 A.M.
Forenoon Watch—8 A.M. to 12 noon
Afternoon Watch—12 noon to 4 P.M.
First Dog Watch—4 P.M. to 6 P.M.
Second Dog Watch—6 P.M. to 8 P.M.

Tradesmen of the sea

On deepwater sailing vessels, there was a category of men known as "idlers." Though idlers didn't have to stand watch—hence the nickname, which was not derisive but rather affectionate—they were indispensable to the operation of the ship. The idlers were the boatswain (who was in charge of rigging and marlinspike seamanship), the sailmaker, the carpenter, and the cook. Usually they berthed separately—that is, neither in the forecastle with the seamen nor in the officers' staterooms.

Watch-keeping at night

Night orders—On large vessels, the master writes out the night orders each evening, specifying exactly what he expects to be done, when and why he expects to be called, what course to steer, etc.
Night order book—the book in which the night orders are written
Standing orders—the expectations of the master concerning procedures in fog, squalls, etc., when sighting other vessels, and in other dangerous circumstances; also, when to call him to the bridge
Special orders—the expectations of the master concerning the immediate events of that particular night: course to steer, changes to course, speed of vessel, landfalls anticipated, etc.

The watch is changed,
The glass is running.
We shall have a good voyage,
If God is willing.
                    —anon.

"A caution, always work the tides."
                    —Frank Cowper

The motion of the sea
Vertical—the rise and fall of the tide
Horizontal—the ebb and flow of the tidal current

"There is a Tide"
by William Shakespeare

There is a tide in the affairs of men,
Which, taken at the flood, leads on to fortune;
Omitted, all the voyage of their life
Is bound in shallows and in miseries.
On such a full sea are we now afloat;
And we must take the current when it serves,
Or lose our ventures.

There is no end to the mystery of the tides.
                    —Hilaire Belloc

Types of tide
Semidiurnal—two high and two low waters each tidal day
Diurnal—one high and one low water each tidal day
Mixed—sometimes diurnal, sometimes semidiurnal, plus large inequality
    in the heights of high and low water

The coming and going of the tides
Some have thought the Earth and Sea to be a living Creature, which by its Respiration, causeth this ebbing and flowing. Others imagined that it proceeds, and is provoked, from a great Whirlpool near Norway, which, for Six Hours, absorbs the Water, and afterwards, disgorges it in the same space of Time.
                    —Bernhardus Varenius

Describing the tide
A coming tide is in flood.
A going tide is in ebb.
The top of the tide is its maximum high.
The bottom of the tide is its maximum low.
Stand of the tide is the period when there is no vertical motion of the tide;
    i.e., the tide is at the top of high water or the bottom of low water.
(Note: Slack water, often used in reference to the tide, actually applies to tidal current. It is the period when there is no horizontal motion of the water; i.e., the tidal current is running neither in nor out.)

A normal tide, unaffected by wind, rises and falls roughly at the following rate
1st hour: $\frac{1}{12}$ of its rise or fall for that day
2nd hour: $\frac{2}{12}$ of its rise or fall for that day
3rd hour: $\frac{3}{12}$ of its rise or fall for that day
4th hour: $\frac{3}{12}$ of its rise or fall for that day
5th hour: $\frac{2}{12}$ of its rise or fall for that day
6th hour: $\frac{1}{12}$ of its rise or fall for that day

In general
The highest tides are usually in funnel-shaped estuaries or bays that are
    directly open to the sea.
A channel open at both ends will usually have minimal rise and fall of the
    tide but strong tidal currents.
If a tide or tidal current does not exactly coincide with the government
    prediction tables, don't blame the government; 99 percent of the
    time, you can blame the wind.

The heights of the levels of the tide
Mean low water—the average height of all low waters at a location
Mean low water springs—the average height of the low waters at the times
    of spring tides
Mean lower low water—the average height of the lower of the two low
    waters of a tidal day
Mean lower low water springs—the average height of the lower of the two
    low waters on the days of spring tides
Lowest normal low water—the average height of the monthly lowest low
    waters, without considering tides produced by storms
Lowest low water—the rock-bottom lowest tide observed in a location
Mean sea level—the average height of the sea over a nineteen-year period

Mean high water—the average height of all high waters over a nineteen-
  year period
Mean high water springs—the average of the high waters on the days of
  spring tides
Mean higher high water—the average height of the higher of the two high
  waters of a tidal day

Tidal extremes
Neap tides—those that rise and fall least from the mean level
Spring tides—those that rise and fall most from the mean level; aka full-
  drain, high coast, and moon tides
In most parts of the world, these tides occur twice in the lunar month.

The highest tides in the world
Sea of Okhotsk
Northern coast of Australia
English Channel
Ungava Bay, Quebec, Canada
Bay of Fundy, New Brunswick and Nova Scotia, Canada
    The highest tides of all are near the town of Wolfville, Nova Scotia,
in the Minas Basin off the Bay of Fundy, where the tidal range runs as
much as 45 feet. The flow of water at midtide in the Minas Channel is
said to equal that of all the rivers, streams, and brooks on earth.

Predicting the tides
In the year 1250, the earliest known tide table was published by St.
Albans Abbey in England. It listed the times of high water at London
Bridge on the River Thames.
    In 1802, Nathaniel Bowditch's *New American Practical Navigator*
contained a chapter on the tides, with tables to determine the state of the
moon and therefore the state of the tide.
    In 1830, the U.S. Coast Survey published the *American Almanac,*
which contained predictions for high tide for Boston, New York, and
Charleston, and time differences for almost 100 other stations between them.
    In 1830, the English astronomer Sir William Lubbock included
tidal predictions in the *British Almanac.*
    In 1872, Lord Kelvin of Great Britain introduced a machine for
predicting tides based on the harmonic analysis method.
    In 1966, the U.S. government switched from the use of mechanical
tide-prediction machines to electronic digital computers.

Factors affecting the height of tide computed from tables

The heights of tide given in the tide tables are predictions, not guarantees.

Heights lower than predicted are likely to occur when the atmospheric pressure is higher than expected, and vice versa.

Strong winds can affect the rise and fall of the tides considerably, even if the wind is far offshore. Strong onshore winds (blowing from the sea toward the land) and a low barometer reading tend to increase the height of high water. Strong offshore winds (blowing from the land toward the sea) and a high barometer reading tend to decrease the height of high water.

During a major storm, the height of the tide can be off by several feet (plus or minus, depending on the direction of the wind), and the time of the tide can be off by as much as an hour.

In places where there is a large inequality between the two high or two low tides during a tidal day, the predictions of height of tide are less reliable than elsewhere.

Wind and tide

Lee tide—The wind blows and the tide runs in the same direction.
Weather tide—The wind blows and the tide runs in opposite directions.

In summer in the Northeast, the wind and tide do this in sounds, bays, and estuaries, generally speaking

The wind usually comes in with the flood.
If the wind and tide come in during the morning, the wind will stay all day.
If the wind and tide come in during the afternoon, the wind will not last long.
If the wind comes in strong against an outgoing tide, expect a long blow.

Tidal symbolism

Flood tide—strength
Ebb tide—weakness
Flood tide—health
Ebb tide—sickness
Flood tide—life
Ebb tide—death

Tidal superstitions

Boys are born on the flood, girls on the ebb.
Sick people who last to the turn of the tide will survive at least to the next one.
Life ends with the ebb.

"He went out with the tide and the sunset," was a phrase I heard from a surgeon describing an old sailor's death under peculiarly gentle conditions.

—Walt Whitman

"The Tide Rises, The Tide Falls"
by Henry Wadsworth Longfellow

The tide rises, the tide falls,
The twilight darkens, the curlew calls;
Along the sea-sands damp and brown
The traveler hastens toward the town,
*   And the tide rises, the tide falls.*

Darkness settles on roofs and walls,
But the sea, the sea in the darkness calls;
The little waves, with their soft, white hands,
Efface the footprints in the sands,
*   And the tide rises, the tide falls.*

The morning breaks, the steeds in their stalls
Stamp and neigh, as the hostler calls;
The day returns, but nevermore
Returns the traveler to the shore,
*   And the tide rises, the tide falls.*

Never go into strange places on a falling tide without a pilot.

—Thomas Gibson Bowles

I saw from the beach, when the morning was shining,
*   A bark o'er the waters move gloriously on,*
I came when the sun o'er the beach was declining,
*   The bark was still there, but the waters were gone.*

—T. Sturge Moore

Out of sight of land the sailor feels safe. It is the beach that worries him.

—Charles G. Davis

An immutable truth
Your boating waters are always limited to those deeper than the draft of your boat.

The joys of tidal waters

To my mind, there is more to be said for sailing in shallow water, making use of the eddies along beaches and watching the current swirl through the sand; or to pole through marsh channels with eel grass stroking the topsides and the smell of mud fairly high.   —Anthony Bailey

Signs of shallow water

Any change in color of the water

Ripples on smooth water

Wading seabirds

In clear water, a suggestion of the bottom appears, usually as blotches of dark and light color.

Water takes on a light-green hue, as green water generally is shallower than blue.

An uncomfortable groundswell arises in smooth water; steeper or break-ing seas in rougher water.

"Suddenly the boy shouted aft that there were ducks ahead. The old man hollered forward: 'Be they walking or be they swimming?'

"When the boy called back that he thought they were walking, the captain yelled: 'All right, then, me lad, ready about and hard alee!' thus taking his vessel back into deeper waters."   —Giles M.S. Tod

Crossing shoal water

Even if the chart and the tide tables indicate enough water over a shoal for your boat, do not forget to take into consideration the state of the sea. A heavy sea or groundswell can cause abnormally shallow water in the trough.

In a sailboat—to pass over a shoal that is slightly shallower than the depth of the keel, sheet her in to heel the boat as much as possible, thus reducing draft.

In a powerboat—don't even think about it.

If you should go aground

Immediately note the heading of the boat, so you will know in which direction the deeper water lies (it's behind you).

In a boat with power, back off. If aground on a sandy bottom, do not use full throttle, as the suck of the propeller is liable to throw sand under the boat, putting her more firmly aground.

In a sailboat without auxiliary power, spin the boat if you can. If that doesn't work, furl all sail.

Get an anchor out to deeper water. Try to pull the boat toward the anchor.

If aground by the bow, move the crew to the stern.

If aground by the stern, move the crew to the bow.

If aground amidships, try to roll her off by swaying on the rigging or running the crew from side to side.

Heel the boat by backing the jib and having the crew lean out on the lee shrouds. The draft can be reduced by nearly a third if the boat can be heeled as much as 45 degrees.

Or try this: Fill the dinghy with water and secure it to the end of the main boom. Swing the boom out as far as it will go. Take up on the main topping lift. The weight of the dinghy will heel the boat.

Sometimes, having the crew jump up and down in unison can shake her off.

If you can't get off and the tide is falling

Pump the bilges to keep bilgewater from getting into the lockers and the bunks as she heels over.

Secure lockers and loose gear below.

Protect with fenders, etc., the side of the hull that will rest on the ground.

Put the best face on it

If you should run aground on a falling tide and can't get her off, climb over the side and scrub the bottom while you wait for the tide to return. Your friends will think you went aground on purpose.

Walking in deep mud

On a tidal mudflat that is too deep and too soft to walk on, strap boards on your feet and use them like snowshoes. Lacking boards, crawl with the full length of your lower leg (knee to instep) in contact with the mud. Keep the weight of your body slightly backward. Wear long pants and gloves to protect your legs and hands against shells, rocks, broken glass, and other debris buried in the mud.

To determine the necessary draft for your next boat

Get out a chart of the waters in which you will use her.
Circle the shallowest waters in which you wish to sail.
Add 2 feet to the shallowest depth indicated inside the circle.
That should be the maximum draft of your boat.

I'm afloat, I'm afloat, on the fierce roaring tide,
The ocean's my home and my bark is my bride.

—anon.

Big tides, strong currents
Weak tides, weak currents.

—anon.

I dip and I surge and I swing
In the rip of the racing tide.

—Rudyard Kipling

EDWARD B.
EDWARDS

Water moving in the sea

Current—horizontal motion of the water, caused by wind and tide. The most famous ocean currents are the Humboldt Current in the Pacific and the Gulf Stream in the Atlantic.

Bore—a tidal current moving so fast that its leading edge forms a wave. The most potent bores are in the Hooghly River, India, where it comes on with the sound of thunder; in the Petitcodiac River on the Bay of Fundy, and in the Fuchun (formerly Tsien Tang) River, China, where the wave can reach as high as 20 feet and the current has been clocked at 18 knots. Other great bores of the world exist in the Amazon River; South Atlantic Ocean; the Turnagain Arm, Cook Inlet, Alaska; and the Severn River, Bristol Channel, England.

Tidal wave—an ocean wave produced by an earthquake, rockslide, volcanic eruption, or submarine subsidence.

Whirlpool—a tight, fast, rotary current, caused by restriction of a current by rocks and ledges. The most famous are Charybdis in the Straits of Messina, described by Homer, and the Maelstrom, off Norway, described in a short story by Edgar Allan Poe.

A whirlpool to remember, the Maelstrom, according to Edgar Allan Poe

The edge of the whirl was represented by a broad belt of gleaming spray; but no particle of this slipped into the mouth of the terrific funnel, whose interior, so far as the eye could fathom it, was a smooth, shining, and jet-black wall of water, inclined to the horizon at an angle of some forty-five degrees, speeding dizzily round and round with a swaying and sweltering motion, and sending forth to the winds an appalling voice, half shriek, half roar, such as not even the cataract of Niagara lifts up in its agony to Heaven.

—from "A Descent into the Maelstrom"

Poe's Maelstrom is not entirely fictitious

Though rumor has greatly exaggerated the importance of the Malstrom [sic], or more properly Moskentraumen, which runs between Mosken and Lofotodden, it is still the most dangerous tideway in Lofoten, its violence being due, in great measure, to the irregularity of the ground.... As the strength of the tide increases the sea becomes heavier and the current more irregular, forming extensive eddies or whirlpools (Malstrom). During such periods no vessel should enter the Moskentraumen.... Fishermen affirm that if they are aware of the approach to a whirlpool and have time to throw an oar or any other bulky body into it they will get over it safely; the reason is that when the continuity is broken and the whirling motion of the sea interrupted by something thrown into it the water must rush suddenly in on all sides and fill up the cavity.

—Sailing Directions for the Northwest and North Coasts of Norway

Memorable tidal waves

August 27, 1667—A 12-foot tidal wave caused by a hurricane struck the English colony of Jamestown, Virginia, and submerged the surrounding countryside.

June 7, 1692—An earthquake and tidal wave destroyed the buccaneer city of Port Royal, Jamaica, which slid into the sea; 3,000 people perished.

May 9, 1877—A tidal wave caused by an earthquake struck the coast of Chile, sinking or destroying in a matter of minutes more than fifteen large sailing ships loading guano for fertilizer.

August 26, 1883—A tidal wave caused by the eruption of a volcano on the island of Krakatoa, in the Sunda Strait between Java and Sumatra, ranged through the islands of the Pacific Ocean, resulting in the deaths of more than 35,000 people.

November 18, 1929—An earthquake centered on the Grand Bank caused a 50-foot tidal wave, which killed twenty-seven people on the coast of Newfoundland.

April 1, 1946—An underwater earthquake near the Aleutian Islands caused a 50-foot tidal wave that ranged through the Pacific Ocean, killing more than 170 people in the Pacific islands.

November 13, 1970—A tidal wave caused by a tropical cyclone with winds of 120 mph struck the Ganges River delta, Bangladesh, resulting in the loss of hundreds of thousands of lives.

The sequence of a tidal current

Flood
Maximum flood
Slack
Ebb begins
Ebb
Maximum ebb
Slack
Flood begins
etc.

Two types of tidal currents

Reversing—The current runs in one direction during the flood and the opposite direction during the ebb; between flood and ebb, there will be a period of slack current.

Rotary—The current changes direction continually; there will be no period of slack.

Fast water

The fastest (and deepest) water in a straightaway of a tidal river is usually in the middle.

In a curving tidal river, the swiftest (and deepest) water usually is near the outer edge of the curve.

Countercurrents and eddies usually are found near points and in bights, as well as near the shores of narrow passageways and straits.

Tidal currents usually reach their greatest velocity in a narrow passage connecting two large bodies of water.

Tide rips—extremely turbulent water in a tidal current—are caused by an irregular bottom, or by a sharp change in the depth of the water, such as at the edges of banks or reefs.

Rough estimate of tidal current

The speed and strength of the tidal current can be estimated by watching buoys. A buoy will lean toward the direction of current flow; how far it leans can indicate how strong the current is.

Do not rely on vessels at anchor to indicate the condition of the tidal current. Unless the air is still, the vessel will be influenced by the wind as well as the current.

The minimum tidal effects (range of tide and strength of current) are usually found in the open ocean and along straight coasts.

The maximum tidal effects are usually found in rivers, bays, harbors, and inlets.

Vessels are sometimes retarded, and sometimes forwarded in their voyages, by currents at sea, which are not often perceived.   —Benjamin Franklin

The effect of tidal currents

A tidal current that is directly against you will slow your speed but not affect your course.

A tidal current that is running directly with your course will increase your speed but not affect your course.

A tidal current that is neither directly against you nor with you will affect
your course and speed to a greater or lesser extent, depending on
the angle of your course to it.

So we beat on, boats against the current, borne back ceaselessly into the past.
—F. Scott Fitzgerald, *The Great Gatsby*

Remembrance of things past

*S*ome day the history of the sea will be divided into two great periods. *The Age of Simplicity and the Age of Complication.* —Felix Riesenberg

American maritime history in the blink of an eye
1492—Christopher Columbus discovered America.
1620—Pilgrims landed in Plymouth.
mid-seventeenth century—Golden Age of piracy in full swing.
early eighteenth century—Whaling as a serious industry underway.
1768—Benjamin Franklin published chart of Gulf Stream.
1773—Bostonians heaved English tea into harbor.
1775—Continental Navy was established.
1776—Washington crossed Delaware River in a rowboat.
1777—*Atlantic Neptune* charts were published.
1779—John Paul Jones had yet begun to fight.
1784—Ship *Empress of China* established America's China trade.
1790—Revenue Cutter Service, forerunner of U.S. Coast Guard, was founded.
1792—Edmund Blunt published *American Coast Pilot.*
1794—U.S. Navy was established.
1798-1800—Quasi-War, primarily naval, fought with France.
1799—East India Marine Society founded, Salem, Massachusetts.
1801—Nathaniel Bowditch published *New American Practical Navigator.*
1801-5—U.S. fought naval war with Barbary pirates.
1807—United States Coast Survey was established.

1807—Robert Fulton's *Clermont* steamed up the Hudson River.

1812–14—War of 1812, primarily naval, fought with Britain.

1818—Transatlantic packet lines underway.

1825—Erie Canal opened for business.

1838—Wilkes's United States Exploring Expedition set sail.

1840—Dana's *Two Years Before the Mast* was published.

1845—United States Naval Academy was established.

1847—Matthew Fontaine Maury's *Wind and Current Charts* was published.

mid-nineteenth century—Golden Age of the clipper ship.

1851—Herman Melville's *Moby-Dick* was published.

1853—Admiral Matthew Perry's fleet arrived in Japan.

1855—Maury's *Physical Geography of the Sea* published.

latter third of the nineteenth century—Golden Age of the downeaster.

1876—Revenue-Cutter Service officer's training school, forerunner of Coast Guard Academy, established.

late nineteenth century—U.S. Navy went steel.

1890—Captain Mahan's *Influence of Sea Power Upon History* was published.

1898—First practical U.S. Navy submarine was launched.

early twentieth century—Golden Age of the fast transatlantic liner.

early twentieth century—Golden Age of the multimasted cargo schooner.

1905—First steam-powered fishing trawler was launched.

1920—First U.S. Navy aircraft carrier was commissioned.

1923—Last McKay clipper ship was destroyed.

1925—Last whaler sailed from New Bedford.

1954—First U.S. Navy nuclear vessel, a submarine, was launched.

1978—First GPS satellite was launched.

The major maritime museums of the Western World

Nationaal Scheepvaartmuseum, Antwerp, Belgium

National Maritime Museum, Roskilde, Denmark

National Maritime Museum, Greenwich, London, England

Musée de la Marine, Paris, France

Nederlands Scheepvaart Museum, Amsterdam, Netherlands

Norsk Sjofartsmuseum, Oslo, Norway

Museu de Marinha, Lisbon, Portugal

National Naval Museum, Admiralty Palace, St. Petersburg, Russia

Museo Maritimo, Barcelona, Spain

Sjofartsmuseet, Goteborg, Sweden

Mystic Seaport Museum, Mystic, Connecticut, USA

The Mariners' Museum, Newport News, Virginia, USA

U.S. museums with significant maritime collections

American Merchant Marine Museum, Kings Point, New York
The Antique Boat Museum, Clayton, New York
Calvert Marine Museum, Solomons, Maryland
Chesapeake Bay Maritime Museum, St. Michaels, Maryland
Cold Spring Harbor Whaling Museum, Cold Spring Harbor, New York
Columbia River Maritime Museum, Astoria, Oregon
Erie Canal Museum, Syracuse, New York
Essex Shipbuilding Museum, Essex, Massachusetts
Great Lakes Historical Society, Vermilion, Ohio
Hawaii Maritime Center, Honolulu, Hawaii
Herreshoff Marine Museum, Bristol, Rhode Island
Hudson River Maritime Museum, Kingston, New York
Hull Lifesaving Museum, Hull, Massachusetts
Independence Seaport Museum, Philadelphia, Pennsylvania
Lake Champlain Maritime Museum, Vergennes, Vermont
Life-Saving Museum of Virginia, Virginia Beach, Virginia
Long Island Maritime Museum, West Sayville, New York
Maine Maritime Museum, Bath, Maine
The Mariners' Museum, Newport News, Virginia
The M.I.T. Museum, Hart Nautical Collection, Cambridge, Massachusetts
Museum of Yachting, Newport, Rhode Island
Mystic Seaport Museum, Mystic, Connecticut
Nantucket Historical Association, Nantucket, Massachusetts
New Bedford Whaling Museum, New Bedford, Massachusetts
North Carolina Maritime Museum, Beaufort, North Carolina
Peabody Essex Museum, Salem, Massachusetts
Penobscot Marine Museum, Searsport, Maine
Portland Harbor Museum, South Portland, Maine
San Diego Maritime Museum, San Diego, California
San Francisco Maritime National Historical Park, San Francisco, California
Smithsonian Institution, Washington, D.C.
South Street Seaport Museum, New York, New York
U.S. Coast Guard Museum, New London, Connecticut
U.S. Naval Academy Museum, Annapolis, Maryland
USS *Constitution* Museum, Boston, Massachusetts
Wisconsin Maritime Museum, Manitowoc, Wisconsin

*An' I don't care if it's North or South
The Trades or the China Sea,
Shortened down or everything set—
Close-hauled or running free—
You paint me a ship as is like a ship…
An' that'll do for me.*
                                        —C. Fox Smith

The two major types of marine art
Ship portraiture
Seascape

The principal elements of a properly executed work of realistic marine art
The scene is plausible and technically accurate.
All ships and boats look like ships and boats.
Details reflect the period of the scene—i.e., a Forbes double topsail is not
    shown on a ship whose time preceded the development of that device.
The feeling, or spirit, of the scene is conveyed through line, color, form,
    and space.

All great marine artists have these qualities
Love of ships and the sea
Knowledge and understanding of ships and the sea
Experience, either as a participant or as an observer
An eye for a sheer

"I want to be a painter," he replied,
"And know the sea and ships from A to Z."
           —from "Dauber," by John Masefield

**A few artists whose marine subjects exhibit both technical
accuracy and "heart"**
George Bellows
Arthur Briscoe
James E. Buttersworth
E.W. Cooke
Fred S. Cozzens
Montague Dawson
William Gilkerson
Gordon Grant
Winslow Homer

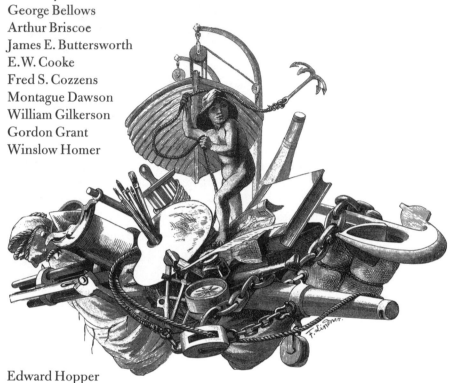

Edward Hopper
Rockwell Kent
Fitz Hugh Lane
Robert Salmon
Warren Sheppard
Arthur Spurling
J.M.W. Turner
Willem van de Velde, the Elder and the Younger
W.L. Wyllie

On the challenges of marine art
There can be no doubt that the sea and ships present the hardest challenges
and many of the insuperable difficulties to the artist, whatever the medi-
um in which he works, because there are so many facets to be mastered.
           —Alex A. Hurst

On the prerequisites for the marine artist

Many are the obstacles to the attainment of a proficiency in drawing
Marine subjects, particularly as it is not only requisite that a person
desirous of excelling in this Art should possess a knowledge of the construction of a Ship, or of what is denominated "Naval Architecture"
together with the proportion of masts and yards, the width, depth and cut
of the sails, &c; but he should likewise be acquainted with Seamanship.

—John Thomas Serres, 1805

On the spirit of marine art

The spirit is the nonliteral or the off-balance quality of the subject, perceived in a flash. It comes across as a feeling of life rather than a feeling
of deadness, or inertness. It is a quality which is not generally found in
banknote engravings. The spirit in a ship picture is that aspect which
cannot be gleaned from models, books, or plans. Spirit stems from direct
observation and experience of the subject and is found more often in the
fast sketch than in the carefully contrived composition. Indeed, by its
very nature it cannot be contrived. It is accidental, perhaps first appear-
ing even as a mistake.   —William Gilkerson

On the representation of ships, I

I wonder why in pictures of vessels at sea they are almost always represented
as under full sail, with a fair breeze. In reality they should be represented
close-hauled in a gale of wind, beating up for port against a head sea.

—Thomas Gibson Bowles

On the representation of ships, II

Too many popular ship paintings are idealistic and romantic: the "blue
water school," with snowy white sails and sunlight dancing on the waves.
Although these images are undeniably attractive, the reality was usually
rather different.   —Vice-Admiral Sir Patrick Bayly

On the representation of ships, III

A marine painter is someone who paints a ship and captures the atmosphere
in its entirety, without concentrating on any one particular point. It must
be a composition which includes the sky, the clouds and the sea. People
want a ship as a point of focus and interest. But I only look on the ship as
part of the whole composition.... To get the painting to live is the most
difficult part. You have to respect your subject, be almost frightened by it.

—Montague Dawson

On ship portraiture as a second-rate redundancy

A ship is a noble thing, and a cathedral a noble thing, but a painted ship
or a painted cathedral is not a noble thing. Art which duplicates art is
necessarily second-rate.   —John Ruskin

On the immortal light of the sea

The light you get at sea never fades. It is not only revealing; it has a suggestion of imperishable origin. You bring a reflection of it ashore with you, without knowing it. —H.M. Tomlinson

On painting the ocean, I

Of all the works of the Creation none is so imposing as the Ocean; nor docs Nature anywhere present a scene that is more exhilarating than a sea-beach, or one so replete with interesting material to fill the canvas of the Painter; the continual change an ever-varying aspect of its surface always suggesting the most agreeable sentiments—whether like the Poet he enjoys in solitude "The wild music of the waves," or when more actively engaged he exercises his pencil amongst the busy haunts of the fishermen, or in the bustle and animation of the port and harbour.

—John Constable, 1833

On painting the ocean, II

Still more striking are the extraordinary patches of indescribable green, "electric green" as I always call it, which appears on the slopes of the larger waves, those which break or at least try to break before they are decapitated by the fury of the wind. This is an "effect" which marine painters find almost impossible to reproduce, as it is essentially luminous; not that there are many who have really seen it. —Marin-Marie

On painting the whole package

If you wish to represent a tempest properly, consider and set down exactly what are the results when the wind blowing over the face of the sea and of the land lifts and carries with it every thing that is not immovable in the general mass.... Let the sea be wild and tempestuous, and between the crests of its waves it should be covered with eddying foam, and the wind should carry the finer spray through the stormy air after the manner of a thick and all-enveloping mist. Of the ships that are there, some you should show with sail rent and the shreds of it flapping in the air in company with the broken halyards, and some of the masts broken and gone by the board, and the vessel itself lying disabled and broken by the fury of the waves, with some of the crew shrieking and clinging to the fragments of the wreck. You should show the clouds, driven by the impetuous winds, hurled against the high mountain tops, and there wreathing like waves that beat upon the rocks; the very air should strike terror through the murky darkness occasioned therein by the dust and mist and thick clouds.

—Leonardo da Vinci

On giving credit where credit is due

I remember being handed a score composed by Mozart at the age of eleven. What could I say? I felt like de Kooning, who was asked to comment on a certain abstract painting, and answered in the negative. He was then told it was the work of a celebrated monkey. "That's different. For a monkey, it's terrific."

—Igor Stravinsky

The poetry of the sea is written on shore.

—Laura Alexandrine Smith

Memorable poems of the sea

Annabel Lee, by Edgar Allan Poe ("It was many and many a year ago, In a kingdom by the sea....")

Crossing the Bar, by Alfred Lord Tennyson ("Sunset and evening star, And one clear call for me!...")

Drake's Drum, by Sir Henry Newbolt ("Drake he's in his hammock an' a thousand mile away....")

L'Envoi, by Rudyard Kipling ("There's a whisper down the field where the year has shot her yield, And the ricks stand grey to the sun....")

My Lost Youth, by Henry Wadsworth Longfellow ("Often I think of the beautiful town, That is seated by the sea....")

The Ocean, by Lord Byron ("There is a pleasure in the pathless woods, There is a rapture on the lonely shore....")

Off Rivière du Loup, by Duncan Campbell Scott ("O ship incoming from the sea....")

Old Ironsides, by Oliver Wendell Holmes ("Ay, tear her tattered ensign down!...")

Over the Sea to Skye, by Robert Louis Stevenson ("Sing me a song of a lad that is gone....")

Psalm 107, the Holy Bible ("They that go down to the sea in ships....")

The Rime of the Ancient Mariner, by Samuel Taylor Coleridge ("It is an ancient Mariner, And he stoppeth one of three....")

Rowers' Chant, by T. Sturge Moore ("Row till the land dip 'neath The sea from view....")

The Shipman, by Geoffrey Chaucer ("A shipman was ther, wonynge fer by weste....")

A Sea Dirge, by William Shakespeare ("Full fathom five thy father lies....")

Sea-Fever, by John Masefield ("I must down to the seas again, to the lonely sea and the sky....")

Stowaway, by Bill Adams ("I crossed the gangway in the winter's raining,
Late in the night, when it was dreary dark....")

The Three Fishers, by Charles Kingsley ("Three fishers went sailing
away to the West....")

Where Lies the Land?, by Arthur Hugh Clough ("Where lies the land to
which the ship would go?...)

Authenticity in nautical literature

The sailor is well aware that the stalls are filled with sea books written by
landlubbers. Rarely, indeed, does he find a work which bears the authentic stamp of seamanship.

How vividly I recall my father's scorn at an incident in one of the
novels of a famous writer of nautical fiction. He was reading the book
aloud one evening, on board the bark *Harvard,* going up the China Sea.
The tale had arrived at the point of love-making; the scene was set on the
quarter-deck of a sixteen hundred ton sailing packet. The heroine
reclined in a deck-chair against the lee rail; a gentle air from the spanker
wafted down upon her, for they were sailing sunny seas. The hero whis-
pered his message; and while she listened, turning her face away, she
trailed her hand idly in the water. "Ha!" snorted my father, when he
reached this passage. "That fellow had better look out for himself—she
has long arms."   —from *An Instrument of the Gods*, by Lincoln Colcord

Advice to young writers

If you cannot get published, go to sea. There is no need to hang about pub-
lishers' offices. Go to sea. If you are eventually successful, you will have the
added advantage of being a mystery. Your publisher will receive your letters
from foreign hotels, from obscure seaports, bearing intriguing postmarks and
the stamps for which children clamor. Better still, you will find fresh material
coming to you, and the sea will evoke from your buried memories an unsus-
pected wealth of copy. The sea will soothe your bitterness and assuage your
grief. Go to Sea!   —William McFee, novelist and marine engineer

The sailor as writer, according to Daniel Defoe

As soon as men have acted the sailor, they come ashore and write books
of their voyage.... Whatever success [most of them] have had in voyage,
they have very little in relation; except it be to tell us that a seaman, when
he comes to the press, is pretty much out of his element, and that a very
good sailor may make but a very indifferent author.

To all you ladies now at land
We men at sea indite;
But first would have you understand
How hard it is to write.
                    —from an old sea song by Charles Sackville

It is no doubt an exaggeration to say that there are more yachting authors
than yachtsmen.   —K. Adlard Coles

W.P. Stephens, boatbuilder and author of *Traditions and Memories of American Yachting*, on the finer side of writing
A yachting writer should possess some sense of honesty and common decency, and he should first of all be a practical yacht sailor, familiar with handling and the rules. He should have a thorough knowledge of yachting history, as the present means nothing unless compared with the past; he should have some knowledge of the principles of yacht design and also of construction.

Milestones of yachting
early seventeenth century—The Dutch adopted *jaghts* for pleasure sailing.
early seventeenth century—Leeboards were in use in Holland to allow shallow-draft *jaghts*.
1660—The Dutch presented Charles II of England the *jaght Mary* to celebrate his restoration to the throne.
1661—Charles II's *Catherine* engaged the Duke of York's *Anne* in the first recorded yacht race.
1718—The Flotilla of the Neva was established in St. Petersburg, Russia.
1720—The first yacht club, the Water Club of Cork, Ireland, was established.
1775—The first English yacht club, the Cumberland Fleet, was established.
circa 1800—James Brown experimented without much success with all-external ballast.
1811—The centerboard was patented in the United States.
early nineteenth century—Centerboards were in use in American yachts.
1844—The first American yacht club, the New York Yacht Club, was established.
1851—The schooner-yacht *America* won the Hundred Guinea Cup at Cowes, Isle of Wight, England, laying the foundation for the America's Cup races.

mid-nineteenth century—Sandbaggers, shallow yachts with movable
ballast for stability, were in use in the United States.

mid-nineteenth century—Louis Winde of Boston became the first
specialist in yacht design to practice in the United States.

1868—The first yacht designer to be so called, St. Clare Byrne of
England, became established.

1870—The first American yacht to be designed totally on paper, with
no use of models, was the 63-foot cutter *Vindex,* by Robert Center
and A. Cary Smith.

1873—The extreme-beam centerboard schooner *Mohawk* capsized at
anchor in New York Harbor.

circa 1875—The jib-headed rig, also known as the Bermudan or Marconi
rig, made its appearance.

1875—The first large yacht with a cutaway forefoot, the *Jullanar,*
designed by E.H. Bentall, was built.

1876—The catamaran *Amaryllis,* designed by N.G. Herreshoff, became
the first multihull to enter an American yacht race, which she won.

circa 1880—External ballast began to gain acceptance.

1883—The Seawanhaka Corinthian Yacht Club adopted a new rating
rule that would dominate yacht racing for years.

1891—Nathanael Herreshoff designed and built the cutter *Gloriana,*
the revolutionary prototype of the modern yacht.

1896—Changes in the yacht racing rules made sandbaggers obsolete.

1925—The first Fastnet Race, from the Isle of Wight, England, to Fastnet
Rock off Ireland, and back, got underway.

1927—The extra-large foresail was first seen at an international racing
regatta in Genoa, Italy, hence the name "genoa."

1983—*Australia II* of the Royal Perth Yacht Club won the America's
Cup and broke the longest winning streak in sports history.

*As far as yachting is concerned, there is not a blasted thing here as good as
it used to be.*   —L. Francis Herreshoff

The glories of yachting

I do not know anything more glorious or exciting than to stand at the tiller
of a noble yacht, with a slashing breeze making her leap through the seas,
the spindrift flying out from her lee side in showers of flaky foam, feeling
oneself the master of her every motion, and she like a thing of life answering every thought of the brain and every movement of the hand; topping
the white crested waves like a bird, gliding swiftly down the hollows, nip-
ping now and again little foam wreaths over her snowy deck, and anon

cleaving through a giant billow, scattering rainbows of sea froth like pearls, and rubies, and sapphires around her; agreeable companions on the quarter-deck; a stalwart, active crew forward, a full bread locker, a brimming beef cask, and the grog tub damp, with a pleasant port and kindly friends looming at the end of the bowsprit.   —Vanderdecken

The meaning of Paradise
Ideas of Paradise are exceedingly various. To the ancients Paradise meant a *dolce far niente* in the Elysian Fields; to the North American Indians it means happy hunting ground and plenty of fat buffalo. The Scythians believed in a Paradise of immortal drunkenness and drinking blood out of the skulls of their enemies.... To some, I believe, Paradise means yachting, and for my own part, I think a 200-ton schooner, a ten-knot breeze, and a summer sea hard to beat.   —Sir Edward Sullivan

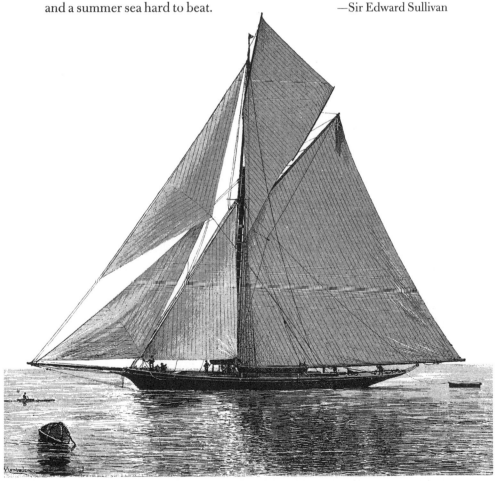

The essential difference between yachting and yacht sailing

For years I have been accustomed to hear remarks implying that a yachtsman's time must be heavy on hand, and hard to kill. It may be in yachting proper, which consists chiefly in promenading on quays, esplanades, and piers, in suitable attire, of course, and in passing to and fro in a steam launch or gig, with colors flying; a delight indulged in only by the extremely affluent, or by those who ought to be so.

Yacht sailing, however, is a very different affair from yachting, and when carried on with spirit, as it is sometimes in large yachts as well as small, is anything but an idle recreation. It is always healthful and exciting, though not always a source of unalloyed pleasure. But even when the work is heavy and continuous, as it must be occasionally, more than ample compensation is found in the contrast of a pretty and quiet anchorage.   —R.T. McMullen

Yachtin' is a gintlemans' sport, an' in daling with gintlemen ye can't be too careful.   —"Mr. Dooley" [Finley Peter Dunne]

By all means join a club, I say.
                         —Captain A.J. Kenealy

The earliest yacht clubs

Flotilla of the Neva, Russia, 1718

Water Club, Cork, Ireland, 1720

Cumberland Sailing Society (later Royal Thames Yacht Club), London, England, 1775

The Yacht Club (later Royal Yacht Squadron), Cowes, England, 1815

Royal Western Yacht Club, Plymouth, England, 1827

Svenska Segel Sällskapet (later Royal Swedish Yacht Club), Stockholm, Sweden, 1830

Royal London Yacht Club, England, 1833

Royal Hobart Regatta Association, Australia, 1838

Royal Southern Yacht Club, Southampton, England, 1838

Société des Régates du Havre, France, 1840

Royal Harwich Yacht Club, England, 1843

Royal Mersey Yacht Club, Liverpool, England, 1844

Royal Bermuda Yacht Club, 1844

New York Yacht Club, USA, 1844

Koninklijke Nederlands Jachtclub, Holland, 1846

Imperial Yacht Club of St. Petersburg, Russia, 1846

*Ladies will be admitted to the main Club House after 3 p.m. on
Thursdays during July and August when there is music.*
—*Rules of the Eastern Yacht Club,* Marblehead, Massachusetts, 1914

**A few rules from the early days of the Water Club of the Harbour of Cork,
Ireland, founded in 1720 and later renamed the Royal Cork Yacht Club**

II. That no Admiral do bring more than two dishes of meat for the entertainment of the club.

IX. Ordered that no long tail wigs, large sleeves or ruffles be worn by any member at the club.

XIV. Resolved that such members of the club or others as shall talk of sailing after dinner be fined a bumper.

Yachting a bit too much? Try rowing

In a rowing craft you find that you are closer to the water than you ever were before, no matter how much boating you have done in other craft. You are much more aware of sea and weather conditions, and see more of your surroundings than you ever did before. You get into places, holes, and creeks you never really knew existed. —R.D. "Pete" Culler

The pleasures of rowing
In a rowboat you are propelled without any noise or expense of fuel; you can explore shallow water regions without damaging your propeller. If it becomes a little cool you can keep yourself warm quite easily. In fact, rowing in temperatures down to freezing is very comfortable. While it is true that rowing races are apt to shorten one's life, still rowing for pleasure will greatly lengthen the life span. But best of all, it will greatly reduce the waistline. —L. Francis Herreshoff

"Is it so nice as all that?" asked the Mole shyly, though he was quite prepared to believe it as he leant back in his seat and surveyed the cushions, the oars, the rowlocks, and all the fascinating fittings, and felt the boat sway lightly under him.
    "Nice? It's the only thing," said the Rat. —from *The Wind in the Willows*, by Kenneth Grahame

Rowing is like life. We don't know where we're going, but we have a clear view of where we have been. —anon.

Rowers leave nothing behind them but the swirls from their oar blades.

—Mac McCarthy

"Rower's Chant"
by T. Sturge Moore

Row till the land dip 'neath
*   The sea from view.*
Row till a land peep up,
*   A home for you.*

Row till the mast sing songs
*   Welcome and sweet.*
Row till the waves outstripped,
*   Give up dead beat.*

Row till the sea-nymphs rise
*   To ask you why.*
Rowing you tarry not
*   To hear them sigh.*

Row till the stars grow bright
*   Like certain eyes.*
Row till the noon be high
*   As hopes you prize.*

Row till you harbor in
*   All longing's port.*
Row till you find all things
*   For which you sought.*

Rowboat terminology
Thwart—the seat on which the rower sits
Single-banked—one rower to a thwart, one rower to an oar
Double-banked—two rowers to a thwart, two rowers to an oar
Gunwale—the outer rail at the top edge of the sheerstrake
Sternsheets—the seat in the after end of the boat, usually for a passenger
Yoke—fitting on the rudderhead to provide leverage for turning the rudder
Steering lines, or yoke lanyards—lines from the yoke used for steering
    the boat

Rowlock, or oarlock—the fitting on the gunwale for holding the oar
Thole pins—wooden or metal pins set in the gunwale instead of
    a rowlock
Painter—a length of rope secured at the bow for towing or tying up the boat

Rowboats for varying conditions
Total exercise, plus speed, flat water—sliding-seat shell
Total exercise, plus speed, choppy water—sliding-seat ocean shell
Harbor crawling, utilitarian—flatiron skiff
Harbor crawling, stylish—round-bottomed skiff
Open water, survival—peapod
Fishing, flat water—punt
Fishing, open water—dory
River travel, quiet flat water—long, straight-keeled round-bottomed skiff
River travel, rapids—Mackenzie River boat
All-around elegance—Whitehall

Notes on rowing
Chin in, back straight, feet against the stretcher.
Rely on the power of your back and legs, not your arms.
Don't dig in; keep the top edge of the blade as close to the surface of the
    water as possible.
Keep the hands more or less at the same level through all positions of the
    stroke, as if they were in a horizontal groove.
Keep the elbows tucked in to the body at the completion of the stroke.
Use short strokes to build up momentum, to maneuver, and to pull into a
    strong wind and/or sea; long strokes when up to speed and "cruising."
When maneuvering, keep the boat moving to maintain control.
When passing through a narrow space, trail the oars or ship them.
When rowing across a current, aim higher than you want to go and
    maintain the stroke at all times.
Pace yourself.

Boat balance, singlehanded rowing
Generally, the center of the rower's weight should be slightly aft of the
    center of buoyancy.
Move weight slightly forward of amidships when rowing into a strong
    wind to allow the stern to "weathervane."
Move weight slightly aft of amidships when rowing with a strong wind to
    prevent the bow from digging in.

Good advice

My mother gave me but two pieces of advice and they were both good. "Never go out in a boat without oars," she said, "even if it's the *Queen Mary;* and don't waste your time on women who can't cook, because they're not likely to be much fun in the other rooms of the house."

—Dashiell Hammett

Oar terminology

Handle—the part gripped with the hands
Loom—the part between the handle and the neck
Throat, or neck—the juncture between the shaft and the blade
Blade—the part dipped in the water
Tip—the end of the blade

A few thoughts about oars

The best softwood oars, for lightness and strength, are spruce.

The best hardwood oars, for strength and durability, are ash.

Other oarmaking woods include clear cedar, fir, maple, and basswood.

Ash oars need not be painted or varnished; spruce must be.

Unfinished ash oars can be kept clean and bright by rubbing them down from time to time with sand and canvas.

If the oars are finished, leave the handles bare, as they will be easier to grip.

Good, utilitarian oars should flex during use—not much, but enough to be noticeable. If they are too stiff, thin them down with a spoke-shave, paying special attention to the lower end of the loom or shaft near the throat, and the throat itself.

To keep track of a pair of oars matched to a particular boat, paint a design on the blades using the color scheme of the boat. Blue and gray boat? Paint blue-and-gray chevrons on the oar blades.

Oar length, according to Shaw & Tenney, professional oarmakers of Orono, Maine

The inboard length of the oar—the distance between the center of the leather and the end of the handle—should be one-half the span between the oarlocks plus two inches.

The total length of the oar should be $1/7$ of the inboard length multiplied by 25. (The distance from the center of the leather to the end of the handle will be $7/25$ of the length of the oar.)

For a boat whose span between oarlocks is 3 feet, for example, the inboard length should be 20 inches and the total length should be 71.43 inches or 6 feet.

**Jury rig in the event an oarlock
is lost overboard and no spare is available**
Jam a wooden pin in the oarlock socket.
Loop a rope strop around the pin.
Insert the shaft of the oar in the strop and row against the pin.
No suitable pin? Jury-rig one from a piece of floorboard.
No suitable strop? Tie a bowline in the end of the painter and use that
     as a strop.
The moral of the story: Always carry either (a) a spare oarlock, or (b) a
     stick of wood that can be used as a pin.

The four components of rowing
Catch—The oar blades are dropped into the water.
Stroke—The oar handles are pulled toward the rower.
Finish—The oar blades are removed from the water.
Recovery—The oar handles are pushed away from the rower.

Great competition rowing traditions

Oxford–Cambridge Boat Race, England, established 1829
Henley Royal Regatta, England, established 1839
Harvard–Yale Race, USA, established 1852
Olympic Rowing Races, inaugurated 1900

Competition rowing, the basic categories

Sweep boats (one oar per rower)
Pair—two rowers, with a coxswain
Straight pair—two rowers without a coxswain
Four—four rowers with a coxswain
Straight four—four rowers without a coxswain
Eight—eight rowers with a coxswain

Sculls (two oars per rower)
Single—one rower
Double—two rowers
Quad—four rowers

Annals of competitive rowing

1315—earliest recorded rowing regatta, Venice
1592—first recorded all-woman boat race, Venice
1716—first Doggett's Coat and Badge race for professional watermen,
    River Thames, England
1775—first rowing regatta in England to be so called, River Thames,
    England
1778—first rowing race in eight-oared boats, London, England
late eighteenth century—introduction of rowing at Oxford University,
    England
1806—introduction of rowing at Eton College, England
1811—first recorded rowing race in United States, Hudson River, New York
1811—first recorded rowing race in Canada, Halifax, Nova Scotia
1829—first University Boat Race between Oxford and Cambridge, River
    Thames, England
1834—first rowing club in United States established, New York Harbor
1839—Henley Royal Regatta established, River Thames, England
1839—Detroit Boat Club, oldest U.S. rowing club still active today,
    founded
1843—first intramural college rowing, Yale University, New Haven, Con-
    necticut

1846—first recorded amateur rowing race in the United States, Hudson River, New York

1852—first Harvard–Yale race, the oldest intercollegiate sporting event in the United States, Lake Winnipesaukee, New Hampshire

1858—Schuylkill Navy, an association of Philadelphia rowing clubs, founded

1859—first intercollegiate rowing regatta in the United States, Lake Quinsigamond, Massachusetts; Harvard, Yale, and Brown

1861—sliding seat developed by Walter Brown of Massachusetts

1867—"Great Five Mile Rowing Match" held for the "Championship of America," Newburgh Bay, Hudson River, New York

1867—first place in a U.S. intercollegiate regatta won by a paper boat

1869—first international intercollegiate rowing race, River Thames, England; Harvard College and Oxford University

1872—National Association of Amateur Oarsmen, now United States Rowing Association, established

1872—first American pair-oared rowing race, in Philadelphia

1877—women's rowing program underway at Wellesley College, Massachusetts

1880—Canadian Association of Amateur Oarsmen founded

1882—Britain's Amateur Rowing Association founded

1895—Intercollegiate Rowing Association established, Poughkeepsie, New York

1900—first rowing regatta at the Olympics, Paris, France

1962—National Women's Rowing Association founded, USA

1974—first Women's World Rowing Championships

1976—first women's rowing competition at the Olympics, Montreal, Canada

1982—National Association for Amateur Oarsmen and National Women's Rowing Association amalgamated to become United States Rowing Association

1997—first transatlantic rowing race, Canary Islands to Barbados, West Indies

On the water no one can hear you scream.
                    —T-shirt slogan seen at a rowing regatta

An emblem of hope

From first to last the seaman's thoughts are very much concerned with his anchors. It is not so much that the anchor is a symbol of hope as it is the heaviest object that he has to handle on board his ship at sea in the usual routine of his duties. The beginning and the end of every passage are marked distinctly by work about the ship's anchors. —Joseph Conrad

An anchor, to be effective, must
Dig in quickly
Hold firmly
Reset itself as the vessel swings
Resist fouling
Break out easily when weighed

The effectiveness of the anchor, according to Thomas Fleming Day
In order to understand the action of the anchor, which is perfect, it is only necessary to take the common pick, such as is employed by laborers in breaking up earth, and drive it into solid ground. Drive the arm of your pick right up to the helve; now pull on it at right angles to the arm. You cannot move it, nor could the strongest man; simply lift the handle up, and the arm will come out of the ground easily. Such is the action of the anchor. Is anything more simple or perfect?

Parts of an old-fashioned anchor
Shank—the main or middle piece of the anchor
Ring—for attaching the rode to the shank

Stock—the piece crossing the shank near the ring end; either of iron or
    wood
Arms—the hooks at the bottom of the shank, one or the other of which
    sinks into and grips the ground
Crown—the point where the shank and the two arms meet
Palm, or fluke—the triangular part at the end of each arm
Pea, or bill—the point at the end of each arm

Names according to use
Bower—general-purpose anchor carried
    in the bow
Stern anchor—general-
    purpose anchor
    stowed aft
Stream anchor—medium-weight anchor
    stowed aft, used to keep the stern from
    swinging in a stream or tideway
Sheet anchor—spare anchor, approximately
    half the weight of the bower
Kedge—small anchor used for kedging off
    when aground, or for warping a vessel
    away from a dock or wharf

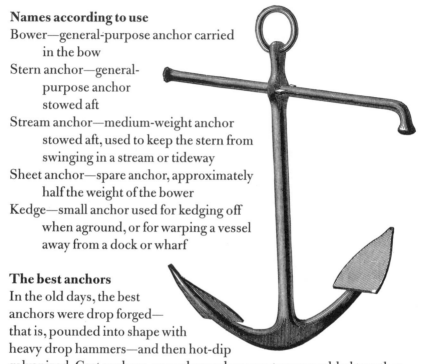

The best anchors
In the old days, the best
anchors were drop forged—
that is, pounded into shape with
heavy drop hammers—and then hot-dip
galvanized. Cast anchors, or anchors whose parts were welded together,
were considered to be not nearly as strong or as long-lasting. Today,
forged anchors are still seen as top of the line, but some anchors fabricated of welded parts, such as the Danforth and Delta types, are right up
there with them.

Carry two anchors
All boats should carry at least two anchors—a lighter one for daily use
    under normal circumstances, and a heavier one for emergency use.
To be safe, choose anchors that are heavier than you think you will need.
Anchors should always be stowed ready for use. An emergency anchor
    stowed at the bottom of a locker under a tangle of loose gear will do
    you no good in an emergency.

Rule of thumb for choosing an anchor

Type of Boat	Rated Holding Power of Anchor
Cruising sailboat	8 percent of the gross weight
Cruising powerboat	7 percent of the gross weight
Launches and light cruisers	6 percent of the gross weight
Centerboard daysailer	5 percent of the gross weight

For example, a cruising sailboat with a gross weight or displacement of 10,000 pounds should carry an anchor with a rated holding power of 800 pounds.

Two more rules of thumb when choosing an anchor
Buy the heaviest you can physically handle.
Hang the expense.

The components of ground tackle
Anchor
Chain
Rode
Shackles
Eyes
Stoppers
Windlass
Anchor buoy

Don't forget the role of the rode
A small anchor on a long rode is more effective than a large anchor on a short rode.

Length or scope of anchor rode
Seven to eight times the distance from chock to harbor bottom, measured at high tide.

Mark the anchor rode
To help keep track of the amount of anchor line that is out, mark the rode at 10-foot intervals, or whatever interval you prefer.

On rope, use color-coded cloth or leather, threaded into a strand and sewed securely.

On chain, use coded wire wrappings on the links at the chosen interval, or use paint on the links (paint, however, can wear off).

A coding system for marking the links of an anchor chain

1 fathom	1 red band
2 fathoms	2 red bands
3 fathoms	3 red bands
4 fathoms	1 white band
5 fathoms	2 white bands
6 fathoms	3 white bands
7 fathoms	1 blue band
8 fathoms	2 blue bands
9 fathoms	3 blue bands
10 fathoms	1 red link
15 fathoms	2 red links
20 fathoms	3 red links
25 fathoms	1 white link
30 fathoms	2 white links
35 fathoms	3 white links
40 fathoms	1 blue link
45 fathoms	2 blue links
50 fathoms	3 blue links

Alternatively, for a small boat, the same coding system can be used with the intervals being feet instead of fathoms (6 feet).

Considerations when anchoring in a strange harbor, according to John "Rob Roy" MacGregor

You sail into a port where in less than a minute you must apprehend by one panoramic glance the positions of twenty vessels, the run of the tide, and set of the wind, and depth of the water; and this not only as these are then existing, but, in imagination, how they will be six hours hence, when the wind has veered, the tide has changed, and the vessels have swung round, or will need room to move away, or new ones will have arrived.

To make an anchor bite in deep water or in difficult holding ground

Under sail—Lower the anchor over the stern while the boat still has way on and tie off the line to a bitt when sufficient rode is out. When the anchor is set, lead the line forward.

Under power—With the boat headed in the direction she will lie when anchored, lower the anchor, drift back until the proper rode is out, tie off the line to a bitt, and back down under power until the anchor is set.

Anchoring a dinghy or rowboat off shore

With the boat pulled up on shore, balance the anchor on the bow of the boat.

Coil the anchor line in the bottom of the boat so it will run out freely.

Make fast a tripline to the crown of the anchor.

While standing on the shore, coil the tripline at your feet so it will run out freely. Make sure the bitter end is secure.

Push the boat away from the shore.

When the boat reaches the proper spot, give the tripline a sharp jerk to pull the anchor overboard.

Make fast the tripline to a tree or rock on the shore.

To retrieve the boat, pull in the anchor by the tripline.

NOTE: This method works only if the tripline is made fast to the crown of the anchor! The best type of anchor for this is a grapnel.

She lies, and grows, well

In seamanlike terminology, the anchor rode is said to grow in the direction it lies, or leads. "I well remember," wrote Commodore B.A. Rogers, "a Hooghly River pilot calling out from the bridge of a British mailship anchoring at Diamond Harbour below Calcutta with the interrogative 'How does she grow?' and the facetious interjection of a passenger on the promenade deck beneath 'with tinkle bells and cockle shells.'"

The three types of load put on ground tackle by an anchored vessel

Wind drag

Current drag

Wave action

To determine if the anchor is dragging

Pick a fixed object on the shore and check every minute or so to see if the bearing to it changes (take into consideration, however, the swinging of the vessel); if the bearing does change, the anchor is dragging.

Put your hand on the rode ahead of the bow chock; if the rode is vibrating, the anchor is dragging.

Lower a leadline to the bottom and, with the line quite slack, secure it to the rail; if the line comes taut, the anchor is dragging (take into consideration, however, the effect of a rising tide).

Solutions for a dragging anchor
Let out more scope.
Deploy a second anchor.
Reset.

Buoy that anchor
If there is any likelihood that the anchor will be fouled by rocks or mooring lines, bend a line with a small buoy on the end to the crown of the
anchor before letting go. The line should be strong enough to raise the
anchor by itself and long enough to allow for the rise of the tide. Such a
buoy line, because of the direction of its pull, will free most fouled
anchors. In the event that the anchor cannot be freed, or in an emergency,
the anchor line can be cut and the buoy will mark the location of the
anchor for later retrieval.

Weighing the anchor, if it will not break out
Under power—Run ahead over the anchor and beyond; if that fails, run
    in a circle around the anchor and work it out.
Under sail—Sail over the anchor and beyond, tacking back and forth to
    work it out.

"Anchors Aweigh," original 1906 version
music by Lt. Charles A. Zimmerman, USN
lyrics by Midshipman Alfred H. Miles, USN

Stand Navy out to sea,
    Fight our battle cry;
We'll never change our course,
    So vicious foe steer shy.
Roll out the TNT,
    Anchors aweigh.
Sail on to victory
And sink their bones to Davy Jones, hooray!

Anchors Away, my boys,
    Anchors aweigh.
Farewell to foreign shores,
    We sail at break of day.
Through our last night on shore,
    Drink to the foam,
Until we meet once more.
Here's wishing you a happy voyage home.

Blue of the mighty deep;
  Gold of God's sun
Let these colors be till all of time
  Be done, done, done,
On seven seas we learn
  Navy's stern call:
Faith, courage, service true,
With honor, ever honor, over all.

Getting underway for home

"All hands up anchor!" When that order was given, how we sprang to the bars, and heaved round the capstan; every man a Goliath, every tendon a hawser!—round, round it spun like a sphere, keeping time with our feet to the time of the fife till the cable was straight up and down, and the ship with her nose in the water.

"Heave and pall! unship your bars, and make sail!" It was done: barmen, nippermen, tieres, veerers, idlers and all, scrambled up the ladder to the braces and halyards. —Herman Melville

Homeward bound

One after another, all hands working with a will, our kites were spread to the gentle land breeze. A course was set, a hand sent to the lookout, and at eight bells came the familiar order: "Go below the watch," and we trooped off to our bunks, with smiling faces and contented hearts— Homeward bound! —Rex Clements

Like unto ships far off at sea,
Outward or homeward bound, are we.
 —Henry Wadsworth Longfellow

There is not anything in all the earth as wonderful as that first scent of shore to sailormen come in from deep-sea voyaging—except it be a woman's kiss, she the right woman. —Bill Adams

The landfall, according to Bowditch

If no fix has been available for several days, considerable doubt may surround the landfall. Often the approximate distance offshore, if not the position, can be determined by means of soundings. Along most of their coasts the continents have a continental shelf of relatively shoal water extending outward for a varying distance. A similar island shelf extends outward from many island groups. At the outer edge, called the continental slope (or island slope), a sharp increase in depth occurs. This is often at about the 100-fathom curve. Therefore the crossing of this curve is often quite abrupt, and gives information on the distance off shore. The position of this and other depth curves may be indicated on the chart.

—The American Practical Navigator

Signs of a landfall

A small cloud, seemingly fixed in position on the horizon, especially if other clouds around it are moving, may indicate an island or high hills or mountains on the mainland.

In cold climates, ice on or surrounding the land may throw a light-colored reflection on the underside of a layer of clouds, especially if it is uniform.

In tropical climates, a light green reflection on the underside of a layer of clouds may indicate the presence of a lagoon surrounded by islets.

Generally speaking, the color of the open ocean is of a dark shade because of the great depth. A lightening color may indicate shallowing water and the presence of land.

Land may be near if birds in large numbers appear. The more birds, the more likely land is nigh.

The direction of land can be roughly determined by the pattern of birds' flight. Generally speaking, birds fly toward the land at dusk and away from it at dawn.

The direction of land can be more accurately determined by studying the pattern of high-level airplane flight.

Generally speaking, the higher the airplanes, the farther the land.

The presence and direction of an island can be roughly determined by studying the pattern of the swell. The swell will bend when it meets an island. Eddies are formed on the backside of an island—the "down-swell" side.

A high swell will produce heavy surf on land, especially if the shore is steep. The surf may be heard at a considerable distance, especially if atmospheric conditions are conducive to the carrying of sound.

Some land has a discernible odor, which will be strongest when the land is approached from downwind.

On soundings

The Marriner having left the vast Ocean, and brought his Ship into Soundings near the Land, amongst Tides or Streams, his Art now must be laid aside, and Pilottage taken in hand, the nearer the Land the greater the Danger, therefore your care ought to be the more.

Being in Tides-ways, narrow Channels, Rocks and Sands, I hope the ingenious Marriner will not take it amiss in recommending this to your Care, your Tides, Courses, Soundings, and the goodness of your Compasses. —Captain Greenville Collins, 1693

Nearing home

The joy of sighting the pilot boat after several months at sea without a single glimpse of land is indescribable. It's a sensation you have to experience to fully appreciate. That square patch of blue bunting above the main topmast [the signal requesting a pilot] has a world of meaning to the sailor. A night ashore just for the novelty of sleeping in a stationary bed, the thought that you don't have to get up and dress every four hours, shore food, theatres and a chance to mingle once more with human beings—what a flood of new ideas that big blue pilot flag brings to mind!

—C.G. Davis

A harbor, even if it is a little harbor, is a good thing.
—Sarah Orne Jewett

And thanks be to God for that

Having found a good haven and being brought safely in sight of land, they fell upon their knees and blessed the God of Heaven who had brought them over the vast and furious ocean, and delivered them from all the perils and miseries of it, again to set their feet upon the firm and stable earth, their proper element.
—William Bradford, of the Pilgrim ship Mayflower

The ship is old, the grub is bad.
　　Leave her, Johnny, leave her.
I'm getting thin, I'm growing sad;
　　It's time for us to leave her.
The sails are furled, our work is done,
　　Leave her, Johnny, leave her,
And now ashore we'll have some fun;
　　It's time for us to leave her.
—old chanty

This is the satisfaction, says Claud Worth

To make an open sea cruise in a seaworthy little yacht, neither courting unnecessary risks nor being unduly anxious as to weather, and having confidence in one's knowledge and skill to overcome such difficulties as may arise, is, to one who loves the sea, the most perfectly satisfying form of sport.

This is the pleasure, says E.F. Knight

To master the art of sailing a fore-and-after is to gain a source of much wholesome pleasure; but the pleasure is greatly enhanced when the amateur sailor has acquired sufficient knowledge to enable him to extend his sailing beyond his home waters, to cruise along shores new to him, finding his way by chart and compass, lead and log, shaping his course across broad seas with no land in sight, employing all the methods of the professional sailor.

This was the way it was, says Rex Clements

A brave sight it was to see some approaching vessel fold her wings one after another as she neared the land, curtsying as she trod down the long swells; to watch her draw nearer, the bubbles breaking in a myriad of fairy bells beneath her sharp forefoot, the long swish of water murmuring against her sides; to hear the clatter of the blocks and the calling out of the men while she swept slowly past; and finally to hear the hoarse roar of the cable as she rounded to and came to rest, squaring her yards and riding to the swell with queenly grace.

This is the way it can be, says G. Christopher Davies

When the stars come out, the herons settle in the shallow pools; the wild duck fly from the sheltered decoys and preserved sanctuaries to more open feeding grounds; a shot rings out on the night from some reed-hidden gunner who has been patiently awaiting the evening flight. In contrast come the notes of a piano and song from a barge; along the bank is a row of lights from cosy cabins; the inn is thronged with boat-sailers eagerly discussing the common sport; then the last cheery good-nights, and silence falls over the lone marsh and winding river.

And now it's time to go...

I am going a long way....
To the island valley of Avilion;
Where falls not hail, or rain, or any snow,
Nor ever wind blows loudly; but it lies
Deep-meadowed, happy, fair with orchard lawns
And bowery hollows crown'd with summer sea.

—from "The Passing of Arthur," by Alfred Lord Tennyson

"L'Envoi"

by Rudyard Kipling

There's a whisper down the field where the year has shot her yield
And the ricks stand grey to the sun,
Singing:— "Over then, come over, for the bee has quit the clover
And your English summer's done."
You have heard the beat of the off-shore wind
And the thresh of the deep-sea rain;
You have heard the song—how long! how long!
Pull out on the trail again!

Ha' done with the Tents of Shem, dear lass,
We've seen the seasons through,
And it's time to turn on the old trail, our own trail, the out trail,
Pull out, pull out, on the Long Trail—the trail that is always new.

It's North you may run to the rime-ring'd sun,
Or South to the blind Horn's hate;
Or East all the way into Mississippi Bay,
Or West to the Golden Gate;
Where the blindest bluffs hold good, dear lass,
And the wildest tales are true,
And the men bulk big on the old trail, our own trail, the out trail,
And life runs large on the Long Trail—the trail that is always new.

The days are sick and cold, and the skies are grey and old,
  And the twice-breathed airs blow damp;
And I'd sell my tired soul for the bucking beam-sea roll
  Of a black Bilbao tramp;
With her load-line over her hatch, dear lass,
And a drunken Dago crew,
And her nose held down on the old trail, our own trail, the out trail,
From Cadiz Bar on the Long Trail—the trail that is always new.

There be triple ways to take, of the eagle or the snake,
  Or the way of a man with a maid;
But the sweetest way to me is a ship's upon the sea
  In the heel of the North-East Trade.
Can you hear the crash on her bows, dear lass,
And the drum of the racing screw,
As she ships it green on the old trail, our own trail, the out trail,
As she lifts and 'scends on the Long Trail—the trail that is always new?

See the shaking funnels roar, with the Peter at the fore,
     And the fenders grind and heave,
And the derricks clack and grate, as the tackle hooks the crate,
     And the fall-rope whines through the sheave;
It's "Gang-plank up and in," dear lass,
It's "Hawsers warp her through!"
And it's "All clear aft" on the old trail, our own trail, the out trail,
We're backing down on the Long Trail—the trail that is always new.

O the mutter overside, when the port-fog holds us tied,
     And the sirens hoot their dread!
When foot by foot we creep o'er the hueless viewless deep
     To the sob of the questing lead!
It's down by the Lower Hope, dear lass,
With the Gunfleet Sands in view,
Till the Mouse swings green on the old trail, our own trail, the out trail,
And the Gull Light lifts on the Long Trail—the trail that is always new.

O the blazing tropic night, when the wake's a welt of light
     That holds the hot sky tame,
And the steady fore-foot snores through the planet-powder'd floors
     Where the sacred whale flukes in flame!
Her plates are scarr'd by the sun, dear lass,
And her ropes are taut with the dew,
For we're booming down on the old trail, our own trail, the out trail,
We're sagging south on the Long Trail—the trail that is always new.

Then home, get her home, where the drunken rollers comb,
     And the shouting seas drive by,
And the engines stamp and ring, and the wet bows reel and swing,
     And the Southern Cross rides high!
Yes, the old lost stars wheel back, dear lass,
That blaze in the velvet blue,
They're all old friends on the old trail, our own trail, the out trail,
They're God's own guides on the Long Trail—the trail that is always new.

Fly forward, O my heart, from the Foreland to the Start—
     We're steaming all too slow,
And it's twenty thousand mile to our little lazy isle
     Where the trumpet-orchids blow!
          You have heard the call of the off-shore wind
          And the voice of the deep-sea rain;
          You have heard the song—how long! how long!
          Pull out on the trail again?

The Lord knows what we may find, dear lass,
And the deuce knows what we may do—
But we're back once more on the old trail, our own trail, the out trail,
We're down, hull down on the Long Trail—the trail that is always new.

Also available from Sheridan House

THE MARINER'S BOOK OF DAYS
Peter H. Spectre

"Will anyone dare to tell me that business is more entertaining than fooling among boats?" Robert Louis Stevenson once asked rhetorically. "He must have never seen a boat, or never seen an office, who says so."

Those of us who do know both – boats and offices, or perhaps more generally, boats, ships, and the sea and any landbound occupation – find our thoughts drifting at the oddest moments. We're sitting in a meeting; the boss is pushing sales quotas; we're thinking about rowing a little skiff deep into a salt marsh. The general manager is talking about production goals; we're in the crosstrees, repairing the rigging.

We're here but we're not here. We're at the helm of our own little ship. We're steaming frames for the boat of our dreams. We're nautical schizophrenics, and there's no known cure short of telling the boss to take a long walk off a short pier and running away to sea. There are medicines, however, and this little volume is one of them.

The Mariner's Book of Days is about Stevenson's entertainment of fooling among boats, a daily reminder of the things we love most about the watery world. The pleasures of building and maintaining our own boats, the development of nautical knowledge, the evolution of a way of life. It is organized in a generally topical manner yet has a labyrinthine quality, not unlike the way we think about the sea while the boss expounds on organizational restructuring. One thing leads to another, and before we know it we're on a rough passage with R.D. Graham or at the drafting table with William Atkin or plotting a course among Caribbean Islands with Hrvclvin Frnger

The Mariner's Book of Days is an annual. Year by year we get together on a 365-day imaginary voyage through time, an encyclopedic passage through what W.P. Stephens called traditions and memories and Joseph Conrad called the mirror of the sea.

America's Favorite Sailing Books
www.sheridanhouse.com

Other books of interest from Sheridan House

THE LO-TECH NAVIGATOR
Tony Crawley

A knowledgable and informative explanation on how to navigate without expensive electronics. Crawley's detailed descriptions make his cost-effective projects easy to carry out.

HARD ON THE WIND
THE TRUE STORY OF A BOY WHO WENT TO SEA AND CAME BACK A MAN
Russ Hofvendahl

Fifteen-year-old Russ Hofvendahl escapes the Great Depression by talking his way onto a four-masted schooner leaving San Francisco. An engaging, maritime bildungsroman.

THE COMPLEAT CRUISER
THE ART, PRACTICE, AND ENJOYMENT OF BOATING
L. Francis Herreshoff

"This charming classic is the only book around on enjoying the minutae of cruising ...that most people do – gadding about one's local bays and islands..." *Next Whole Earth Catalog*

THE COAST OF SUMMER
SAILING NEW ENGLAND WATERS FROM SHELTER ISLAND TO CAPE COD
Anthony Bailey

"In prose as gentle as the breezes that push his craft, Bailey tells of his summer voyage aboard the good ship LOCHINVAR...[He]pulls you right to his side on a most amiable walking/boating tour: an inspired guide in a fascinating locale with a rich past." *Kirkus Reviews*

THE UNLIKELY VOYAGE OF JACK DE CROW
A MIRROR ODYSSEY FROM NORTH WALES TO THE BLACK SEA
A.J. Mackinnon

"...will have you alternately laughing and shaking your head in disbelief at the brilliant insanity of the ill-defined quest." *Cruising World*

America's Favorite Sailing Books
www.sheridanhouse.com